Global Leaders Praise for
The Faith Book

Every Christian is challenged to run the race of faith during his/her lifetime. In *The Faith Book*, Dr. James O. Davis, shows us how to begin, build, and broaden our life of faith over the span of our lifetime. Your Christian life will be enriched after reading and studying this phenomenal resource!

—**Rev. Doug Clay**
General Superintendent
Assemblies of God

The Faith Book is for this generation. Dr. James O. Davis has creatively written a power-packed book to help both younger and older alike to live the life of faith with God. You can learn how to see the invisible, believe the impossible, and receive the indescribable! Be sure to purchase enough copies for you and your team today!

—**Dr. Glenn C. Burris**
President Emeritus
Foursquare Church

In a time of great fear, Dr. James Davis has given us *The Faith Book* that will inspire our faith and give us hope. The Bible tells us that "perfect love casts our fear" (1 John 4:8). But the way we know that love is through faith. This study of the Hall of Fame of Faith will encourage each of us as we serve the Lord in our times."

—Dr. Doug Beacham
General Superintendent
International Pentecostal Holiness Church

Faith is the assurance of things hoped for and the conviction of things not seen. In his latest book, *The Faith Book: The Master Key To A Grand Life Of Faith,* Dr. James O. Davis teaches the God-given path to the faith-filled life. When you read and reap from this book, your life will be enriched forever!

—Dr. Gustavo Crocker
General Superintendent
Church of the Nazarene

The Faith Book by Dr. James O. Davis is the quintessential book on faith for our time. Through his global leadership travels, combined with his dynamic exposition of Hebrews 11, Dr. Davis will inspire you to believe for incredible answers to prayer in your life. Be sure to get enough copies for you and your team!

—Dr. Timothy Hill
General Overseer
Church of God

At the very core of every believer's walk with the Lord, you will find faith. Throughout Scripture we find Jesus teaching His followers on matters of faith, reminding them that with faith "nothing is impossible." In *The Faith Book*, Dr. James O. Davis masterfully provides a comprehensive look at some of the Bible's most inspirational characters and how they lived a faith-filled life. No doubt your faith will increase as you read the pages of this powerful book!

— Bishop Sam Clements
General Overseer
Church of God of Prophecy

The Faith Book is a dazzling achievement, a classic book on faith for this generation, and indeed all generations. Dr. James O. Davis creatively introduces us to the grand heroes of faith and clearly shows us the path from a rogue's gallery to a hall of champions.

— Dr. Leonard Sweet
Best-selling Author (*Rings of Fire*)
Professor (Drew University, Tabor College,
Evangelical Seminary, George Fox University)
Founder of preachthestory.com and
The Salish Sea Press

Every life-challenge can be addressed by our faith in God. It is paramount for Christians to grow in their faith throughout their lives. In *The Faith Book*, Dr. James O. Davis shows us the success path to living, learning, and leading a grand life of faith for Christ. Every Christian leader will greatly benefit from this valuable resource!

— Dr. Tommy Barnett
Founder, The Dream Center
Dream Center Church

Many have read it. Some have declared it. Few know how to do it. We know we should, but do we really know how to "walk by faith and not by sight?" Dr. James O. Davis has provided the quintessential book to help Christians to live the life of faith. In *The Faith Book: The Master Key To A Grand Life Of Faith*, Dr. Davis states, "If you please the Lord, it does not matter who you displease; but, if you displease the Lord, it does not matter who you please." Throughout this life-changing book, you will learn how to walk by faith in every circumstance in life."

—**Kenneth C. Ulmer, DMin, PhD**
Global Church Divinity School
Faithful Central Bible Church

Faith Walking is at the center of our Christian experience. We cannot obey Christ ... serve Christ ... or become like Christ unless we exercise faith in Him. Our faith walk is dependent upon the Word of God and the best way we can learn to walk by faith is found in Scripture. Dr. James O. Davis, in his latest book, *The Faith Book: The Master Key To A Grand Life Of Faith*, has walked us into God's hall of fame, and those who are there exhibited perfect faith in God.

—**Dr. Elmer Towns**
Cofounder/Liberty University
Lynchburg, VA

Dr. James Davis has done it again! He's written another encouraging book designed to supercharge your life of faith. Romans 10:17 tells us, "faith comes by hearing and hearing by the Word of God," and this book does just that. Dr. Davis takes us through an amazing study of the power of faith by walking us, step by step, with the heroes of faith in Hebrews 11. You'll never ever see this faith-filled chapter the same and trust me, your faith in God will definitely reach new heights.

—**Rev. Jeff Jones**
Lead Pastor, Valley Family Church

We know "the just shall live by faith," and "without faith it is impossible to please God." So how important is faith? We are to abide in Faith, Hope, and Love. Faith is right up there. In his book, *The Faith Book: The Master Key To A Grand Life Of Faith*, Dr. James O. Davis, a man who has lived and continues to live a life of faith, lays out in this book the value, the keys, and the principles of faith. Utilizing Hebrews chapter 11, Dr. Davis opens up insight that few have seen. Dr. Davis, who has ministered many decades, who has seen more than most, who is eloquent in words of faith and grounded in the word of faith, in his book pens some of the inspirations on faith that we all long for. I know this book will stir your faith, help grow your faith, and bring you up into the "Grand Life of Faith."

—**Pastor Peter Mortlock**
Senior Pastor, City Impact Church International
Auckland, New Zealand

Very few leaders have been able to write a book on Faith as a result of a walk of faith. Dr James O. Davis has walked by faith both in his personal life, surmounting incredible trials and obstacles, as well as in his service in God's Kingdom, always undertaking great things for God! Dr. Davis is one of the best expository preachers I know and I am impressed on how he is able to bring his expository principles in writing into this incredible book. *The Faith Book: The Master Key To A Grand Life Of Faith* is a book that every Christian leader who wants to live by faith must have on his desk!

— **Dr. Guy Sottile**
Italy for Christ
President and Founder

The Faith Book by Dr. James O. Davis is a must read. Why? Because Dr. Davis is a man of great faith. He is an inspiration to many. His ministry has expanded exponentially as a direct result of his taking leaps of faith through every season of life.

Hebrews 11:6 teaches you cannot please God without faith. I am confident that your heart's desire is like mine, to please God to a greater degree than ever. Let's begin today by reading *The Faith Book* and receive a deeper understanding of Hebrews 11:1-12:3.

— **Rev. Terry G. Bailey**
District Superintendent
Tennessee Assemblies of God Ministry Network

With *The Faith Book: The Master Key To A Grand Life Of Faith*, Dr. James O. Davis reveals the secret of the Global Church Network and the secret of his worldwide ministry: It is just doing what Paul has written in 2 Cor. 4:13: "But having the same spirit of faith, according to that which is written, I believed, and therefore did I speak; we also believe, and therefore also we speak." Dr. James O. Davis invites the readers to open their mind for this wonderful spirit of faith and to speak and act according to the examples of the heroes of faith in Hebrews 11:1–12:3.

— **Daniel Schmid, DTh, Founder and Leader**
LiFe Evangelism International

It is my privilege and joy to call Dr. James Davis my friend and gospel partner for twenty years. He was a faithful confidant and servant of one of the greatest men of God in church history — Dr. Bill Bright, who was a man of unbelievable faith. Following in his steps and in his spirit his latest book, *The Faith Book: The Master Key To A Grand Life of Faith*, is a book that will indeed fortify your faith, strengthen your soul, and lift your life to new heights. When you read this book, you will find yourself soaring with wings like eagles and you will never be the same.

— **Dr. James Merritt**
Lead Pastor, Cross Point Church
Duluth, GA
President Emeritus
Southern Baptist Convention

Expressed as a simple equation, the Book of Hebrews = Pentateuch + 4 Gospels. Dr. James O. Davis in *The Faith Book* expresses this most vividly through the lens of twenty-two different-colored jewels in Hebrews 11. Strongly recommended for those who wish to find the most precious jewel in life.

— **Dr. Byoungho Zoh**
Founder of Bible Tongdok Movement
Adjunct Professor (Drew University & Youngnam
Theological University and Seminary in S. Korea)
Best-selling Author

Dr. James O. Davis, in his latest book entitled, *The Faith Book: The Master Key To A Grand Life of Faith*, teaches us how to take the biblical steps of faith into victory. Dr. Davis walks us through the hall of fame of faith in Hebrews 11, showing us how to believe God for the impossible to be released in our lives. I encourage you to buy a box of books and pass them out to the key leaders on your team.

— Dr. David Sobrepena
Founder, Word of Hope Church
Manila, Philippines
General Superintendent
Philippines Assemblies of God

Dr. James O. Davis and I have ministered and served together for more than twenty-five years. In his latest book, *The Faith Book: The Key To A Grand Life of Faith,* he carefully describes the key of faith, which opens all doors in the Kingdom of God. While you read this powerful book, your faith will soar as you walk out God's plan for your life. You will learn how to live by faith, bringing together vision and provision and obstacles and opportunities for godly success!

— Rev. Carl Stephens
Lead Pastor, Faith Assembly of God
Orlando, Florida

The Faith Book will help to you to hear God's voice, receive His vision, and live in victory. This powerful book, written by Dr. James O. Davis, will enlarge your faith and equip you for your God-given mission.

— Dr. Carla Sunberg
General Superintendent
Church of the Nazarene

FOREWORD BY DR. SAMUEL RODRIGUEZ

THE FAITH BOOK

THE MASTER KEY TO A GRAND LIFE OF FAITH

DR. JAMES O. DAVIS

BILLIONSOUL PUBLISHING®

Orlando, Florida

The Faith Book
The Master Key To A Grand Life Of Faith

Copyright © 2021 by Dr. James O. Davis

ISBN: 978-0-578-85349-9

Billion Soul Publishing
Orlando, Florida
www.billionsoulpub.com

In Dedication To

Dr. Tommy Barnett and Dr. Elmer Towns
who have daily demonstrated
living, learning, and leading
a grand life of faith.

Table of Contents

Foreword

The opening words of Hebrews 11, "Now faith is the substance of things hoped for, the evidence of things not seen" (KJV), sometimes perplexes Christian leaders. The author of Hebrews is not analyzing faith into its component parts; rather, he is telling us how faith operates. Faith is the substance, that is, the assurance, the steady confidence of mind, even the "title deed" of what we hope for. We have a heavenly deed in the next world!

The term "hope" ("things hoped for") is not wishful thinking but something that is certain but not yet fully realized in our present experience. Faith is not wishful thinking; it is not faith in faith or just speaking positively. It is the hope of which Paul speaks in Romans 5:5 where he says that the hope of glory will not let us down because we have already tasted the love of God in our hearts through the Spirit.

Faith is also the evidence, that is, the conviction of the reality of what we do not yet see. It is the characteristic of those who live "as seeing him who is invisible" (Hebrews 11:27 KJV). Faith permits us to see the invisible, believe the incarnational, and receive the impossible!

Faith, then, in its present activity, is always looking forward to the future and exercising it always means that we do not view life and its events through spectacles from the lens crafters of this world but through the divine prescription that enables us to have the long-look, spiritual vision in this world because we view it from the perspective of another world. We have chosen to take the long look instead of the short look in this life.

All of this sounds so grand, so deeply theological that we are surely entitled to ask the author of Hebrews what this means in practical terms. Dr. James O. Davis states in *The Faith Book* that "Faith is belief with legs on it. We are not called to sit on our faith but to stand on it."

The rest of Hebrews 11 is taken up with showing us what this kind of faith means, not in the happy by-and-by but in the nasty now-and-now. Dr. Davis leads us on a grand tour through an amazing portrait gallery of men and women of faith. With each of the heroes of faith, he teaches power-packed lessons to encourage and equip us to keep on keeping on in our race. With Abel, we learn the worship of faith; with Enoch, we learn the walk of faith; with Noah, we learn the wages of faith; with Abraham, we learn the ways of faith; with Moses, we learn the wealth of faith; with Joshua, we learn the walls of faith; with Rahab, we learn the worth of faith; with Gideon, we learn the war of faith; with Jesus, we learn the win of faith! As I said, we will learn power-packed lessons that will impact every area of our lives!

Only when we reach the end do we realize that Dr. Davis has been leading us all along to the person of our Lord Jesus — the Author and Finisher of our faith! His faith also, indeed supremely as Hebrews 12 makes plain, was "the substance of things hoped for, the evidence of things not seen."

I believe the heroes of the faith had two things in common. They looked *beyond the present* (to things hoped for) and *beyond the visible* (to the invisible). They defied the wisdom of the world that told them to live for today and that what they saw was what was real. Instead, they lived in the present in the light of the future and handled everything that was visible in the light of the invisible. For example, Moses compared all of the treasures of Egypt to the treasures of Christ and the heavenly world. As a result, he made his decision to forsake his earthly inheritance to receive his future heavenly reward.

There are many Old Testament examples of this. It is worth noting in passing how the Hebrew writer draws all his illustrations of faith for New Testament believers from the Old Testament. He could hardly make clearer his conviction of the harmony of the Bible, of the way of salvation, and of the work of the Spirit. Even though Hebrews 11 takes us through thousands of years of the family of faith, Dr. Davis focuses our attention at greater length on two figures: Abraham and Moses. Here were two men who supremely exemplified these twin characteristics of genuine faith.

What explains their wonderful faith? We can sum their faith up with they heard and trusted God's Word or, perhaps even better, they trusted the God who speaks through His Word. The voice comes first, and the vision comes second. We first hear and then we see.

In other words, to live by faith is not to live by what we can see and feel and touch — on the basis of our sense experience — but to live on the basis of what God has already said and promised. That is faith. Our faith's epicenter is found in our Lord Jesus Christ. It takes its practical shape from what God has said and promised in His Word.

We need to be aware of strange ideas of what faith is in our generation. Dr. Davis has prayed that this book will be the "Faith Book" for both the younger and older of this timeframe on earth. Faith is more than looking for the extraordinary or the miraculous. Living by faith means doing what the Lord did — living by every word that proceeds from God's mouth (Matthew 4:4 citing Deuteronomy 8:3). This is the Bible's key to the life of faith — to be so deeply fed and nourished by the Word of God that it energizes us to live in faith, trusting God's Word, living now in the light of God's certain kingdom. From beginning to end, "Faith comes by hearing, and hearing by the word of God" (Romans 10:17 NKJV).

I wish to challenge us to take the grand tour of walking through the Hall of Fame of Faith. As you take this Spirit-inspired tour, take the time to allow the leaders high-lighted in Hebrews 11 to deeply influence, inspire, and impact your spiritual life. We are to know the promises and trust them and know the Word and live on its basis, being guided by its wisdom.

I am most grateful that Dr. James O. Davis has prepared this watershed book on the life of faith. For decades, Dr. Davis has lived, learned, and led by faith for the glory of Christ. He believes that it is not great faith in God but faith in a great God that makes the ultimate difference! You will be enriched by this book for years to come!

Dr. Samuel Rodriguez
President
National Hispanic Christian Leadership Conference
January, 2021

Acknowledgments

The Faith Book would have only remained a dream without the tireless creative leadership of Allison Ward, Jackie Chrisner, and Natalie Velazquez.

I am grateful for Allison Ward, who brought imaginative energy, for Jackie Chrisner, who built with inspirational edits, and for Natalie Velazquez, who broadened with intentional efforts.

Introduction

Indiana Jones (Harrison Ford) in *The Last Crusade* movie (released in 1989), stands looking across a great chasm. Somehow, he has to cross this huge chasm, to reach the Holy Grail, the Cup of Christ, on the other side. Indiana holds in his right hand, his Dad's diary for the quest of the Holy Grail. As he looks across the chasm, he reads from his Dad's diary, "Only a leap from the Lion's mouth, will he prove his worth."

Even though we cannot see the path forward, we take the first step on God's path in the right direction.

While Indiana is gathering his courage to take this bold leap, his Dad (Dr. Henry Jones, Sean Connery) some distance away, is dying from a gunshot to the stomach. Dr. Jones exclaims, "You must believe boy! You must believe."

Then, Indiana looks at the chasm one final time and says, "It is a leap faith." With his heart pounding in his chest, he takes the leap of faith to discover that there was a hidden, solid rock path for him to walk on. Before he took the leap of faith, this solid rock path was hidden due to being made of exactly the same kind of rock of the chasm walls. The leap of faith revealed the path to cross success-fully to the other side.

In Hebrews 11:1, we read, "Now faith is the assurance of things hoped for, the conviction of the things not seen. We take the leap of faith, because we have the assurance of the things hoped for and the conviction (the title deed) of the things not seen. Even though we cannot see the path forward, we take the first step on God's path in the right direction. The God-given path is revealed day by day, as we continue to follow the Lord. We do not always have to know where we are going, but we must know who we are following. When we are following the Lord, He will lead us to the "promise land" of our lives.

The Lord called me into fulltime ministry at the young age of fourteen. I had sensed his calling developing in my life for several months. Then, at an altar at the Alabama Assemblies of God Youth Camp in July 1975, I yielded my life with the confession, "Lord, I will be who you want me to be and will do what you want me to do." On August 19, 1979, I took a small leap of faith, by driving to Montgomery, Alabama, to speak at Evangel Temple, for the Wednesday evening worship service.

Even though I took a small leap faith on August 19, 1979, it put me on a daily revealed path that has taken me more than 10 million miles, to nearly 140 nations, speaking to millions of people. As we continue to walk by faith, we will be required at many points in life, to new larger leaps of faith. And, just as in our first leap of faith, we have things that are hoped for and the title deed of the evidence not yet seen. We have claimed it; but have not yet conquered it.

Several decades ago, I made a decision, that while trav-eling to new towns, cities and nations, I would make it a point to visit cemeteries and churches, where world class men and women are buried. These personal and family walks through the corridors of time, have been some of the most inspiring moments of my life. Most people usually just visit the "tourist sites" but do not take the time or even have the interest in visiting the gravesites of the people who actually built the cities or sites, they have chosen to tour. I will not be able to highlight the scores of sacred places visited over the years; but will bring into focus a few of them as we prepare to "walk through the hall of faith" together.

It has been reported that **Pilgrim's Progress** *is the second most-read Christian text, after the Bible.*

Many years ago, a friend called me on my cell phone and said, "James, if you had 8 hours in London, before catching your next flight, what would you do in that span of time?" I answered, "I would use my time to visit two cemeteries: Norwood and Bunhill Fields."

Across the street of Bunhill Fields, is the home of Dr. Jonathan Wesley. Behind his home is where this powerful faith-filled man of God is buried. Dr. Wesley took the leap of faith to begin the Methodist Church, to write hundreds of worship songs, to preach to large crowds in open fields and to train thousands of pastors. The first Methodist church he planted still meets every Sunday! Today, millions of people call themselves, Methodists.

In Bunhill Fields cemetery, Rev. John Bunyan, the famed author of Pilgrim's Progress is buried. He was the son of a Bedfordshire tinker with little education. At first, he followed his father's trade. He served for three years in the Parliamentary Army during the Puritan Revolution but saw little fighting. In about 1649 he married an Anglican and embraced her Christianity. Afterwards, Rev. Bunyan, had an intense spiritual awakening, seeing visions of Jesus watching him through the roof, and the Devil tugging at his clothes as he prayed. After being baptized in the River Ouse in 1653, he took a leap of faith and began to preach and to write.

In 1660 the Monarchy was restored, and non-Anglican or unlicensed preaching became a crime. Rev. Bunyan was sentenced to three months in Bedford Jail for avoiding Anglican services, and refusing to be silenced. Then, three months stretched to twelve years, during which he wrote one of his first major works, "Grace Abounding" (1666). He also wrote the first part of his most famous book, "The Pilgrim's Progress", but decided not to publish it because of its then a controversial fictional format.

After the Declaration of Indulgence in 1672, Bunyan was freed, and became a licensed preacher in Bedfordshire. but the respite was brief, and he was again imprisoned for six months when the Declaration was repealed in 1673. During this timeframe, he completed "The Pilgrim's Progress", which was published in 1678, immediately becoming popular, with thirteen editions published before Bunyan's death. It is an allegory of an ordinary man's spiritual journey, told in language derived from the Bible. It has been said to be the second most-read Christian text, after the Bible. The last ten years of Bunyan's life were spent writing and preaching. Rev. Bunyan shook his known world and continues to influence our world today! John Bunyan is buried close to Daniel Defoe, the author of Robinson Crusoe and Susanna Wesley, Jonathan Wesley's mother!

In Norwood Cemetery, Dr. Charles Haddon Spurgeon is buried. Charles Haddon Spurgeon, Victorian England's best-known Baptist minister, was born on June 19, 1834 in Kelvedon, Essex and spent his childhood and early teenage years in Stambourne, Colchester, and Newmarket.

In 1856 he married Susannah Thompson; their only children, twin sons Thomas and Charles, were born on September 20, 1857.

Some regard Spurgeon as the greatest orator since Whitefield. Today, many homileticians consider him to be one of the finest preachers since the Apostle Paul.

Spurgeon had no formal education beyond Newmarket Academy, which he attended from August 1849 to June 1850, but he was very well-read in Puritan theology, natural history, and Latin and Victorian literature. His lack of a college degree was no hindrance to his remarkable preaching career, which began in 1850, when he was only fifteen years old. A few months after his conversion to Christianity, he took a leap of faith to begin his preaching at Teversham. The next year, he accepted his first pastorate, at the Baptist Chapel in Waterbeach. The church quickly grew from fewer than a dozen congregants to more than four hundred, and Spurgeon's reputation as a preacher caught the attention of New Park Street, London's largest Baptist church. He was invited to preach there in December 1853 and, following a brief probationary period, he agreed to move to London and become the church's new pastor.

Spurgeon's New Park Street congregation grew rapidly, soon becoming too large for the 1200-seat auditorium. On August 30, 1854, the membership agreed to enlarge the chapel; during the remodeling, services were held at the 5,000-seat Exeter Hall, a public auditorium on Strand Street. When the renovations to the New Park Street Church were complete in May 1855, the church was still too small. Thus, a committee was formed to oversee the construction of the church's new home, the 5,000-seat Metropolitan

Tabernacle. The congregation moved once again, meeting in Exeter Hall and the 8,000-seat Surrey Gardens Music Hall until the Tabernacle was dedicated on March 18, 1861.

Spurgeon's preaching was both enormously popular and highly controversial. Some regarded him as the greatest orator since Whitefield. Today, many homileticians consider him to be one of the finest preachers since the Apostle Paul. Tens of thousands of preachers have studied and read his sermons from around the world. He preached his final sermon at the Metropolitan Tabernacle on June 7, 1891. He died in France on January 31, 1892. On February 9, over 60,000 people filed past his casket in The Metropolitan Tabernacle. He was buried at Norwood Cemetery on February 11.

When our family visited Plymouth, Massachusetts, to see where the Pilgrims had landed on November 21, 1620, we also took time to walk through the Pilgrims Cemetery. Most people do not visit the Pilgrims Cemetery because it is located up on a hill, not very accessible by automobile. Think about the leap faith that William Bradford and the Pilgrims took to finally make it to America.

On September 16, 1620, the *Mayflower* sets sail from Plymouth, England, bound for the New World with 102 passengers. The ship was headed for Virginia, where the colonists—half religious dissenters and half entrepreneurs—had been authorized to settle by the British crown. However, stormy weather and navigational errors forced the *Mayflower* off course, and on November 21 the "Pilgrims" reached Massachusetts, where they founded the first permanent European settlement in New England in late December.

Thirty-five of the Pilgrims were members of the English Separatist Church, who traveled to America to escape the jurisdiction of the Church of England, which they found corrupt. Ten years earlier, English persecution had led a group of Separatists to flee to Holland in search of religious freedom. However, many were dissatisfied with economic opportunities in the Netherlands, and under the direction of William Bradford, they decided to immigrate to Virginia, where an English colony had been founded at Jamestown in 1607.

Because it the Mayflower Compact established constitutional law and the rule of the majority, the compact is regarded as an important precursor to American democracy.

Along the way, the settlers formulated and signed the Mayflower Compact, an agreement that bound the signatories into a "civil body politic." Because it established constitutional law and the rule of the majority, the compact is regarded as an important precursor to American democracy. After a 66-day voyage, the ship landed on the tip of Cape Cod at what is now Provincetown, Massachusetts.

While we stood at William Bradford's grave, I explained to my daughters, the faith required by Bradford and the Pilgrims to leave the land of the familiar, to cross the seas of the unknown to claim the future. Their tombstones are a testimony of their faith in God's Word!

Every time I have been fortunate to visit, Rome, Italy, I have made it a priority to visit the Mamertinum Prison. I am quite confident that 90 percent of the Christians who visit the iconic Colosseum, do not take the time to visit the Mamertinum Prison. The Colosseum is located at one end of the Roman Forum and the Mamertinum Prison is located at the opposite end. As you may recall, it was at the Colosseum where the Roman leaders who fed Christians to the lions, while the crowds cheered it on. However, you most likely do not know that while Christians were being fed to the lions in the Colosseum, the Apostle Paul was writing letters in the Mamertinum Prison!

The Mamertinum Prison was the oldest prison in Rome. It is the place where according to tradition, the Apostles Peter and Paul lived their last days before their martyrdom.

The entrance to the prison records the tradition that it is the place where Saint Peter and Saint Paul were imprisoned. The Prison was constructed around the time of the First Sack of Rome by Gauls, about 386 BC. It was originally created as a cistern for a spring in the floor of the second lower level. There were two levels, the lower of which was where prisoners were kept by lowering them through the floor of the upper room. However, eventually a passage between the cistern drain and the Cloaca Maxima was constructed for flushing out dead bodies.

Typically, only higher profile prisoners were kept in the prison; usually foreign commanders who were defeated and became the centerpiece in a Roman triumphant procession. They usually remained incarcerated there until they were paraded and strangled in public, unless they happened to die of natural causes first.

The Mamertinum Prison was the oldest prison in Rome. It is the place where according to tradition, the Apostles Peter and Paul lived their last days before their martyrdom.

It was a maximum-security prison for enemies of Rome awaiting execution. It is situated at the foot of the Capitol Hill and in front of the Roman Forum, a clear symbol of the implacable justice of Rome.

When I stood deep inside this prison, the darkness crept into my mind and the coldness of the walls touched my spirit. While standing there the last time, with my daughters, I read out loud some of the final words of Paul, that would have been written in this prison:

> *For I am already being poured out as a drink offering, and the time of my departure has come. I have fought the good fight, I have finished the course, I have kept the faith; in the future there is reserved for me the crown of righteousness, which the Lord, the righteous Judge, will award to me on that day; and not only to me, but also to all who have loved His appearing* (2 Timothy 4:6-8).

Do these words grab ahold of your faith and pull you forward? Many years earlier, the Saul of Tarsus, took a leap of faith to become the Apostle Paul. He did not know at the beginning where his faith walk would take him. Yet, he could testify at the end he had kept the faith and was about to cross the finish line. Not too far from the Mamertinum Prison, the Roman guards took Paul just outside the city walls and cut his head off. I have stood at the grave the Apostle Paul, inside the Basilica Papale San Paolo fuori le Mura, Rome, Italy.

Over the years, as stated earlier, I have been fortunate to visit scores of famous gravesites of faith-filled leaders worldwide. With this in mind, we will walk together through the grand hall of fame of faith. As we walk together, I will highlight nearly thirty visionary faith leaders, who "heard the promise" given to them and took a leap of faith, believing the invisible path would become visible as they walked it out day by day and year by year. Are you ready for your spirit to be enlightened and for your faith to be enlarged? Here we go!

The Definition of Faith

We live in an age where we have a lot of people who are called music stars and movie stars. We have a lot of people who are called idols — sports idols and music idols. In my humble opinion, we have too many stars and too many idols and not enough heroes.

In Hebrews 11, we will walk and talk with the visionary giants of faith who touched God and transformed their world. Chapter 11 is set up by Chapter 10.

In Hebrews 10:38 we read, "But My righteous one shall live by faith." This is a quotation from Habakkuk 2:4. Habakkuk was perplexed. He lived in a day of violence, a day of degradation, a day of apostasy, a day of danger. He bombarded heaven, pleading with God to give him an answer. He wanted God to explain things so he could get along in life as it was day by day. God said, "Habakkuk, you couldn't understand if I told you what I am up to. You think I am not working? I am working; and Habakkuk, here is your responsibility. You are to live in this uncertain age by faith."

How are we to live? We do not live by explanations; we live by faith. Faith is the spiritual steel and concrete of our lives. "But My righteous one shall live by faith." This is the only way to live.

As a matter of fact, this scripture is quoted three times in the Word of God. I wonder if God is trying to tell us something. I know He is! "My righteous one shall live by faith."

We do not live by explanations; we live by faith.
Faith is the spiritual steel and concrete of our lives.

We all have problems, but there is not a problem we have that does not relate itself someway to faith as the answer. For example, there is worry. All of us at some point worry. I think there is almost a pandemic of worry in our society. Well, why do we worry? Lack of faith. Worry is a mild form of atheism. Worry is a way of saying, "God, this problem is too big for us; or if there's a God at all, you're not able to handle it." Worry is just faith turned inside out. If we are prone to worry, we need to strengthen our faith.

What is faith? Faith is our acceptance of God's acceptance of us. God receives us not because of our own goodness but when we come to Him in faith. Therefore, being justified by faith, we have peace with God through our Lord Jesus Christ.

Why do we have trouble obeying the Word of God? We do not believe it. For example, the Bible says, "'Bring the whole tithe into the storehouse, so that there may be food in My house, and test Me now in this,' says the LORD of hosts, 'if I do not open for you the windows of heaven and pour out for you a blessing until it overflows'" (Malachi 3:10).

There is no one who does not want the heavens to open and God to pour out such blessings we cannot even contain them all. Everyone wants that, but not everyone tithes. Why? Because we do not believe that promise.

What do we do when we pass a wall with a sign on it that says, "WET PAINT—DO NOT TOUCH"? We touch it. Why? We simply do not believe the sign. Why do we disobey? Because we do not believe the Word of God.

WE NEED TO HEED THE PRESENT EXPLANATION OF FAITH (HEBREWS 11:1-2)

The key of faith is the master key that opens all of the doors in the house of salvation. Faith is the only way to live. "My righteous one shall live by faith" (Hebrews 10:38). God describes faith In Hebrews 11:1-2: "Now faith is the assurance of things hoped for, a conviction of things not seen. For by it the men of old gained approval."

It is very important we understand what faith is not before we learn what faith is. Faith is not blind superstition. I am amazed not only at what people will not believe but what they will believe.

Faith is not positive thinking or a feeling of optimism. I like to be around positive thinkers; I like to be around optimists. I do not like to drive behind a person who thinks the light is going to turn red before they get there. By the time they do, it has.

I do not like to be around negative people. I know people who brighten up a room by leaving it. I like to be around optimistic people. Faith and optimism may be in some way tangential, but they are not the same. Faith is not positive thinking or optimism.

Faith is not a leap in the dark. To the contrary, it is stepping into the light. Faith is not faith in faith. Jesus says to "have faith in God" (Mark 11:22); He does not say have faith in faith. Sometimes people say, "just believe"; however, believing will not make it so.

What Is FAITH? The writer of Hebrews tells us that faith has three elements:

The Confidence Required

First, it is a **confidence** that rests in hope. "Now faith is the assurance of things hoped for" (Hebrews 11:1). Why did I call it confidence? Because Hebrews 10:35 explains it as "confidence." This word is akin to substance, and substance is an acceptable translation meaning assurance.

Substance means a confident expectation. Faith is the confident expectation that what we hope for and what is unseen, we already have. Faith is not simply hoping for something but saying, "I have it already."

Faith is the confident expectation that what we hope for and what is unseen, we already have.

The term for "confidence" was used in the language for a title deed. If we had a piece of property or an inheritance that we had not yet seen but had the deed, we would have the assurance of that which we had not yet seen, but we want to have it. Our hope is the unseen. Faith is a confidence. It is not a will-o'-the-wisp sort of a thing; it is substance. "Sub-stand" — something beneath that we stand on. We are not walking around on eggshells and Jell-O. Faith is a substance or confidence.

Furthermore, it is the confidence that rests in hope. The word "hope" does not mean "perhaps" nor does it even mean "wish" or "desire."

Biblically, the word "hope" means rock-ribbed assurance based on divine revelation. For example, the Second Coming of Jesus is called what? The "Blessed Hope."

Is this a "maybe hope?" No! It is rock-ribbed assurance based on the promises of the Word of God.

Now faith, therefore, is the title deed — the confidence that what God has said is true and God will perform it. There is no legitimate faith without hope, and there is no legitimate hope without faith. Faith and hope cannot be separated. Faith is the substance of things hoped for.

The Conviction Realized

Now think not only of confidence but also of **conviction**. Faith is a conviction that sees the invisible. Faith is the evidence of things not seen. The word "evidence" may remind us of a detective looking for evidence, yet this word "evidence" literally means a conviction. Jesus Christ used this same word when He challenged those who were challenging Him: "Which one of you convicts Me of sin?" (John 8:46). Who could convict Him of sin? Of course, no one could. The term has the idea of conviction.

What does it mean if we have faith in our heart with a conviction of something that we have not yet seen? It is an absolute confidence that leads to a conviction even though we have not yet seen it. We do not have to see it for it to be real.

There is an invisible world. That invisible world is electronically all around us right now. There are movies, newscasts, internet, and music in the air; but we are not tuned in all the time.

In Colossians 1:16, we read, "For by Him [Jesus] all things were created, both in the heavens and on earth, visible and invisible." We must never make the mistake of thinking that everything that is real is communicated to us by the five senses. We need to have a sixth sense. There is another world; there is an invisible world.

Now what does faith do? It is the only way to live. Faith enables the believing soul to treat the future as present and the invisible as seen. We can treat the future as present, and we can treat the invisible as seen by faith. We are to live by faith!

The Communication Received

The third element of faith is a **communication** that comes from heaven. "For by it [that is, by faith] the men of old gained approval" (Hebrews 11:2).

"Gained approval" does not mean they made straight A's. As a matter of fact, it does not talk about what they did at all. It talks about what happened to them. They gained approval. God spoke to them out of heaven. It does not deal with their reputation. The good report means they heard from heaven. It is not their reputation but God's revelation that is spoken of in this passage. They were conscience of God's testifying to them.

When we put confidence, conviction, and communication together, we have something in our heart that is glorious and wonderful; and it is called faith. This is the only way to live. We live by faith.

When we put confidence, conviction, and communication together, we have something in our heart that is glorious and wonderful; and it is called faith. This is the only way to live. We live by faith.

When we put these things together, we should understand that faith should not be:

Altered by Appearances

"Faith is the assurance of things hoped for" (Hebrews 11:1). When we live by faith, we live above "see level" — above the level of what we can see. We live in a world that says seeing is believing, but the Bible says believing is seeing.

In John 20:29, we read, "Jesus said to him, 'Because you have seen me, have you believed? Blessed are they who did not see, and yet believed.'" Thomas examined the nail prints in Jesus' hand and the wound in His side. Jesus said, "Blessed are they who did not see, and yet believed."

Speaking of Jesus, Peter said, "And though you have not seen Him, you love Him" (1 Peter 1:8). By faith we see the invisible, so faith should not be altered by appearances. We must not allow any so-called appearance to make a lie out of the Word of God in our hearts and minds.

Fettered by Feelings

Faith is confidence that goes beyond emotions. Our emotions are the shallowest part of our natures. Faith is the deepest work of God, and God does not do the deepest work in the shallowest part. We must not live our lives under the tyranny of emotions—by feelings. It feels good to feel good, and there is nothing wrong with feeling good; yet feelings are fickle. Sometimes we wake up with a dull headache. Sometimes things will happen, and we will get all bent out of shape because of feelings.

Sometimes this happens to preachers. When I am speaking, I always try to look like I am having a good time. However, there are times I do not feel well at all. Maybe I did not get any sleep last night. Maybe I have an upset stomach. Maybe I have a dull headache and go to the pulpit to preach.

There are times we think we are going to have a good service; but then while we are preaching, we get our foot in a lard bucket and cannot get it out. The ushers will not usher. The choir or praise team sounds like a couple of calves dying in a hailstorm.

When we as preachers are in that kind of nightmare situation, we may think God is light-years from the sanctuary. Then heaven comes down. Our emotions had nothing to do with it. Faith is not altered by appearances. Faith is not fettered by our feelings.

Limited by Logic

Faith is not contrary to logic; faith just goes beyond logic.

If I am walking towards a ditch, there will come a point when I must leap over it. Taking it step-by-step in the right direction is logical; however, I will come to a place where logic ends. I need to get to the other side of the ditch. I need to take a leap of faith, but I will cross the ditch only by taking a leap of faith. Faith is rooted in logic, yet faith goes beyond logic. Faith becomes its own best logic.

Faith is not contrary to logic;
faith just goes beyond logic.

The people who were following Jesus became tired and hungry, so He called Philip and said, "How are we going to feed these people? There are 5,000 here."

Philip got out his pocket calculator and said, "Well, it would take a laboring man a year's wages to feed them." Technically, Philip was correct; however, any good atheist could have done the same thing. When Jesus asked Philip, "How we going to feed these people?" He was not asking for information because the Bible says He knew what He would do. He just wanted Philip to learn something about a miracle.

There was a little boy there with a lunch, and Jesus fed the whole multitude with a couple of fish and five loaves.

If we are adding up an equation, we are never going to get the right answer if we leave out one of the elements. What Philip did was leave out God. He figured his numbers without God. Philip was correct logically, but faith is not limited by logic.

WE NEED TO HEAR THE PERSUASIVE EVIDENCE FOR FAITH

There are things that we will never understand apart from faith.

Spiritual Wisdom

"By faith we understand that the worlds were prepared by the word of God, so that what is seen was not made out of things which are visible" (Hebrews 11:3). The visible was made out of the invisible.

In the Bible, God is not explained. God is not argued. God is just simply presented. God must be accepted by faith: "And without faith it is impossible to please Him, for he who comes to God must believe that He is" (Hebrews 11:6).

We are talking about wisdom. The skeptic will say, "Prove there is a God." Do not ever try it. The finite cannot prove the infinite. Merely say to the skeptic, "Well, I can't." He or she will smirk, but it is not over yet.

We then say, "Now, friend, prove there is no God." Of course, the sceptic cannot prove there is no God for he or she accepts there is no God by faith. All people are believers—those who believe in God and those who believe there is no God; however, all are believers.

What is science? Science is the study of phenomena now existing. God asked Job: "Where were you when I laid the foundation of the earth?" (38:4).

9

There were no scientists then. There was no way they could explain the universe. How do we understand it? By faith. They say, "Well, that takes a lot of belief." I say it takes less belief than to believe that nothing times nobody equals everything.

No wonder the Bible says, "The fool has said in his heart, 'There is no God'" (Psalm 14:1). God is the supreme fact, and the man who denies it is the supreme fool. For a scientist to go into the laboratory to try to prove God would be like tearing a piano apart to try to find a tune. Faith is required to understand the origin and the order of the universe.

Spiritual Worship

Look again at Hebrews 11:6: "And without faith it is impossible to please Him [worship is pleasing to God] for the one who comes to God must believe that He is."

We might be tempted to say, "God, prove yourself to me; and I'll serve You." God is not going to prove Himself to us. He is not under any obligation to prove Himself to us. Faith is not a response to proof. That is what Thomas demanded. Jesus responded, "Because you have seen me, have you now believed? Blessed are they who did not see, and yet believed" (John 20:29).

What is faith? Faith is the heart's response to the character of God.

What is faith? Faith is the heart's response to the character of God. When Jesus Christ came to this earth, He left all the splendor and all the glory of heaven. When He came to this earth, He came in a very ordinary, nondescript way.

"He had no form or majesty that we should look at him, and no beauty that we should desire him" (Isaiah 53:2 ESV). What did Jesus look like? Like the paintings that the masters painted? Like He just stepped out of a beauty salon? If that is the way He looked, then why did Judas have to point Him out so they could take Him away?

There is no beauty that we should desire Him. However, there was in Him all the glory, all the serenity, all the dignity, all the majesty, all the purity, all the character of God in human flesh. He did not come down to this earth in a jeweled chariot nor was he born in a palace. He was born in a stable. When He did miracles, they were not publicity stunts. He would often say, "Don't tell anybody about this" (Matthew 8:4, 9:30; Mark 7:36; Luke 8:56).

When our eye is right, it responds to light. When our ear is right, it responds to sound. When our heart is right, it responds to God; and that response is called F-A-I-T-H.

Faith is the heart's response to the character of God. When our eye is right, it responds to light. When our ear is right, it responds to sound. When our heart is right, it responds to God; and that response is called F-A-I-T-H.

Spiritual Wealth

Look again in Hebrews 11:6. "And without faith it is impossible to please Him, for he who comes to God must believe that He is . . ." now watch this ". . . and that He is a rewarder of those who seek Him."

How do we seek Him? By faith. Jesus said, "It shall be done to you according to your faith" (Matthew 9:29). Jesus did not say be it unto to us by our fame, feeling, future, fortune, friends, or fate according to our faith.

Faith is the medium of exchange in the kingdom of heaven. If we pray without faith, we do not receive an answer. "All things for which you pray and ask, believe that you have received them, and they will be granted" (Mark 11:24). Pray, believe we will receive. Pray in doubt, we do without.

God is a rewarder of those who diligently seek Him. Faith is the dynamic of spiritual wealth. How spiritually strong are we? How wealthy are we? What kind of reserves do we have? It is all according to our faith.

We will walk with the champions of faith. We are going to live by faith, and we will not live without faith. We can exist without faith, but we will never live without faith. Jesus said, "I came that they may have life" (John 10:10). We put our faith where God has put our sins—on Jesus Christ.

2

The Dedication of Faith

In Hebrews 11:4, we read: "By faith Abel offered to God a better sacrifice than Cain, through which he obtained the testimony that he was righteous, God testifying about his gifts, and through faith, though he is dead, he still speaks."

Abel, being dead, still speaks today. He preached his own funeral. What we see in Abel is a shadow of the crucifixion of our Lord and Savior Jesus Christ.

The Old Testament is a book of shadows that points to New Testament truths. For example, Colossians 2:17 tells us that the Old Testament is a shadow of things to come. A shadow must have light, and it must have something to shine upon. The light is the Old Testament scripture, and the body that the shadow shines upon is the Lord Jesus Christ.

The Old Testament is a book of shadows that points to New Testament truths. For example, Colossians 2:17 tells us that the Old Testament is a shadow of things to come. A shadow must have light, and it must have something to shine upon. The light is the Old Testament scripture, and the body that the shadow shines upon is the Lord Jesus Christ.

The angle of the light determines the sharpness of the shadow. In the early morning, the shadows are not really clear; they are somewhat distorted. By midmorning, the shadows become clearer. At high noon, there are no shadows at all. In the Old Testament, we have shadows pointing toward the Lord Jesus Christ. However, when Calvary came in the New Testament, then it is high noon. What we are going to see in this story of Abel is the beginning of these shadows that are pointing to the coming of our Lord and Savior Jesus Christ.

In Genesis 4:1-8, we read the story of Adam and Eve, obviously the first humans on the earth. "Now the man had relations with his wife Eve, and she conceived and gave birth to Cain, and she said, 'I have gotten a manchild with the help of the Lord.' Again, she gave birth to his brother Abel" (vv.1-2).

"Abel was a keeper of the flocks, but Cain was a tiller of the ground" (v.2). One was a shepherd, and one was a farmer. "So it came about in the course of time that Cain brought an offering to the LORD of the fruit of the ground. Abel, on his part also brought of the firstlings of his flock and of their fat potions. And the LORD had regard for Abel and for his offering; but for Cain and for his offering He had no regard. So Cain became very angry and his countenance fell" (vv.3-5).

What we have here is a shadow of the cross in the offerings that Cain and Abel made. Two offerings: Cain offered the fruit of the ground; he offered vegetables to the Lord. Abel offered a slain lamb of the firstlings of the flock to the Lord. The Bible says that God accepted the offering of

Abel not the offering of Cain. We are going to learn some powerful contrasts from Genesis 4 and Hebrews 11.

WE NEED TO LEARN THE CONTRAST IN THEIR WORSHIP

They are young men worshipping God. One is worshipping in Spirit and in truth; the other is worshipping by His own ingenuity. In Hebrews 11:4, we read, "By faith Abel offered to God a better sacrifice."

What was the difference? All religions are not of the same value. In the world today, we are looked upon as politically incorrect if we do not put our arms around everybody else and say, "Your religion is just as good as mine." It is not true. God had respect unto Abel's offering but not unto Cain's.

We divide Christianity into thousands of different denominations and fellowships, yet there are only two religions in the entire world: true and false. There is the religion of grace and the religion of works.

All people, particularly Christians, are supposed to be tolerant today. I believe in tolerance in some areas but not in tolerance that sacrifices truth. Furthermore, there is nothing today so intolerant as the intolerance against those who say there is a fixed standard of right and wrong. There is a true religion, and there is a false religion. Our world does not need more religion. It has too much religion. This world needs Jesus!

There are approximately 9,900 different religions. Some of these religions have many gods. The Hindus have 300 million gods.

We divide Christianity into thousands of different denominations and fellowships, yet there are only two religions in the entire world: true and false. There is the religion of grace and the religion of works. There is the religion of Cain and the religion of Abel.

Hebrews 11:4 states, "By faith Abel offered to God a better sacrifice than Cain." What was the way of Cain? The way of good works. It was salvation by his own effort. He was a tiller of the ground. God said, "By the sweat of your face you shall eat bread" (Genesis 3:19). Cain offered what was his own toil, sweat, and effort when he came to God with this offering of vegetables and fruits.

No doubt, there was fragrant fruit, lovely flowers, and tasty vegetation. Cain offered all of this to God because he had been out there plowing the ground. The Bible says, "Cursed is the ground because of you; in toil you will eat of it all the days of your life" (Genesis 3:17). Cain offered his own work to God.

"Woe to them! For they have gone the way of Cain" (Jude 11). What is the way of Cain? It is to try to save ourselves by our own good works rather than by the grace of God. It represents culture rather than Calvary.

"Without shedding of blood there is no forgiveness" (Hebrews 9:22). There is no salvation apart from the shedding of blood. What did Cain offer? Vegetables.

People may say, "We have our own religion." So did Cain. Others may say, "I'm looking for a religion that suits me." So did Cain. Cain died and went to hell. "Woe to them! For they have gone the way of Cain." Most of the people in the world do not need religion. They need to turn from religion to Jesus Christ. A lot of people are egomaniacs strutting to hell, thinking they are too good to be lost.

What did Abel offer? The firstling of his flock. "Abel, on his part also brought of the firstlings of his flock" (Genesis 4:4). Abel's offering was based on a blood atonement.

I said previously that people need to turn from religion to Jesus Christ. Religion is what sinful people do for a holy God. The Gospel is the good news of what a holy God has already done for sinful man. "By faith Abel offered to God a better sacrifice than Cain" (Hebrews 11:4).

Religion is what sinful people do for a holy God.
The Gospel is the good news of what a holy God has
already done for sinful man.

Where did Abel get the idea of bringing a blood offering to Almighty God? It was just a shadow of the Lord Jesus Christ. When Adam and Eve sinned against God, they tried to clothe themselves with fig leaves. What is that? The fruit of the ground. What did God do? God came into the Garden of Eden and made them coats of animal skin. How did they get coats of skin? Blood had to be shed. Where did Abel learn the idea that it takes the shedding of blood for remission? He learned it from his parents.

Abel was a prophet of God. "For this reason also the wisdom of God said, 'I will send to them prophets and apostles, and some of them they will kill and some they will persecute, so that the blood of all the prophets, shed since the foundation of the world, may be charged against this generation, from the blood of Abel to the blood of Zechariah" (Luke 11:49-51). Abel is called a prophet of God. Abel was a martyr who died for his faith.

Adam and Eve had two sons: one a martyr; one a murderer. Abel was a prophet. He understood the Word of God. We ask, "Did he really understand about the Lord Jesus Christ?" In Acts 10:43, we read, "Of Him all the prophets bear witness." Now if Abel was a prophet — and he was, the Bible also says, "that through His name [the name of Jesus] everyone who believes in Him receives forgiveness of sins."

Just outside the gates of the Garden of Eden was a man named Abel who offered a spotless lamb that is a picture, a prophecy, of Jesus who was to come. Isn't the Bible a wonderful book? Do not get the idea that these people are just plowing with sticks and did not know anything. The blood of the Lord Jesus Christ was not an afterthought. It was not an emergency action.

People say, "Christ is my example." No, He has to be our Savior. We are not saved by learning lessons from the life of Christ but by receiving life from the death of Christ.

God had the redemption by blood in His heart before He ever made the world. "All who dwell on the earth will worship him, everyone whose name has not been written from the foundation of the world in the book of life of the Lamb who has been slain" (Revelation 13:8). Jesus was in the heart and mind of God from the foundation of the world. Before He placed this world into space, God had redemption by blood in His mind.

People say, "Christ is my example." No, He has to be our Savior. We are not saved by learning lessons from the life of Christ but by receiving life from the death of Christ. God says when I see the what? The blood . . . I will pass over you. Without the shedding of blood is no remission of sins.

Throughout the Old Testament, God was pointing toward Calvary. All of the shadows, types, and lessons were leading to Calvary. The river of blood begins in the Garden of Eden and ends at Calvary. When Jesus bows His head and dies, His blood redeems the world.

WE NEED TO LISTEN TO THE CONSEQUENCES OF THEIR WORSHIP

"But for Cain and for his offering He had no regard. So Cain became very angry" (Genesis 4:5). In plain English, he was ticked off; He was angry. "And his countenance fell. Then the LORD said to Cain, 'Why are you angry? And why has your countenance fallen?'" (Genesis 4:5b-6).

God did not have any respect for Cain and all his good intentions and all his good works. The difference between Cain and Abel is the difference between righteousness and unrighteousness.

No doubt some people think that God should have said to Cain, "Well, you tried, and you don't get a hundred percent for your grade on the test; but I'm going to grade on the curve." God does not grade on the curve. God does not just give an "A" for effort. God will not overlook sin.

There are others who say, "Well, God's too good to punish sin." However, God is too good NOT to punish sin. If we had to go through all the lectionaries and dictionaries of the world to get a word that would describe God in one word, that would, of course, be impossible. However, if we had to choose one word above all other words, it would be the word "holy." Holy means that God is a holy God. God never has, never can, and never will overlook sin. If God overlooked sin, God would topple from His throne of holiness. God would cease to be a righteous God.

The Apostle Paul says, "For all have sinned and fall short of the glory of God" (Romans 3:23).

What is the definition of sin? Coming short of the glory of God. The gap between the glory of God and us — that is sin.

"Being justified as a gift by His grace through the redemption which is in Christ Jesus; whom God displayed publicly as a propitiation in His blood through faith. This was to demonstrate His righteousness, because in the forbearance of God He passed over the sins previously committed" (Romans 3:24-25).

Our sin will be pardoned in Christ or punished in hell. When a guilty man is acquitted, the judge is condemned. If God were to let sin go unpunished, God himself would become a sinner. We are saved by grace.

What does the word "propitiation" mean? It means "satisfaction." Nothing can satisfy the righteousness of God — the holiness of God — except the shed blood of the Lord Jesus Christ.

Our sin will be pardoned in Christ or punished in hell. When a guilty man is acquitted, the judge is condemned. If God were to let sin go unpunished, God himself would become a sinner. We are saved by grace.

Abel was killed by Cain, but he did not cease to exist. "Though he is dead, he still speaks" (Hebrews 11:4). For the child of God, death is not a period but a comma. Abel still lives on.

WE NEED TO LOOK AT THE CONFLICT OF THEIR WORSHIP

"But for Cain and for his offering He had no regard. So Cain became very angry and his countenance fell. Then the Lord said to Cain, 'Why are you angry? And why has your countenance fallen? If you do well, will not your countenance be lifted up? And if you do not do well, sin is crouching at the door" (Genesis 4:5-7).

Sin is like an animal crouching at the door. God says, "If you do what I tell you to do, you'll do well." God is no respecter of persons. "Sin is crouching at the door; and its desire is for you" (Genesis 4:7). Sin is ready to devour us.

"But you must master it" (Genesis 4:7). That is, if you will do right. "Cain told Abel his brother. And it came about when they were in the field, that Cain rose up against Abel his brother and killed him" (Genesis 4:8).

The first murder was over religion. A religious crowd crucified the Lord Jesus Christ. Adam and Eve had two sons: one was a murderer; the other was a martyr.

Why did Cain kill Abel? Because his heart was not right with God. No man can be wrong with God and right with his brother. False religion is characterized by force. Our faith is characterized by love.

Take a moment to think about what is happening in the world today. We think of the people who are being murdered in the name of religion. Perhaps Cain was too refined to offer a blood sacrifice, but he was not too refined to plunge a knife or whatever into his brother's bosom.

Jesus said:

These things I have spoken to you so that you may be kept from stumbling. They will make you outcasts from the synagogue, but an hour is coming for everyone who kills you to think that he is offering service to God. These things they will do because they have not known the Father or Me. But these things I have spoken to you, so that when their hour comes, you may remember that I told you of them. These things I did not say to you at the beginning, because I was with you. (John 16:1-4)

The word "martyr" and the word "witness" are the same word in the Greek language. Death does not make martyrs; it just simply reveals them. What is our true faith? True faith is never based upon force.

Islam is an idea like Communism is an idea, and you cannot kill an idea with a bullet or a bomb. The only thing that will kill an idea is a better idea. The greatest idea is the gospel of our Lord and Savior Jesus Christ. I believe there are times when we need to go to war but not to spread the Christian faith. We spread the Christian faith with love.

Dr. Ravi Zacharias wrote:

> The teaching of Jesus is clear. No one ought to be compelled to become a Christian. This sets the Christian faith drastically apart from Islam. In no country where the Christian faith is the faith of the majority is it illegal to propagate another faith. There is no country in the world that I know of where the renunciation of one's Christian faith puts one in danger of being hunted down by the powers of the state. Yet, there are numerous Islamic countries where it is against the law to publicly proclaim the gospel of Jesus Christ. And where a Muslim who renounces faith in Islam to believe in anything else risks death (Synergize 2016 Conference, Orlando, Florida).

That is the difference between true religion and false religion. The salvation of Jesus Christ is by grace through faith based on the shed blood of the Lord Jesus Christ.

Cain slew Abel. Cain was the loser, not Abel. He won the martyr's crown. There are two religions in the world:

the true and the false. The difference between these two religions is the difference between heaven and hell.

A person may say, "I believe there is another way other than the shed blood of the Lord Jesus Christ." If there is another way other than the shed blood of the Lord Jesus Christ, then why did Jesus die? The Bible says if righteousness comes by the law, Christ is dead in vain. If a man, a woman, a boy, or a girl could be saved any other way, then Calvary was a blunder.

There is a red river of blood that flows through all the Bible. What can wash away my sin? Nothing but the blood of Jesus. What can make me whole again? Nothing but the blood of Jesus.

Why did God let Jesus die on that cross if there was another way? Why not take the other way? Why did He allow His Son to die in agony in blood if there was another way? There is no other way. "Without shedding of blood there is no forgiveness" (Hebrews 9:22). There is a red river of blood that flows through all the Bible. What can wash away my sin? Nothing but the blood of Jesus. What can make me whole again? Nothing but the blood of Jesus.

If you please the Lord, it does not matter who you displease. Yet, if you displease the Lord, it does not matter who you please.

3

The Departure Through Faith

Enoch is an unusual character who appears three times in the Word of God and is an important figure in studying the Second Coming. In Genesis 5:21-24, we are told of his birth, that he walked with God, that he gave birth to a son, and that he was raptured into heaven. In Hebrews 11:5, we read that he pleased God and that he was translated into heaven. In Jude 14-15, we learn that he preached to the ungodly of his day and warned them of the coming of the Lord in judgment:

> And about these also Enoch, in the seventh gener-ation from Adam, prophesied, saying, "Behold, the Lord came with many thousands of His holy ones, to execute judgment upon all, and to convict all the ungodly of all their ungodly deeds which they have done in an ungodly way, and of all the harsh things which ungodly sinners have spoken against him" (Jude 14-15).

In these two short verses, Jude refers to the Book of Genesis and what Enoch saw concerning the Second Coming of Jesus as well as what he saw six thousand years later about the Lord's coming "with many thousands of His holy ones, to execute judgment upon all."

In Enoch's day, there were two kinds of people on the earth—the descendants of Seth and the descendants of Cain. The descendants of Cain lived for this world. They are found in Genesis 4 in the marketplaces and cities of art, science, and industry. They lived a life of "doing man's thing" to build a pain-free, pleasure-filled society.

The descendants of Seth did not live for this world but for the things of God and the world to come. Genesis 5 does not take us to the marketplace but to the morgue. In fact, throughout the chapter, we read over and over, "And he died...and he died...and he died..."

Satan had told Adam and Eve, "You will surely not die!"
(Genesis 3:4); but God had told them that if they broke
the commandment of the Lord, they would die.
Every time we see "and he died," we are reminded
that the devil is a liar.

Satan had told Adam and Eve, "You will surely not die!" (Genesis 3:4); but God had told them that if they broke the commandment of the Lord, they would die. Every time we see "and he died," we are reminded that the devil is a liar. Even though Genesis began in a garden, it ended in a grave. It started with a beginning but ended with a burial. Genesis ended with Joseph's dying and being buried. The point is that when man sins, man dies.

The Bible makes two comments of the Sethites that it does not make of the Canaanites. Of the godly people in the line of Seth, we read, "he lived" and "he died." In between the deaths, there was always life. The Word never says the Canaanites "lived" because they chose a mere existence on the planet, not the abundant life that God provided. The Canaanites were always dying; whereas, even though the Bible records deaths, we read of God's people that "they lived."

We also never find in Genesis 4-5 that God recorded any of the Canaanite deaths as precious in the sight of God. Any time a child of God passes away, however, God makes a record and knows the passing of every saint of God who is precious to Him.

Enoch was the seventh from Adam. Instead of a tomb, he experienced translation. Instead of death, he experienced departure. Instead of a grave, he made it to glory. The life of Enoch is a type of the Second Coming of the Lord Jesus Christ.

The characteristics of the man named Enoch had several similarities with his day, time, and life as compared with our day, time, and lives.

OUR FAITH PREPARES US FOR SURROUNDING GLOOM

At Enoch's birth, Adam was 622 years old, Seth was 492 years old, and Jared was 162 years old. As a matter of fact, Enoch, the great-great-great-great-grandson of Adam lived alongside Adam for 308 years. Enoch was 65 years old when he left the earth, just a young man. The age of 65 for that period of history was just a child because people then were living above 900 years; but because man sinned, man's life was shortened and he eventually experienced death.

An Age of Permissiveness

Enoch lived in a time of social permissiveness. There were no restraints on crime, lawlessness flourished, and immorality was rampant. Marriage was only a convenience, not a commitment. Polygamy was the lifestyle of the day. It sounds familiar to our day!

An Age of Presumptuousness

It was an age of presumptuousness when men were trying to create their own paradise based on science rather than following or obeying the Lord. Secularism was the rule of the day. The people were occupied with the necessities of life, eating, and drinking. They were also bent toward the niceties of life, marrying, and giving in marriage.

People were interested in the present world more than the world to come, in gold more than God, in silver more than the Savior, money more than the Messiah, and in the kingdom now more than the Kingdom to come.

Secularism was as much an influence then as it is today. People were interested in the present world more than the world to come, in gold more than God, in silver more than the Savior, money more than the Messiah, and in the kingdom now more than the Kingdom to come. In addition, it was a day of spiritualism. It was a time when ancient myths were forged. The love stories of the gods became so prominent they influenced the religions of the Greeks. The occult was prevalent, and occult practices that were started then are still practiced today.

An Age of Progressiveness

Scientifically, Enoch's day was an age of progressiveness when men began to build great cities that flourished. Populations exploded. It was an age of technological and scientific sophistication, much like our own today; but the people had no heart for God.

Enoch lived in surrounding gloom. It was during this time that Enoch was translated from earth to heaven. He did not see a tomb, but he did see the face of God. We are living in a day and hour much like his when we are going to be caught away and will also see the face of our God. As we look around, the signs of the times tell us that Jesus is coming soon. The signs of His coming have already been fulfilled!

OUR FAITH PROVIDES SAVING GRACE

Enoch walked with Almighty God and had a righteous relationship with Him. Enoch knew God and God knew him. The Bible tells us that Enoch was blessed when God took him up without experiencing death, but he was also blessed on earth with new birth. He "begat" Methuselah who lived long enough to see the end of this permissive age due to the great flood.

Enoch experienced the saving grace of God. Every day we can thank God for the grace He has bestowed upon us. Not only did Enoch experience the simple, saving grace of God, but he also knew how to walk with God. We need to learn how to walk with God if we are going to be ready when the Lord Jesus returns. Those who walk with God are those who are going to be with God. Those who are half-hearted, apathetic, cold, carnal, critical, and could care less are not walking with God. If we are going to be ready when the Lord Jesus returns, we must learn how to walk with God day in and day out.

OUR FAITH PERCEIVES THE SIMPLE GOSPEL

Enoch had a simple gospel to share. The gospel he shared with his lips was the same gospel he preached with his life. When we are walking with God, our lips and our life must coincide. What we say must line up with the way we really are.

The Force of His Faith

Enoch is an example of one who both professed and lived the life of a believer. Not only did he know how to walk with God, but he also showed others how to walk with God. We read of the force of his faith as Hebrews 11:5 states that he was "pleasing to God."

He lived a life that was pleasing to God — a God-fearing, God-worshipping, and God-serving life. There must be a distinction in the life and walk of those who have experienced the grace of God.

In some circles, it is socially acceptable for Christians to live immoral lives, to live a compromising lifestyle. Sometimes it is very difficult to tell the difference between the lost and the saved, yet no one doubted the life of Enoch.

He lived a life that was pleasing to God — a God-fearing, God-worshipping, and God-serving life. There must be a distinction in the life and walk of those who have experienced the grace of God. When we are walking with God, we are not walking with the world. When we are walking with God, there is a difference in our lives.

The Forthrightness of His Faith

To the people of his day and time, Enoch said, "Behold, the Lord came with many thousands of His holy ones, to execute judgment upon all" (Jude 14-15). Enoch did not hesitate to share the gospel and judgments of God with others. We also can share the simple gospel that Jesus saves, heals, and fills with the Holy Spirit. We can tell about the soon coming of Christ and the judgments of God on those who refuse to accept Christ as Savior.

The Fundamentals of His Faith

Enoch learned the fundamentals of the faith: "Without faith it is impossible to please Him" (Hebrews 11:6). We know Enoch had faith because we know he was "pleasing to God."

As Christians and believers, we also can learn to exemplify faith. "Without faith it is impossible to please Him" means just that! There must be a stretching, a building up, and an increasing of our faith. To build our faith, we must get into God's Word and into prayer.

Enoch learned that if he were going to please God, he would have to have faith. He got faith by walking with God. The more we walk with God, the more faith in God we have.

There is a great *impossibility*. Enoch learned that if he were going to please God, he would have to have faith. He got faith by walking with God. The more we walk with God, the more faith in God we have. The better we get to know God, the more faith in God we have. The more time we spend with our creator, the more we trust our creator.

There was a grand *imperative.* "For he who comes to God must believe that He is and that He is a rewarder of those who seek Him" (Hebrews 11:6). Many in the "Great Hall of Faith" of Hebrews 11 did tremendous exploits. Toward the end of the chapter, we read of others who experienced persecution, pressures, and problems; but they never gave up their faith. They died believing. As long as we serve Christ, we constantly and continually build our faith in Almighty God. The more we walk with God, the greater our faith will become.

In order to be ready for the Second Coming of the Lord Jesus Christ, we must experience the saving grace of the Lord Jesus Christ. The more we walk with God, the more faith we will have in God.

OUR FAITH PLANS FOR SUDDEN GLORY

"Enoch was taken up so that he would not see death" (Hebrews 11:5). Enoch was not only marked, but he was also missed. Genesis 5:24 states, "He was not" while Hebrews 11:5 states, "He was not found." People went out looking for him and could not find him.

People will miss the believers on the day the Church is caught away, the day when God will reach down for His church and for a champion. He will not only reach for a bride but for His body. When He takes us, people will know we are gone and will miss us.

People went everywhere looking for Enoch, but Enoch could not be found because God took him. There is soon coming a day when God will reach down and take us all away to be with Him in glory. It is going to be the greatest day of our lives when the captain of the conquerors, the head of the heroes, the leader of the legislators, the Prince of princes, the King of kings, the Lord of lords, and the

Master of the mighty comes back and we are raptured from this earth to spend eternity with our Lord.

Just as Enoch experienced sudden glory, we will experience sudden glory. Just as Enoch was transformed, we will be transformed. In that day we will exchange our mortality for His immortality. We will lay aside our corruption for His incorruption. There will be no more disease, discouragement, depression, or devil to plague the bodies of God's people. There will be no more pressures, problems, pain, or agony. On that day, we will experience sudden glory. Our bodies will be changed as we shall see Him as He is. It is going to be the greatest day of our lives when Jesus takes us all away!

There will be no more disease, discouragement, depression, or devil to plague the bodies of God's people.

There is coming sudden glory. We are living in that day and time. Just as Enoch experienced sudden glory, before we realize it, our bodies will be changed and we shall go to be with the Lord.

More than a century ago, a mother was tucking her little girl into bed when the young daughter asked, "Mother, can you tell me the greatest day of your life?"

The mother thought for just a second and then said, "Honey, I can tell you the greatest day in my life. I remember it as though it were yesterday. As you know, my father fought in the Civil War. My mother and I were sitting on the porch one warm day several months after we had received word that he had been killed in battle. I was playing with my kitten as my mother and I were sitting in the swing. Ever since Mother lost Father, she had missed him very much.

33

"On that day, we saw someone coming down the long, dusty road that ran in front of our small house. My mother said, 'Oh, there's a man coming down the road.'

"A moment later she said to me, 'Sweetheart, I declare that man kind of favors your father.'

"After another moment, she said, 'Darling, I really do think that is your father!'

The greatest day of our lives will be when our commander in chief, the Lord Jesus, comes back for us. We will look into the face of Jesus and see the scars of battle He suffered for us.

"At that, she leaped off the porch, ran across the front yard, through the picket fence gate, and down the road toward the open arms of my father. I was right behind her. I jumped for my father's arms as I often had done as a little girl when he would swing me. However, all I found was an empty coat sleeve. I saw the scars of battle on my daddy's face, and I saw that his body was bruised from the war. I saw that he was missing an arm from the war he'd fought.

"With tears in her eyes, the mother said to her daughter, "Little girl, the greatest day in my life was when your daddy came back home."

The greatest day of our lives will be when our commander in chief, the Lord Jesus, comes back for us. We will look into the face of Jesus and see the scars of battle He suffered for us. The only manmade things we will find in heaven will be the scars on the Lord's body. We will recognize that He fought a terrible battle to save us from our sins. The greatest day of our lives is yet to come when Jesus comes back to take us home to be with Him!

4

The Deluge of Faith

"By faith Noah, being warned by God about things not yet seen, in reverence prepared an ark for the salvation of his household, by which he condemned the world, and became an heir of the righteousness which is according to faith" (Hebrews 11:7).

The Titanic set sail in 1912, the same year my grandmother was born. It was coined as being unsinkable, but about the only thing it ever really did was sink. It was filled with the lavish splendor of ballrooms and theatres and beauty salons and tennis courts and sauna baths and much more. The sinking of the Titanic is a great object lesson for our age.

The Titanic was marked by **confidence**. How confident they were! The engineers said because of the watertight compartments on the Titanic, it was unsinkable. If one compartment would leak, then another would keep it up. Sir J. Bruce Ismay, the White Star Chairman of the Board, said: "I cannot imagine any condition that would cause the ship to founder. I cannot imagine any disaster happening to this vessel. Modern shipbuilding has gone beyond that." Every sailor on board said confidently, "It cannot sink." One sailor said flippantly, "Even God couldn't sink this ship."

One sailor said flippantly,
"Even God couldn't sink this ship."

The Titanic was also marked by **carelessness**. People were not thinking about the ship sinking. They were all just having a good time. Mrs. Irene Harris, one of the passengers on the ship, said, "We were out on a lark and revelry was the keynote. The weather was superb. The comfort and luxury aboard were all that had been promised. The days passed too quickly. I felt as if I could go on until the end of time. And those who were keeping watch on the ship, every now and then would sound the hour and they would say, 'All's well, and the lights are burning brightly.'"

Yet on April 14, 1912, as this ship was gliding along on an ebony sea as smooth as silk, there was no moon out, but it was a clear night with the stars lighting the heavens. The ship was moving along very carelessly thinking she was an unsinkable ship.

Moving along at 22 knots, the Titanic was marked by **calamity** because on that night at 11:40 p.m., it hit an iceberg. A 300-foot gash was ripped along the side of the ship. One of the passengers on board said it felt as if someone had taken a giant finger and drawn it along the side of that ship. Suddenly, one compartment, two compartments, three compartments, four compartments, and five water-tight compartments were cut open. No alarms sounded at first. For those who were a little frightened, a soothing word of assurance was given that there was no danger, so they went right on with their amusements.

At 12:45 a.m., a rocket was fired, the first of eight attempts to signal another ship for help. However, all of these attempts were futile for no one saw the rockets that were fired into the air. Finally, it became apparent that they should board the lifeboats. Consequently, an urgent call went down through the corridors—women and children first. By 1:30 a.m., that dream cruise had turned into a terrible nightmare. There were over two thousand persons on board and only lifeboats for half that many. People were crowding into the lifeboats. Men even disguised themselves as women and tried to get on to the lifeboats! The lifeboats that could be filled were filled, and they drifted away from the Titanic and got in a circle around it.

One observer said it was like relatives standing around the deathbed of a dying loved one. They watched the ship as it began to fill with water and slivered into a watery grave. The impossible had happened! The Titanic had sunk! Only a handful of survivors made it!

When the Titanic set sail, there were all classes of people on board: upper class, middle class, and lower class. After the ship sank, there were only two classes of people recorded in New York City: saved and lost.

What a stark contrast between the sailing of the Titanic under Captain Smith and the sailing of the good ship grace under Captain Noah. We are going to learn life lessons from Noah's ship, the unsinkable ship of faith.

WE NEED TO RECOGNIZE NOAH AND HIS FAITH

"By faith Noah, being warned by God about things not yet seen, in reverence prepared an ark" (Hebrews 11:7). Noah prepared this ark by faith—a **working faith**. Read carefully these words: "By faith, Noah . . . prepared an ark."

37

His faith led him to do something. James 2:26 states that "faith without works is dead." When we studied Abel who offered the proper sacrifice, his faith was a **worshipping faith**. When we studied Enoch who walked with God, his faith was a **walking faith**. It is a beautiful order that God is giving us. We worship, walk, and work for God.

*It is a beautiful order that God is giving us.
We worship, walk, and work for God.*

Noah could have said that he had faith; but had he not built the ark, he would have had no faith. He showed his faith by his works. Noah built the ark with concrete evidence of his faith. We cannot say we have faith in God if our faith in God is not enough faith to cause us to study the Bible, if our faith is not enough faith to cause us to worship Him, if our faith is not enough faith to get us to go to church, if our faith is not enough faith to get us into the baptistery, or if our faith is not enough faith to transform our lives! One of these days a lot of people are going to die and go to hell because their faith was not real! Faith without works is dead! Noah's faith was a working faith.

Moreover, Noah's faith was a **warning faith**. "By faith Noah, being warned by God" (Hebrews 11:7). God had spoken to Noah. Noah did not just decide, "Well, I think I'll build an ark because I want to have faith to build an ark." We cannot have faith for anything that God does not first of all speak to us about. Faith is not merely positive thinking. It is not faith in faith or faith in ourselves. It is faith in God! All true faith is rooted in the Word of God: "So faith comes from hearing, and hearing by the word of Christ" (Romans 10:17).

Before we can have any kind of faith, God must first of all speak. If we do learn anything else in this series of lessons on faith, we must learn this: True faith, real faith, lasting faith, biblical faith is rooted in the Word of God. We must hear the voice of God before we can have faith.

Furthermore, true faith can **wait** on God. Noah prepared an ark, but it was 120 years before the flood came. Noah waited all of that time for the fulfillment of the promise. Real faith waits on God. Faith rests in the promises of God. Sometimes faith does not see the fulfillment right away. Our faith needs to be a working faith, a warning faith, and a waiting faith.

We should get our eyes off the crowd and on Christ!
Real faith is faith that can stand alone.
Real faith does not depend upon appearances.

Do we have the kind of faith that gets hold of God and will not let go of Him until the answer comes because He has spoken and cannot lie? Noah's faith was a faith that could stand alone. The time is coming when those who want to kill Christians will think they are doing God a favor. We will have to be willing to stand alone in this world that crucified our Lord and would be willing to crucify Him again. Yet in a godless age like that, Noah stood for God and his faith did not waver.

We should get our eyes off the crowd and on Christ! Real faith is faith that can stand alone. Real faith does not depend upon appearances. "By faith Noah, being warned by God about **things not yet seen**" (Hebrews 11:7). There is no evidence that it had ever rained up until this point. To the contrary, the Bible tells us that "a mist used to rise from the earth and water the whole surface of the ground" (Genesis 2:6). There had been no rainbow up until this time.

Noah did not say to God, "Now, God, you say it's going to rain. Just put a few clouds out there, let me feel a few drops, and then I'll believe." Faith is the evidence of things not seen. Noah had not seen these things. All he had was the Word of God! God said it, and that settled it! We are not to walk by sight; we are to walk by faith! It may have been a cloudless day when God gave this announcement to Noah; nonetheless, he obeyed God.

WE NEED TO REALIZE NOAH AND HIS FEAR

"By faith Noah, being warned by God about things not yet seen, in reverence prepared an ark" (Hebrews 11:7). Noah was moved with fear, and he prepared an ark. Noah resolved that he was not going to drown. He resolved that he was going to save his own life.

When God created us, He put within us an instinct called "self-preservation." Everybody is motivated by fear. Doctors use fear to motivate us by saying, "You better lose some weight, or you'll have a heart attack."

Insurance people use fear to motivate us by saying, "You'd better drive safely or you'll have an accident." We do a lot of things simply out of fear! We wear an overcoat because we are afraid that we will catch a cold. When we cross the road, we look both ways because we are afraid that we will be hit by a vehicle. There is nothing wrong with this kind of fear; it is just plain common sense.

We are motivated by fear every day in hundreds of ways except in the greatest way—the spiritual way! Our greatest danger is not the danger of being hit by a vehicle or starving to death or catching a cold. Jesus told of our greatest danger: "Do not fear those who kill the body but are unable to kill the soul; but rather fear Him who is able to destroy both soul and body in hell" (Matthew 10:28). Our greatest danger, our supreme danger, should be that one day we will stand before God unpardoned, unforgiven, and uncleansed!

Some people accuse preachers of using fear to motivate people. I would rather frighten people into heaven than tranquilize them into hell! There is something to be warned about. "The fear of the Lord is the beginning of wisdom" (Proverbs 1:7). Are we ready to meet God? Do we know that we are saved? If not, we ought to be motivated like Noah was — by faith and by fear.

WE NEED TO REMEMBER NOAH AND HIS FORESIGHT

Noah "prepared an ark" (Hebrews 11:7). He made preparation, he had foresight, and he did not wait until it started to rain before starting to build the ark.

What is God telling us about Noah's faith? Like Noah, we should get ready! One of these days it will be too late. Had Noah not made preparation before the flood, it would have been too late when the flood came.

Noah moved with fear! He had some foresight! It is amazing how many people have wisdom about the future in so many things but no wisdom when it comes to getting right with God. I want us to see what Jesus had to say about the lack of foresight of Noah's generation. In Matthew 24:36, Jesus talks about His Second Coming: "But of that day and hour no one knows, not even the angels of heaven, nor the Son, but the Father alone." No one knows when Jesus Christ is returning. The angels in heaven do not even know, but notice: "For the coming of the Son of Man will be just like the days of Noah" (Matthew 24:37). Jesus gives us an indication of what the days are going to be like just before Jesus Christ comes back to this earth.

There are identifying marks of Noah's day. "For as in those days before the flood they were eating and drinking, marrying and giving in marriage, until the day that Noah entered the ark, and they did not understand until the flood came and took them all away; so will the coming of the Son of Man be" (Matthew 24:38-39).

What were the three marks of Noah's day? The first mark was **indifference**! "They were eating and drinking, marrying and giving in marriage." What does that mean? It means that they were going on with the same routines of life. They were thinking about physical and material things rather than spiritual and eternal things.

We are interested in material things rather eternal things. We live in a materialistic age, and people are indifferent to spiritual truths.

Take time to listen to what people talk about today. If we listen to the conversations in the barber shop or in the office, we will find that 90 percent of those conversations is built around such things as buying and selling, eating and drinking, marrying and getting married, and building and tearing down. We are interested in material things rather eternal things. We live in a materialistic age, and people are indifferent to spiritual truths. It is not that most people are anti-God; they are just indifferent!

Another mark of Noah's time was **immorality**. "They were . . . marrying and giving in marriage" (Matthew 24:38). There is nothing wrong with getting married or giving someone to be married, but scholars tell us this is a term that speaks not of normal marriages but of the multiplicity of marriages. It speaks of sexual promiscuity and immorality. The Bible links the days of Moses and days of Noah with the days of Lot. In Lot's day, it was sexual perversion — sodomy. "It was the same as happened in the days of Lot" (Luke 17:28).

It is unbelievable some of the things that are being presented as entertainment today. If we want to find out the level of any particular society, see what amuses them — what they laugh at. When people start laughing at sin and finding their amusement and titillation from laughing at the breaking of God's seventh commandment, "Thou shalt not commit adultery" (Exodus 20:14 KJV), we can mark it down — we are in the days of Noah!

The last mark of Noah's day was **ignorance**. "And they did not understand until the flood came" (Matthew 24:39). They should have known, but they did not. It was not that they had not been warned; it was not that they did not hear!

One of the stunning marks of our age is people's intellectual abilities and spiritual ignorance. Men and women today worship at the shrine of their computers. People have all their degrees and all of their accoutrements of knowledge all around them, yet they are spiritually ignorant!

Noah was different from everyone else. In the midst of indifference, immorality, and ignorance, Noah made preparation. Have we made preparation? Are we ready for Jesus Christ to come? If not, why not?

WE NEED TO REFLECT ON NOAH AND HIS FAMILY

Noah not only saved himself but also got his family into the ark. "By faith Noah, being warned by God about things not yet seen, in reverence prepared an ark for the salvation of his household" (Hebrews 11:7).

Not only was Noah saved, but his wife along with their sons and their sons' wives were also saved. Are our children in the ark of safety? Do we have the kind of faith that Noah had—a household faith? Noah said, "I'm going to heaven, and I'm going to take my children with me!" Are our children going to hell while we go to heaven, or are we going to hell and taking our children with us?

Do we have the kind of faith that Noah had—
a household faith?

I can imagine a little boy in Noah's time coming up to his dad and saying, "Daddy, may I ask you a question?" And the dad, a very kind dad, says, "Why, sure, son. Sit down; what's on your heart?"

"Well, Daddy, you know Mr. Noah, the man who's building the big thing he calls an ark?" The father says, "Yes, I know him." "Well, Daddy, some of the boys were over there playing today, and Mr. Noah sat down on a sawhorse and began talking with us. He said that God is very angry with everybody and is getting ready to destroy the world by a flood. He said if we are going to be saved, we are going to have to put our faith in God and come aboard that ark! I was just wondering, Dad, what do you think about all of that?"

The boy's father begins laughing. "Son, forgive me for laughing. I'm not laughing at you; I was just thinking. It's so funny that you would ask me that today because, you see, here's the funny part. When I was a little boy, I went over to play around that ark also. He's been building that boat for a long time. That old man came out and told me the same story. It scared the wits out of me, but that's not the funniest part. Here's the funniest part: I went home and told my daddy, your granddaddy. Do you know what? Your granddaddy said that old fool told him the same story and scared him when he was a little boy. Son, don't pay attention to that old religious fanatic! Noah has been saying something about a flood for years! Don't worry about it; just run out and play. Remember, Daddy loves you. Have a good time today!"

Are there any fathers like that around today? "Oh, don't you let those preachers warn you about the Second Coming of Jesus Christ! Don't you go down there and become a religious fanatic! Remember, Dad loves you and wants you to have a good time."

Noah brought his family into the ark! Why do we think God put this in the Word? We are not only to be saved, but we should also get our kids on board!

WE NEED TO REVIEW NOAH AND HIS FORECAST

Noah—a weather forecaster? "By faith Noah, being warned by God about things not yet seen, in reverence prepared an ark for the salvation of his household, by which he condemned the world" (Hebrews 11:7). How did he condemn the world? He condemned the world by warning the world.

God had spoken to that generation. Noah had preached a 120-year-long sermon with a hammer. "Then the Lord said, 'My Spirit shall not strive with man forever'" (Genesis 6:3). Do not think that they did not know. It was probably only fifteen or sixteen hundred years from the time of Adam when the flood came.

When we do some arithmetic, we will discover that Methuselah's life overlapped Adam's life by two hundred years! Methuselah, who lived right up until the time of the flood, had talked with Adam! He knew about the fall in the Garden of Eden! He knew about the coats of skin!

He would have heard about Abel's offering and Cain's offering! He knew that Enoch had been taken! God had spoken to these people! God had warned these people!

How did Noah condemn the world? He forecasted the judgment that was to come! He told about the flood, but they would not believe him! What is the judgment of this generation going to be? "This is the judgment, that the Light has come into the world, and men loved the darkness rather than the Light, for their deeds were evil" (John 3:19).

Noah spoke to that generation and warned them, but they would not hear; therefore, they were condemned. They could not come to God and say, "Oh, God, I didn't know." They did know. The Bible makes it clear that through His preachers, God's Holy Spirit had spoken unto them. When was the last time we warned our friends or colleagues of the judgment to come?

WE NEED TO RECEIVE NOAH AND HIS FORTUNE

Noah "became an heir of the righteousness which is according to faith" (Hebrews 11:7). Noah had an inheritance. He became an heir of the righteousness which is by faith.

However, that is not all he inherited. Have we ever thought about the time, the effort, the money, and the labor that Noah put into that ark? Have we ever thought what it would have taken to build a ship of such immense proportion? I do not know how many carpenters he had to hire nor how much it cost. The ark was Noah's life's work. The entire time Noah was investing in the ark, the rest of the people were buying and selling and marrying and giving in marriage. They must have thought Noah was a fool. They were investing in stocks and bonds and real estate, but there came a turning point when all of their so-called real estate was not very real because it was all covered with water and they lost it all.

What about Noah? Did he lose it all? No, he gained it all! He stepped off of that boat, and the whole world was before him. He owned it all! "Blessed are the gentle, for they shall inherit the earth" (Matthew 5:5). We cannot outgive God. We must not worry about what we have invested for the Lord Jesus Christ.

We cannot outgive God. We must not worry about what we have invested for the Lord Jesus Christ.

Real wealth is not found in this world. The wealth of this world is just a pittance compared to the real fortune that I am talking about. Noah became an heir of righteousness! He did not earn righteousness but inherited righteousness by faith! We need to be righteous today, and the only way that we can be made righteous is not by good works nor by keeping the Ten Commandments but by trusting the Lord.

Peter tells us that the ark was a type or a picture of Christ. Noah's faith has been for all time a picture of faith in the Lord Jesus Christ. The reason the ark only had one door is because Jesus said, "I am the way, and the truth, and the life; no one comes to the Father but through Me" (John 14:6). Jesus said, "I am the door; if anyone enters through Me, he will be saved" (John 10:9). There was one door. The gangplank was faith. We enter that door by faith!

When Noah went in, God shut the door. "Then the LORD said to Noah, 'Enter the ark, you and all your household'" (Genesis 7:1). God did not say to Noah, "Noah, go into the ark." To the contrary, God said, "Enter the ark." That meant that God was already in the ark.

47

That may not make a difference anyone else, but it makes a big difference to me. If I say, "Go into that room," that means I stay out here and someone else goes in there. However, if I say, "Come into the room," that means the person comes in where I am. When Noah went into that ark, he went in where God was.

How safe was Noah and his family? He was as safe as God was. When will I go down? When Jesus goes down for I am in Christ. He is my ark of safety. God said to Noah, "Enter the ark"; and when he went into the ark, God shut the door. Ephesians 1:13 says that "having also believed, you were sealed in Him with the Holy Spirit."

Security is not in a place; security is in a person.
His name is Jesus.

Noah may have fallen down many times in the ark, but he never fell off the ark. He was in the ark, and God shut the door! All the storm and all the wind and all of the waves and all of the water battered against that ark! It was Jesus who took our judgment, but inside we are safe! Inside we are secure! Inside we are satisfied! Inside of Christ, we are made righteous!

Some people do not believe in eternal security. They do believe they are going to be secure, but they believe they will be secure when they get to heaven. They think they are going to step into heaven, slam the door behind them, and say, "Whew, I made it. I'm secure!" Yet the angels fell from heaven. If we are not secure down here, we would not be secure up there.

Security is not in a place; security is in a person. His name is Jesus. The ark is a picture of the Lord Jesus Christ. He is our ark of safety. We come into Him by faith.

What was Noah's fortune? He became an heir of righteousness! That means that his sins were forgiven! God gave him a new heart! He was not just merely saved from a flood but was saved for all eternity, and one day we will meet Noah in heaven. When Noah and his family went into the ark, they were the minority in the world. When they came out of the ark, they were the majority!

─∞∞∞─

One of the stunning marks
of our age is people's
intellectual abilities and
their spiritual ignorance.

5

The Disciplines of Faith

Charles Haddon Spurgeon said, "Little faith will bring your soul to heaven, but great faith will bring heaven to your soul." Wouldn't we all like to have great faith? When we came to Jesus Christ, God enrolled us in the School of Faith. Life is the classroom, the Bible is the textbook, the prophets and the apostles are the professors, and Abraham would have to be the dean of the School of Faith.

Abraham was an amazing man. His name is loved and revered by Jews and Christians alike. He is called "Abraham, who is the father of us all" (Romans 4:16). In Hebrews 11:8-15, we read:

> By faith Abraham, when he was called, obeyed by going out to a place which he was to receive for an inheritance; and he went out, not knowing where he was going. By faith he lived as an alien in the land of promise, as in a foreign land, dwelling in tents with Isaac and Jacob, fellow heirs of the same promise; for he was looking for the city which has foundations, whose architect and builder is God. By faith even Sarah herself received ability to

conceive, even beyond the proper time of life, since she considered Him faithful who had promised. Therefore, there was born even of one man, and him as good as dead at that, as many descendants AS THE STARS OF HEAVEN IN NUMBER, AND INNUMERABLE AS THE SAND WHICH IS BY THE SEASHORE.

All these died in faith, without receiving the promises, but having seen them and having welcomed them from a distance, and having confessed that they were strangers and exiles on the earth. For those who say such things make it clear that they are seeking a country of their own. And indeed if they had been thinking of that country from which they went out, they would have had opportunity to return.

I cannot emphasize enough the importance of faith. We are not talking about something that is incidental. "Without faith it is impossible to please Him" (Hebrews 11:6). If you please God, it does not matter whom you displease; and if you displease God, it does not matter whom you please. There is no way to please God without faith. Faith is the mark of a Christian. Christians were called believers before they were called Christians. We will never succeed in our Christian life without believing God.

Abraham was a pagan and an idolater. He lived in a place called Ur of the Chaldees when God spoke to him, and he 75 years of age when he enrolled in the School of Faith two thousand years before Christ. We are never too evil or too old to begin to walk with God.

Pause and ponder this: Abraham packs up his bags and leaves the land of the familiar to go a strange land. He leaves it all to go to a country he has never seen. He has sealed orders. God does not tell him where he is going nor does He tell him how long it is going to take to get there. God does not tell him what he is going to do when he gets there or how long he is going to stay there. God just says, "Get up and go." Abraham leaves and enrolls in the School of Faith.

If you please God, it does not matter
whom you displease; and if you displease God,
it does not matter whom you please. There is no way
to please God without faith.

Abraham and Sarah were strangers and pilgrims in the land of Canaan. Abraham was not a fugitive; he was not running away from home. Abraham was not a vagabond; he was not looking for home. He was a pilgrim heading home.

Many faith-powered and life-changing principles will come out of our passage to help us have that dynamic faith that will bring heaven to our souls.

WE SHOULD EMBRACE GOD'S VOICE

We must hear God. "By faith Abraham, when he was called, obeyed by going out to a place which he was to receive for an inheritance; and he went out, not knowing where he was going" (Hebrews 11:8).

The operative phrase here is he heard the voice of God. "So faith comes from hearing, and hearing by the word of Christ" (Romans 10:17). We must hear God. Notice how God comes to Abraham: "Now the LORD said to Abram, 'Go forth from your country, and from your relatives and from your father's house, to the land which I will show you" (Genesis 12:1).

God follows with four "I will's" to Abraham: "And I will make you a great nation, and I will bless you, and make your name great; and so you shall be a blessing; and I will bless those who bless you, and the one who curses you I will curse. And in you all the families of the earth will be blessed'" (Genesis 12:2-3).

He hears the voice of God saying: "I will, I will, I will, I will." We are reading about the root of faith. In Genesis 11, we find people who tried to build a massive tower to heaven called the Tower of Babel. Compare Genesis 11:1-4 with Genesis 12:1-3:

Now the whole earth used the same language and the same words. It came about as they journeyed east, that they found a plain in the land of Shinar and settled there. They said to one another, "Come, let us make bricks and burn them thoroughly." And they used brick for stone, and they used tar for mortar. They said, "Come, let us build for ourselves a city, and a tower whose top will reach into heaven, and let us make for ourselves a name, otherwise we will be scattered abroad over the face of the whole earth" (Genesis 11:1-4).

Now the Lord said to Abram,
   "Go forth from your country,
   And from your relatives
   And from your father's house,
   To the land which I will show you;
   And I will make you a great nation,
   And I will bless you,
   And make your name great;
   And so you shall be a blessing;
   And I will bless those who bless you,
   And the one who curses you I will curse.

And in you all the families of the earth will be blessed" (Genesis 12:1-3).

In Genesis 11, man said, "let us, let us, let us" — let us make for ourselves a name. In Genesis 12, God says to Abraham, "I will, I will, I will, I will" — I will make your name great.

I submit that most people in the cities around the world are in the "let us" mode trying to build high-rises to hell, trying to build utopias; but faith hears the voice of God saying, "I will." The people in Genesis 11 were going to make a name for themselves. Do we know even one of their names? We all know the name of Abraham because God said to him, "I will make your name great."

The best way to pray is saying, "Lord, this is Your will and I thank You for it and I stand on it."

We are learning about voice principle. How can we hear the voice of God?

We often pray, "Lord, if it is Your will." Lord, if it is Your will, heal; Lord, if it is Your will, show us what to do; Lord, if is Your will, keep us safe." If we do not know the will of God, that is a good way to pray but not the best way to pray. The best way to pray is saying, "Lord, this is Your will and I thank You for it and I stand on it."

"This is the confidence which we have before Him, that, if we ask anything according to His will, He hears us" (1 John 5:14). Do we have the confidence to say, "God, this is Your will"? That is where great faith comes from. Great faith does not come from guessing at the will of God.

God spoke to Abraham and others in ways that He may not use today. God appeared to Abraham through an angel, the angel of Jehovah. "The LORD appeared to Abram and said, 'To your descendants I will give this land.' So he built an altar there to the LORD who had appeared to him" (Genesis 12:7). God has never appeared to me like this.

God spoke to Moses out of a burning bush. I have never seen a burning bush, at least not one that burned supernaturally. God spoke to Saul, who became the Apostle Paul, while he was on the road to Damascus to put Christians to death. The Lord appeared to him in a vision. I have never experienced this. Simon Peter was on a rooftop when an angel came to him and he had a vision. All of these people heard the Word of God in a supernatural way.

Is that what we are waiting on today? No. That is not the norm for us today. Does that mean we cannot hear the voice of God? No. Does that mean that we are less? No, it means that we are more. Do we have less advantage? No, we have greater advantage. To know God, to know the will of God, we have the greater advantage.

How can we know the will of God? When our hearts are clean and our motives clear and we are walking in the Spirit, we can assume that what we think and desire is the will of God.

"God, after He spoke long ago to the fathers in the prophets in many portions and in many ways, in these last days has spoken to us in His Son, whom He appointed heir of all things, through whom also He made the world" (Hebrews 1:1-2). How does God speak to us? By His Son. The Bible teaches that we have three things: the written Word of God, the mind of Christ, and the guidance of the Holy Spirit. We have the greater advantage.

Before they had the Bible and before they knew what we know by the indwelling of the Holy Spirit, the Old Testament characters had to wait for God to break in with open revelation or vision. However, we can open the Bible and hear the inspired, infallible, inerrant Word of God. When we were born again, we received what the Bible calls the mind of Christ. "But a natural man does not accept the things of the Spirit of God, for they are foolishness to him; and he cannot understand them, because they are spiritually appraised. But he who is spiritual appraises all things, yet he himself is appraised by no one. For WHO HAS KNOWN THE MIND OF THE LORD, THAT HE WILL INSTRUCT HIM? But we have the mind of Christ" (1 Corinthians 2:14-16).

Our responsibility is not to understand totally but to obey readily.

How can we know the will of God? When our hearts are clean and our motives clear and we are walking in the Spirit, we can assume that what we think and desire is the will of God. However, when we walk out-of-bounds, the Person of the Holy Spirit will blow the whistle and encourage us to get back inbounds. When we want to go to a particular place and it is not God's will, He can speak to us like He did to the Apostle Paul and direct us to another place. If we are puzzled, we need to wait on the Lord to give clear direction. "But the path of the righteous is like the light of dawn, that shines brighter and brighter until the full day" (Proverbs 4:18).

The Word of the Lord came to Abraham, and God will speak to us. However, before someone makes the statement, "I don't know the will of God," let me ask this question: Are you living by what you already know in the Bible?

If not and you are asking God to guide you, you are a big hypocrite. Why should God give you more light when you are not obeying what is in the revealed Word of God?

WE SHOULD ENLIST FOR GOD'S VENTURE

We must hear the voice of God and obey what He says. "By faith Abraham, when he was called, obeyed by going out to a place which he was to receive for an inheritance; and he went out, not knowing where he was going" (Hebrews 11:8). He did not know where it was going to end. Our responsibility is not to understand totally but to obey readily. Abraham was leaving all he knew and all he loved and was going out in sheer obedience. God gives us the choice. If we do not obey what we know, we should not ask God for more light. God is not going to give it to us.

Are we having a faith problem? If we are, we are probably having an obedience problem. Is there confession that needs to be made? Is there restitution that needs to be performed? Is there a gift that needs to be given? Is there a testimony that needs to be offered? Is there a place we need to go? Do we want faith? The voice principle — hear from God. The venture principle — obey God.

What is amazing about this story is that Abraham did not know where he was going. I do not know many people who venture out and have no idea where they are going. We surely do not take vacations this way. We do not take a flight on a plane without knowing where we are going. We usually do not even leave the house in the car without knowing where we are going, yet Abraham did not know where he was going, and he was leaving everything and everyone he knew except for his wife and his nephew, Lot.

However, we do not have to know where we are going if we know whom we are following. If we know whom we are following, we can make sure we arrive at the right place. In this instance, Abraham did not have to know where he was going since he knew he was following God. If we are following God, He will make sure we get to the right place on time!

WE SHOULD EXPAND GOD'S VALUES

We must establish priorities. "By faith he lived as an alien in the land of promise, as in a foreign *land*, dwelling in tents with Isaac and Jacob, fellow heirs of the same promise; for he was looking for the city which has foundations, whose architect and builder is God" (Hebrews 11:9-10).

The reason so many of us do not have faith is because our priorities are wrong. We think that faith is some way to get our will done in heaven when faith is God's way to get heaven's will done on earth.

Abraham was a stranger away from home and a pilgrim heading home. Canaan was not his home at that time. He was looking for a city that had foundations whose builder and maker was God. He was living in a tent, but he would not put the tent pegs down too deeply because his motto was, "This world is not my home. I'm just a passing through" ("This World Is Not My Home," Albert E. Brumely, 1937). Abraham had a different priority.

The reason so many of us do not have faith is because our priorities are wrong. We think that faith is some way to get our will done in heaven when faith is God's way to get heaven's will done on earth. "Thy kingdom come, thy will be done on earth, as it is in heaven" (Matthew 6:10 KJV). Consequently, Abraham was living in a tent.

Our citizenship is in heaven; and we dare not, we must not, get too attached to this world. "For our citizenship is in heaven, from which also we eagerly wait for a Savior, the Lord Jesus Christ" (Philippians 3:20). If we are living for this world, we will not have faith. Furthermore, we will be in the junk business. The Bible warns about friendship with the world: "You adulteresses, do you not know that friendship with the world is hostility toward God? Therefore whoever wishes to be a friend of the world makes himself an enemy of God" (James 4:4).

Do we have a worldly mindset? Do we think God is going to give faith to His enemies? Abraham was not a friend of the world. When we become a friend of the world, we begin to live like the world. "Do not love the world nor the things in the world. If anyone loves the world, the love of the Father is not in him. For all that is in the world, the lust of the flesh and the lust of the eyes and the boastful pride of life, is not from the Father, but is from the world. The world is passing away, and also its lusts; but the one who does the will of God lives forever" (1 John 2:15-17).

When we become a friend of the world, we begin to love the world and be conformed to the world. "And do not be conformed to this world, but be transformed by the renewing of your mind, so that you may prove what the will of God is, that which is good and acceptable and perfect" (Romans 12:2).

If this world is squeezing us in, molding us or shaping us through Madison Avenue, television, the Internet, Bank of America, General Motors, or whatever it may be, then we need to pause and ponder this path. It could be a football team or a fashion designer. What is it that molds us or conforms us? Then we wonder why we do not have the mind of Christ and why we do not understand the will of God.

Abraham had his nephew, Lot, with him. Lot was following Abraham, and the Bible tells us that Abraham was living in a tent, and Lot pitched his tent toward Sodom. He moved into the world. Perhaps Lot's wife moved up the social ladder in Sodom's society and maybe his daughters were cheerleaders at Sodom High. Lot became a businessman and a Sodom councilman. Lot looked at Sodom, lived in Sodom, and became a leader in Sodom; however, Lot lost everything.

We hear so much today about the separation of church and state. We need to hear messages about the separation of church and the world— not isolation but insulation.

We hear so much today about the separation of church and state. We need to hear messages about the separation of church and the world—not isolation but insulation. Look at average Christians today vs. the world—they look alike, they dress alike, they talk alike, they smoke the same things, and they drink the same things. We should be different. "'Therefore, come out from their midst and be separate,' says the Lord" (2 Corinthians 6:17). If we were arrested for being a Christian, would there be enough evidence to convict us?

Do we want faith? Abraham had a pilgrim character. That does not mean he was a dropout. Abraham was in business. He had a family. He even had to go to war several times, but Abraham was not molded by this world. Even though he was very wealthy, he lived in a tent. He was not moved by the pleasures, treasures, and measures of the world.

What are our personal goals? To make enough money to retire and have a nice house and live in ease and have certain things? What are our goals for our children? To be successful and famous, or are we more concerned about their spiritual walk with God? Are we more concerned about the character of our children growing in Christ and the kingdom of heaven? Would we leave our present job and take a job with less pay if it were better for the character of our children? What is our goal? To impress other people? In whose home would we rather visit—the rich and the famous or the godly and the pure? Most of us are so squeezed in by this world that it is no wonder we do not have faith. Abraham was a man to whom this world meant very little "for he was looking for the city which has foundations, whose architect and builder is God" (Hebrews 11:10). He had a pilgrim character.

WE SHOULD ENCOURAGE GOD'S VISION

"All these died in faith, without receiving the promises, but having seen them and having welcomed them from a distance, and having confessed that they were strangers and exiles on the earth" (Hebrews 11:13). It is so easy to lose the focus that we have of the right values and become earthly- and worldly-minded. The Apostle Paul states, "Therefore if you have been raised up with Christ, keep seeking the things above, where Christ is, seated at the right hand of God. Set your mind on the things above, not on the things that are on earth" (Colossians 3:1-2).

Our definition of faith: "Now faith is the assurance of *things* hoped for, the conviction of things not seen" (Hebrews 11:1). "All these died in faith, without receiving the promises, but having seen them and having welcomed them from a distance" (Hebrews 11:13). They saw the invisible; they saw things that were not seen. Faith is seeing the invisible.

"While we look not at the things which are seen, but at the things which are not seen" (2 Corinthians 4:18). Is that double-talk? Paul says we are not looking at what we can see but at what we cannot see. Faith sees the invisible, knows the unknowable, and does the impossible. Our vision will focus with faith.

They saw the invisible; they saw things that were not seen. Faith is seeing the invisible.

There is an invisible world, a world that is more real than this world. All the heroes of the faith were people who could see the invisible world. Most of us live a life where all we see is what is before us — our car, our house, our job. We never get a vision. We never look upward. We never look onward.

We think of the people who make a mark in the material world — the explorers, the novelists, the artists, the creators, the inventors. All of these had the ability to see the invisible. When Disney World was being dedicated in Orlando, Florida, in October 1971, they opened it with a grand procession. Walt Disney had already passed away, and Lillian Disney, his widow, was sitting alongside one of the executives. A lady sitting next to Mrs. Disney said, "It's a shame Walt is not here to see all of this." Mrs. Disney replied, "Oh, he saw it; that's why it's here."

What are we setting our eyes on? We are going in the direction of our main focus. Faith brings focus. Every day Abraham focused his eyes on the city that God was building. Is it any wonder he was not interested in Sodom? Sodom was not on the path to the heavenly city! Each morning we should begin our day by placing our mind and our spiritual eyes on what God is building. We need to take the long look instead of the short look.

WE SHOULD ENLARGE GOD'S VIGILANCE

"By faith even Sarah herself received ability to conceive, even beyond the proper time of life, since she considered Him faithful who had promised" (Hebrews 11:11).

God gave Abraham a promise, but he got his eyes off God as did Sarah. They did some terrible things that have impacted our world ever since. Abraham went down to Egypt when God had put him in Canaan. God tested him, and he failed the test at first.

God will test our faith. A faith that cannot be tested cannot be trusted.

Abraham went to Egypt because of the famine in Canaan. He did not pray about his decision. He got off the faith-path and became sexually involved with Hagar who bore him a son, Ishmael. God had given a promise to Abraham that he and Sarah would have a child; but when the years began to roll by, they doubted God and took matters into their own hands. What is the big deal about this?

Fourteen years later, Abraham and Sarah had a son, Isaac. God kept His promise! However, Isaac and Ishmael did not get along with each other. God commanded Abraham to send Hagar and Ishmael away when Ishmael was 17 years old. Isaac and Ishmael did not get along together then, and the Jewish world and the Muslim world do not get along today. The Muslim world believes Ishmael went up with Abraham to Mount Moriah to offer a sacrifice, and the Jewish world believes Isaac was the one chosen by Abraham to travel up with him to offer a sacrifice. If Abraham would have waited until the Lord fulfilled His promise of a son, it would be a completely different world today!

God will test our faith. A faith that cannot be tested cannot be trusted. The Bible speaks of the trial of our faith (1 Peter 1:7). When we live the life of faith, it is not all honey and no bees. Our faith will be tested. Abraham should have stayed in the land of Canaan even though there was a famine. If he knew God had put him there, he should have said, "Even if I starve, I'm going to stay here. If God put me here, God is going to take care of me."

Our faith is going to come under attack. Never think there will be no heartaches or tears in life for there will be problems. Abraham returned to Canaan to live the life of faith. I encourage anyone who has gotten off the "faith path" to get back on it as quickly as possible.

WE SHOULD ENTER INTO GOD'S VICTORY

We are to enjoy the blessings. "By faith even Sarah herself received ability to conceive, even beyond the proper time of life, since she considered Him faithful who had promised. Therefore there was born even of one man, and him as good as dead at that, as many descendants AS THE STARS OF HEAVEN IN NUMBER, AND INNUMERABLE AS THE SAND WHICH IS BY THE SEASHORE" (Hebrews 11:11-12).

Abraham's name is great; his descendants are great. Abraham has been a blessing to the world. God gave Abraham the land and did many things through Abraham. From Abraham came the Jewish nation, the prophets, the Bible, and the Lord and Savior Jesus Christ.

There is the victory principle; however, there is no way we can live in victory apart from faith. This is the victory that overcomes the world, even our faith; and all of these things are right there in the School of Faith for us.

Imagine God and Abraham walking together while the sun was setting over Canaan. God says to Abraham, "I am going to bless you like the stars."

Abraham says, "Like the stars? What do you mean?"

God responds, "After the sun sets, the stars will begin to appear. I encourage you to count the stars as they appear. However, I warn you; the stars begin appearing slowly but eventually will pick up speed in their appearance."

Abraham states, "I will be happy to count the stars. Math was my best subject at Ur High School."

It is the victory principle. When we walk by faith, we can look back over the shoulder of time and see God's blessings like the stars and the sand.

As the stars appear, Abraham counts them one at a time. Finally, he says, "God, the stars are now appearing faster than I can count!"

The next morning God and Abraham are walking along a seashore. God says to Abraham, "You were unable to count the stars last night. This morning I would like for you to count the grains of sand on this beach."

Who could imagine trying to count grains of sand? How many grains are in a handful? A cupful? A bucket full? A truck full? It would be impossible to count sand on one beach much less all the coasts worldwide.

God said to Abraham, "I am going to bless you like the stars and the sand." In other words, he will experience so many blessings that he will be unable to count them.

Do we have this testimony? Is it not true that God has given us more blessings in our lifetime than we are able to count? It is the victory principle. When we walk by faith, we can look back over the shoulder of time and see God's blessings like the stars and the sand.

—⟨≋⟩—

When our hearts are clean
and our motives clear and we
are walking in the Spirit, we can
assume that what we think and
desire is the will of God.

6

The Defense of Faith

A faith that cannot be tested cannot be trusted. For example, how would we like to get on an airplane that had never been tested? How would we like to have a doctor perform surgery on us who had not passed every test in medical school? I heard a story about man who was having surgery; and the doctor said to him, "You seem nervous." The patient said, "Yes, this is my first surgery" to which the doctor responded, "I know how you feel; it's mine also."

"By faith Abraham, when he was tested, offered up Isaac, and he who had received the promises was offering up his only begotten son; it was he to whom it was said, 'In Isaac your descendants shall be called'" (Hebrews 11:17-18).

How could Abraham offer Isaac up as a sacrifice? "He considered that God is able to raise people even from the dead, from which he also received him back as a type" [in a type, he received him] (Hebrews 11:19). God will give us trials and tests to see if our faith is real just as He did to Abraham when He said to "offer up Isaac."

Tests, trials, and temptations come in two kinds. The devil solicits and tempts us to do evil in order to cause us to stumble while God tests us to do good in order to cause us to stand and make our faith strong and pure.

The devil solicits and tempts us to do evil in order to cause us to stumble while God tests us to do good in order to cause us to stand and make our faith strong and pure.

God will put our faith in the fire. Some of us are going through a test, an ordeal. God means us no harm but wants us to understand whether or not we have the real thing. The temptations from Satan are pretty well standardized, but the trials that come from God are tailor-made. God knows where we are as well as our circumstances and may put us through a test.

Now it came about after these things, that God tested Abraham, and said to him, "Abraham!" And he said, "Here I am." He said, "Take now your son, your only son, whom you love, Isaac, and go to the land of Moriah, and offer him there as a burnt offering on one of the mountains of which I will tell you." So Abraham rose early in the morning and saddled his donkey, and took two of his young men with him and Isaac his son; and he split wood for the burnt offering, and arose and went to the place of which God had told him. On the third day Abraham raised his eyes and saw the place from a distance. Abraham said to his young men, "Stay here with the donkey, and I and the lad will go over there; and we will worship and return to you."

Abraham took the wood of the burnt offering and laid it on Isaac his son, and he took in his hand the fire and the knife. So the two of them walked on together. Isaac spoke to Abraham his father and said, "My father!" And he said, "Here I am, my son." And he said, "Behold, the fire and the wood, but where is the lamb for the burnt offering?" Abraham said, "God will provide for Himself the lamb for the burnt offering, my son." So the two of them walked on together.

Then they came to the place of which God had told him; and Abraham built the altar there and arranged the wood, and bound his son Isaac and laid him on the altar, on top of the wood. Abraham stretched out his hand and took the knife to slay his son. But the angel of the LORD called to him from heaven and said, "Abraham, Abraham!" And he said, "Here I am." He said, "Do not stretch out your hand against the lad, and do nothing to him; for now I know that you fear God, since you have not withheld your son, your only son, from Me." Then Abraham raised his eyes and looked, and behold, behind *him* a ram caught in the thicket by his horns; and Abraham went and took the ram and offered him up for a burnt offering in the place of his son. Abraham called the name of that place The LORD Will Provide, as it is said to this day, "In the mount of the LORD it will be provided. (Genesis 22:1-14)

What an incredible story! God had never before commanded human sacrifice, but now He has commanded Abraham to take the son of promise, the beloved son, and put him to death.

Remember that Isaac was the son of miracle birth, the son of promise, and the beloved son; but with no hesitation whatsoever, Abraham set out for Mount Moriah: "And Abraham rose up early in the morning" (v.3).

Imagine with me that before starting up the mountain, Abraham and Isaac were sitting around the campfire. What must Abraham have been feeling as he looked into the face of his son, wondering what he would say to him? How would he tell him? What memories Abraham must have been having about raising young Isaac. Was he wondering what Isaac's last look at him would be like?

Not are we willing to give up our sins for God but are we willing to give our blessings back to God.

Just as He did with Abraham, God is going to test our faith by asking us to do something that may surprise us — not surprise us by giving up the wrong things but by giving up the good things. It would be relatively easy if God asked us to give up the wrong things such as lying, stealing, cheating, and pride to show that we loved Him; but that is not what God is asking. God had given Abraham a possession, a wonderful son. God had given Abraham a program, to make of him a great nation. He was going to bless the whole world; and that program was going to come through his possession, Isaac.

God had given Abraham a promise, "I will do it." Now it seems that God was saying, "Now Abraham, give all of this back to me."

There are some things we give up for the Lord, but the test of faith Abraham was facing was not what he was giving up for the Lord but what he was giving back to the Lord.

The question we must wrestle with is, "Am I able to give my blessings back to God?" Not are we willing to give up our sins for God but are we willing to give our blessings back to God. Abraham was asked to give his blessing back to the Lord. Following are three questions, and how we answer these questions will confirm whether or not we pass the test of our faith.

CAN WE TRUST GOD WITH THE POSSESSIONS HE HAS GIVEN US?

"By faith Abraham, when he was tested, offered up Isaac, and he who had received the promises was offering up his only begotten son" (Hebrews 11:17).

The test was over a gift that God had given to him. Why the test? Could it have been that Abraham was coming to love Isaac more than he loved God? Could it have been that he was coming to love the gift more than the giver? Could it have been that God was being moved into second place? The angels said the test was to find out whether or not that was true. We must remember that God will never take second place to anything or to anyone in our lives.

Many of us want to give God a place in our lives, but God does not want a place in our lives nor does He want prominence in our lives. God desires, deserves, and demands preeminence in our lives. He will not be a part-time God with a duplex for a throne.

Many of us like to have God in our lives; however, how many of us say, "God, I love You supremely"? We must be very careful that our blessings do not become curses. "'If you do not listen, and if you do not take it to heart to give honor to My name,' says the Lord of hosts, 'then I will send the curse upon you and I will curse your blessings'" (Malachi 2:2). God goes on to say, "Indeed, I have cursed them already, because you are not taking it to heart."

What is wrong in our God-blessed America today? God is beginning to curse our blessings. America has been blessed like no other nation on the face of the earth yet we spit in the face of God with more vileness, more immorality, more slaughter of the unborn, more disregard for God, and more arrogance strutting through our nation. Sadly, we have put God aside and concentrated on our blessings. I fear God is going to turn our blessings to curses unless we turn back to Almighty God. God says He will not take second place to anyone or anything.

Anything God has given us, we can trust Him with; and anything God has not given to us, we do not need.

It was not wrong for Abraham to love Isaac. I love my children with all of my heart, but we cannot truly love our children until we love God as we ought. God was not asking Abraham if he loved Isaac; He knew Abraham loved Isaac. What God wanted to know was whether Abraham loved Him more than he loved Isaac.

After the resurrection, Jesus asked Simon Peter, "Simon, son of John, do you love Me more than these?" (John 21:15). Some think Jesus was asking if Peter loved him more than all the other disciples loved Him; however, I do not think that is what He meant. I believe Jesus was standing by the seashore saying, "Simon, do you love me more than these your brothers? Do you love me more than you love these fish and these nets and these boats and this way of life? Do you love me more than these things? Simon, I will not take second place in your life." The test of faith is not primarily between love and hate but between two loves — those things we love dearly and that which we must love supremely. Do we have in our hearts any love that is greater than our love for Jesus Christ?

If we consider there may be a love greater than a love we have for God, God's message from this passage of scripture is to "get up to Moriah and put it on the altar and sacrifice it as a burnt offering."

Is there anything we would not give back to God that God has already given to us if He asked us for it? Anything God has given us, we can trust Him with; and anything God has not given to us, we do not need. God said, "Abraham, I gave you Isaac. Now take him up to the mountain and sacrifice him to Me." We are talking about the testing of our faith.

CAN WE TRUST GOD WITH THE PURPOSE HE HAS FOR US?

We have talked about the possessions God has given to us, but what about the purpose He has for us. "By faith Abraham, when he was tested, offered up Isaac, and he who had received the promises was offering up his only begotten son; it was he to whom it was said. 'IN ISAAC YOUR DESCENDANTS SHALL BE CALLED'" (Hebrews 11:17-18).

Faith is not primarily believing God in spite of the evidence; it is obeying God in spite of the consequences. Obedience is the great proof of our trust and our faith.

God had given Abraham a purpose; and Abraham said, "Yes, I understand. I know what's going to happen. I'm going to have a son and this son is going to have sons and their sons are going to have more sons; and I'm going to have innumerable descendants, a people of faith." Then God said, "Put it to death."

In our thinking, that did not make sense. Faith is not primarily believing God in spite of the evidence; it is obeying God in spite of the consequences. Obedience is the great proof of our trust and our faith. When we know that we know that we have a word from God, we do not pass it through the judgment bar of our understanding. We just simply obey. There is only one alternative to obedience: disobedience.

We need to serve Jesus Christ with a burning, blazing, passionate, emotional love for Him.

We are to have an **informed obedience**. We do not go out and make some sort of sacrifice to show God how much we love Him. That would be a horrible mistake. We must be in tune with God. Abraham heard God speak. Many Christians are endeavoring to do things for God that God does not want done. God has not promised to bless any endeavor He has not commanded. We must hear God in order to obey God. It must be informed obedience.

We are to have an **intentional obedience**. We might say, "Well, I'm not informed." Did we report to God for duty? Real obedience is not merely an absence of doing wrong but actively seeking the will of God. Ignorance of God's will is not an excuse if we do not have intentional obedience.

As soon as God gave the command to Abraham, he got up in the morning and got started. We are to have an **immediate obedience**. No delay. As soon as possible, Abraham got on the road to do exactly what God told him to do. Procrastination is a form of disobedience. If God has told us to say something, give something, or do

THE DEFENSE OF FAITH

something, why are we waiting? Real obedience is immediate obedience.

We are to have an **impassioned obedience**. No reluctance, no pouting, no dragging our feet. We need to serve Jesus Christ with a burning, blazing, passionate, emotional love for Him. Most assuredly, it was a struggle for Abraham; but thank God he passed the test.

CAN WE TRUST GOD WITH THE PROMISES HE HAS MADE TO US?

"By faith Abraham, when he was tested, offered up Isaac, and he who had received the promises was offering up his only begotten son" (Hebrews 11:17). That is antithetical to the promise because the promise said it was in Isaac that Abraham was going to be blessed. "It was he to whom it was said. 'IN ISAAC YOUR DESCENDANTS SHALL BE CALLED'" (Hebrews 11:18). How did he do it? "He considered that God is able to raise people even from the dead, from which he also received him back as a type" (Hebrews 11:19).

Abraham had already learned that God was the God of the impossible. God had given him a son when he was a hundred years of age. Can't we just see him coming out of the maternity ward on a cane saying, "It's a boy!" Sarah was ninety years of age. Her womb was dead. Abraham knew that God was a God of miracles, and his faith was steadfast to believe God.

Abraham did not know how God would do it; he simply knew that God would. God did not let Abraham sacrifice Isaac because it was not Isaac that God wanted; it was Abraham. God wanted to know that Abraham loved Him more than anything else. The heart of the message is that if we love it, let it go; if it is ours, we will get it back. If not, we will be saved from a fate worse than death; that is, holding on to something that would be an impairment to our spiritual lives. Jesus said, "He who has found his life will lose it, and he who has lost his life for My sake will find it" (Matthew 10:39).

---

*Remember, we do not live
by explanations but by promises.*

Abraham was "accounting that God was able to raise him up, even from the dead" (Hebrews 11:19 KJV). The word "accounting" literally means "considered, to calculate." It is the Greek word from which we get the words "logic" and "logistics." Abraham was calculating; he was saying, "God look, you gave me this boy. I can trust you with him. Lord God, you have a purpose, and I can trust you with it. Lord God, you made a promise, and I reckon on it. You are going to keep your word; you cannot lie. I don't have to understand; I don't have to parade it pass the judgment bar of my knowledge." God gave Abraham his son back, and Abraham called the name of that place "Jehovah Jireh" — God will provide.

There was a ram in a thicket to take Isaac's place (Genesis 22:13) — no sooner and no later than it was needed for God is always on time. Is there any good gift we are unwilling to surrender? Not the bad things but the blessings. It may be our finances or our health or our grandchildren. Is there any obedience we are not willing to perform even though it seems contradictory to what we think God's way is for us? Is there any promise that we cannot trust God with even when it does not make sense? Remember, we do not live by explanations but by promises.

We may say, "God, I don't want this kind of test!" The faith that cannot be tested cannot be trusted. God wants us to be strong in faith for without faith it is impossible to please God. Abraham saw the coming Messiah. Jesus said, "Abraham rejoiced to see My day, and he saw it and was glad" (John 8:56).

The Messiah that Abraham trusted is the one we must trust today. He is the one who wants to save us and help us. On the authority of the Word of God, He will forgive every sin and fulfill every promise.

A faith that cannot be tested
cannot be trusted. If you want
a testimony you will have
to pass the test.

7

The Destiny of Faith

"By faith Isaac blessed Jacob and Esau, even regarding things to come" (Hebrews 11:20).

There was a student who was finishing up his examinations just before the Christmas holidays. He had not really studied very hard, and the professor asked an exceptionally difficult question. The student did not have the foggiest idea what the answer was; but he thought perhaps he could get by because of the spirit of the season, so he wrote on his examination paper, "Only God knows the answer to this question. Merry Christmas!" The professor looked at it; and before returning the student's paper wrote, "God gets 100, and you get 0. Happy New Year!"

Even though God is all-knowing, He chooses not to leave us in confusion and darkness; however, we need not get a zero because when it comes to these questions that are so perplexing, God chooses to reveal certain things to us so we can face the future with faith.

WE NEED TO LEARN ABOUT ISAAC
AND HIS FUTURE

Isaac was one of the great patriarchs of the Old Testament. "Patri" meaning father, "arch" meaning ruler—a father ruler. Isaac was the son of Abraham, the progenitor of the Jewish nation. It was also through Isaac that the promised Messiah would come. Isaac had twin sons. Esau was the firstborn, a redhead who became a brawny sort of man while Jacob was very smooth-skinned and the younger of the two.

Isaac prayed to the Lord on behalf of his wife, because she was barren; and the Lord answered him and Rebekah his wife conceived. But the children struggled together within her; and she said, "If it is so, why then am I this way?" So she went to inquire of the Lord. The Lord said to her,
"Two nations are in your womb;
And two peoples will be separated from your body;
And one people shall be stronger than the other;
And the older shall serve the younger." (Genesis 25:21-23).

Before Esau and Jacob were born, God had a divine plan for them. Paul said, "And not only this, but there was Rebekah also, when she had conceived twins by one man, our father Isaac; for though the twins were not yet born and had not done anything good or bad, so that God's purpose according to His choice would stand, not because of works but because of Him who calls, it was said to her, 'The older will serve the younger.' Just as it is written, 'Jacob I loved, but Esau I hated'" (Romans 9:10-13).

The word "hated" gives us trouble; however, it does not mean that God despised Esau but can be translated as, "Jacob have I chosen; Esau have I not chosen." The strange thing is that before they were ever born, God said, "This son is going to do this, and the other son is going to do that."

We call this "divine election." Sometimes when we talk about God's foreknowledge, God's predestination, and God's election, we wrinkle our brows a little bit because it is something that is very difficult to understand. There are some things we do not understand about divine election, but God is sovereign and has a plan for history. He predetermines certain things that are going to happen and does that by what the Bible calls divine election.

There are some things we do not understand about divine election, but God is sovereign and has a plan for history.

Some people get a little worried about divine election because they get the idea they may somehow be predestined to go to hell. They believe God predetermines that some people are going to heaven and nothing can stop it and that some people are going to hell and nothing can stop that. Do not believe it. Anyone who wants to be saved can be saved. "The Lord is not slow about His promise, as some count slowness, but is patient toward you, not wishing for any to perish but for all to come to repentance" (2 Peter 3:9). "This is good and acceptable in the sight of God our Savior, who desires all men to be saved and to come to the knowledge of the truth" (1 Timothy 2:3-4).

The world has never gotten out of control nor gone where God cannot control it. Man proposes, but God disposes. Man may rule, but God overrules. It is like being aboard a great airplane such as a 777. We are flying overseas; and on the flight deck is a pilot, co-pilot, and navigator. We are in the back of the plane either sitting or standing, reading or sleeping, talking or praying, eating or not eating. We make a lot of decisions and live by the repercussions of those decisions while the whole time that airplane is going to a predetermined destination.

God the Father is the pilot; God the Son is the co-pilot; and God the Holy Spirit is the navigator. There will not be a hijacking for God is in control. He is bringing us to a divine destination, and we call that the predetermined will of God.

God the Father is the pilot; God the Son is the co-pilot; and God the Holy Spirit is the navigator. There will not be a hijacking for God is in control. He is bringing us to a divine destination, and we call that the predetermined will of God. On the other hand is the free will of man, and we make our decisions and live by them. However, where man rules, God overrules. God is moving history to its predetermined climax. In God's sweep of history, He saw these two sons: Esau who would be the progenitor of the Edomites and Isaac who would be the progenitor of the Jews. God said that the younger, Jacob, would have the ascendancy over the older, Esau.

God planned it that way. There is nothing we can do about it and nothing we ought to want to do about it for God revealed His plan for the future to Isaac and Rebekah.

WE NEED TO LISTEN TO ISAAC AND HIS FAMILY

Those who come from a dysfunctional family should not worry about it because we are about to study a family

84

that consisted of a misleading mother, a scheming son, a failing father, and a broken brother.

> Now it came about, when Isaac was old and his eyes were too dim to see, that he called his older son Esau and said to him, "My son." And he said to him, "Here I am." Isaac said, "Behold now, I am old and I do not know the day of my death. Now then, please take your gear, your quiver and your bow, and go out to the field and hunt game for me; and prepare a savory dish for me such as I love, and bring it to me that I may eat, so that my soul may bless you before I die." Rebekah was listening while Isaac spoke to his son Esau. So [when] Esau went to the field to hunt for game to bring home" (Genesis 27:1-5).

In that era, the father, the patriarch ruler who had received the covenant promises from Abraham, would pass those covenant promises down. That covenant promise was called the birthright, and it included material and spiritual blessings. Through these descendants would come the Scriptures and ultimately the Savior. This birthright was something to be sought after and greatly desired. Esau was about to receive the birthright, but this was not God's plan. God's plan was that Jacob receive it. Genesis 25:23 says that Jacob, the younger, should have the ascendancy and receive the birthright. Isaac was about to give the birthright to the wrong son for the wrong reason.

Isaac said, "Esau, go out into the woods, find and kill a deer, prepare it, cook it really well, and bring it to me. We're going to have a feast. Then, Esau, I'm going to lay a great blessing on you."

As the plot began to unfold, enters the **misleading mother**.

> Rebekah said to her son Jacob, "Behold, I heard your father speak to your brother Esau, saying, 'Bring me some game and prepare a savory dish for me, that I may eat, and bless you in the presence of the Lord before my death.' Now therefore, my son, listen to me as I command you. Go now to the flock and bring me two choice young goats from there, that I may prepare them as a savory dish for your father, such as he loves. Then you shall bring it to your father, that he may eat, so that he may bless you before his death." Jacob answered his mother Rebekah, "Behold, Esau my brother is a hairy man and I am a smooth man. Perhaps my father will feel me, then I will be as a deceiver in his sight, and I will bring upon myself a curse and not a blessing." But his mother said to him, "Your curse be on me, my son; only obey my voice, and go, get them for me" (Genesis 27:6-13).

In essence, Rebekah was saying, "We'll fool your father, and you can get the blessing." She was a mother teaching deceitfulness and sneaking around trying to fool her husband by conniving and cheating, trying to get what God had already promised. She was fighting a battle already lost when she could have been enjoying a victory already won!

God had already said it was going to happen. Rebekah did not need to help God. Have we ever been guilty of trying to help God? God does not need our help. The Almighty is quite sufficient. The strange thing was that by not leaving the matter in God's hands and by not giving her sons to God, she lost Jacob from this point on when he left home never to return again. The way to keep our children is to give them to God.

The next part of the plot is the **scheming son**. "So he went and got them, and brought them to his mother; and his mother made savory food such as his father loved. Then Rebekah took the best garments of Esau her elder son, which were with her in the house, and put them on Jacob her younger son. And she put the skins of the young goats on his hands and on the smooth part of his neck" (Genesis 27:14-16).

Have we ever been guilty of trying to help God? God does not need our help. The Almighty is quite sufficient.

Have you ever seen a man with hair all over his shoulders? That is the way Esau was. Jacob now had hair all over his shoulders, only it was goat skin. "She also gave the savory food and the bread, which she had made, to her son Jacob. Then he came to his father and said, 'My father.' And he said, 'Here I am. Who are you, my son?' Jacob said to his father, 'I am Esau your firstborn; I have done as you told me. Get up, please, sit and eat of my game, that you may bless me" (Genesis 27:17-19).

Jacob was a liar; he was not Esau. Why was he lying, conniving, and cheating to try to get what God already wanted him to have? How we wish Jacob could have just trusted the Lord. It is amazing how some people do not seem to be able to appropriate the things already given to them.

Every Christian already has a birthright: "Blessed be the God and Father of our Lord Jesus Christ, who has blessed us with every spiritual blessing in the heavenly places in Christ" (Ephesians 1:3). We already have the blessing; and when we start enjoying our blessings and start trusting, our Christianity is going to move into a new dimension. So many Christians are fighting, warring, scheming, planning, and conniving when they ought to be trusting. We must learn to live the Christian life by faith.

Our feelings can deceive us. We have all been blinded by sin and will be deceived if we live in the realm of the five senses. Feelings are fickle, and we will never get anywhere in the Christian life when we live for the flesh and our feelings!

It seems the worst person in the family was Isaac himself. I call him the **failing father.** Why did Isaac love Esau more than Jacob? For one reason: "Because he did eat of his venison" (Genesis 25:28 KJV). Esau was a hunter, and Isaac loved venison! Esau ruled over his father because he made merchandise of his father's appetite. Esau was a profane man, but Isaac was a carnal man. Isaac lived in the realm of the flesh!

We cannot depend upon our senses. "Isaac said, 'Behold now, I am old and I do not know the day of my death'" (Genesis 27:2). He thought he was about to die, but he lived for forty more years. His senses deceived him.

"Isaac said to his son, 'How is it that you have it so quickly, my son?'" (Genesis 27:20). Isaac thought the goat meat was venison!

"So Jacob came close to Isaac his father, and he felt him and said, 'The voice is the voice of Jacob, but the hands are the hands of Esau.' He did not recognize him because his hands were hairy like his brother Esau's hands" (Genesis 27:22-23). He thought the goat skin was Esau's hair. He did not understand the difference.

"Then his father Isaac said to him, 'Please come close and kiss me, my son.' So he came close and kissed him; and when he smelled the smell of his garments, he blessed him and said, 'See the smell of my son is like the smell of a field which the LORD has blessed'" (Genesis 27:26-27).

Isaac was deceived and led by feeling rather than by revelation. Our feelings can deceive us. We have all been blinded by sin and will be deceived if we live in the realm of the five senses. Feelings are fickle, and we will never get anywhere in the Christian life when we live for the flesh and our feelings!

The Apostle Paul states: "For those who are according to the flesh set their minds on the things of the flesh, but those who are according to the Spirit, the things of the Spirit. For the mind set on the flesh is death, but the mind set on the Spirit is life and peace" (Romans 8:5-6).

Isaac was not spiritually minded; he was carnally minded. Some people trust their feelings as to know whether they are saved. Feelings are not necessarily the result of forgiveness. We do not depend upon our assurance of our salvation because of the way we feel. Nowhere in the Bible are we told to feel a certain way to know we are saved. The word "feeling" is only used twice in the New Testament while the word "faith" is used over and over and over again. What a foolish decision Isaac made. He said, "That voice! Sounds like Jacob, but the feeling is Esau." We had best learn to go by the voice of God rather than by our feelings.

Then there is the **broken brother**. Esau comes in to see Isaac.

Now it came about, as soon as Isaac had finished blessing Jacob, and Jacob had hardly gone out from the presence of Isaac his father, that Esau his brother came in from his hunting. Then he also made savory food, and brought it to his father; and he said to his father, "Let my father arise and eat of his son's game, that you may bless me." Isaac his father said to him, "Who are you?" And he said, "I am your son, your firstborn, Esau." Then Isaac trembled violently, and said, "Who was he then that hunted game and brought it to me, so that I ate of all of it before you came, and blessed him? Yes, and he shall be blessed." When Esau heard the words of his father, he cried out with an exceedingly great and bitter cry, and said to his father, "Bless me, even me also, O my father!" (Genesis 27:30-34).

Why was he so sorrowful? He did not want the spiritual blessing as he "despised his birthright" (Genesis 25:34); however, he wanted the material blessings because he was a "profane person" (KJV). "That there be no immoral or godless [profane] person like Esau, who sold his own birthright for a single meal" (Hebrews 12:16).

God does not change us so He can love us; He loves us in order to change us. God loves us just as we are.

The word "profane" comes from two Latin words: "pro" and "fanum." The fanum was the holy place located in the front of the temple. It means not having entered into the temple. We can live a profane life—just living for the things of this world. What was the problem with Esau? He was earthbound! Esau cared for present things, not future things; for material things, not spiritual things! His life ended in misery.

We would be hard-pressed to pick the worst one of this family. Every one of them blew it! We wonder what kind of faith Isaac could have had after this; but in the New Testament, he is singled out as an object of faith. In the midst of all of this, God kept on working His plan. God does not change us so He can love us; He loves us in order to change us. God loves us just as we are. Consequently, God kept loving Isaac's family, pouring His love out on them and fulfilling His promise!

WE NEED TO LIVE LIKE ISAAC AND HIS FAITH

God does not need our help on either end. On the one hand, Jacob and Rebekah were trying to make God's plan come into being! On the other hand, Isaac and Esau were trying to keep it from coming into being! However, the plan of God stood sure! "Many plans are in a man's heart, but the counsel of the LORD will stand" (Proverbs 19:21). Regardless of the Esaus and the Jacobs or the Isaacs and the Rebekahs, the counsel of the Lord shall stand.

"By faith Isaac blessed Jacob and Esau, even regarding things to come" (Hebrews 11:20). We learn of **the realization of the will of God** that came to Isaac. It finally began to dawn on Isaac when Esau came in and said, "Dad, I'm ready for the blessing," and Isaac realized that he had blessed Jacob instead. "Then Isaac trembled violently" (Genesis 27:33). For the first time in a long time, Isaac began to discern that God was the one in business and that God was overruling all of Isaac's plans. He began to see the hand of God and started to tremble! This was the trembling of conviction! In essence, Isaac was saying, "I almost blew it! I was placing myself at cross-purposes with the plan, the will, and the wisdom of God!" He saw how God in His providence overruled his willfulness and plans. We had better tremble lest we miss the plan of God for our lives.

There was a **resignation to the will of God**. "Then Isaac trembled violently, and said, 'Who was he then that hunted game and brought it to me, so I ate of all of it before you came, and blessed him?'" (Genesis 27:33). Esau "cried out with an exceedingly great and bitter cry" (Genesis 27:34) and tried to get his father to change the blessing; but Isaac said, "I blessed him—and indeed he will be blessed!" (Genesis 27:33 NIV). Isaac was moving into a new dimension! Once he had seen the will of God, he said, "I'm taking my stand on the Word of God; and your tears, your protestations, and your pleadings will not change me!"

Will we take our stand on the will of God? When God shows us something, will we plant both feet firmly on it and say, "Here I stand, and I shall not be moved!" That was the faith of Isaac: a realization of the will of God and a resignation to the will of God.

What followed was **a reliance on the will of God**. Isaac did not worry about it.

> So Isaac called Jacob and blessed him and charged him, and said to him, "You shall not take a wife from the daughters of Canaan. Arise, go to Paddan-aram, to the house of Bethuel your mother's father; and from there take to yourself a wife from the daughters of Laban your mother's brother. May God Almighty bless you and make you fruitful and multiply you, that you may become a company of peoples. May He also give you the blessing of Abraham, to you and to your descendants with you, that you may possess the land of your sojournings, which God gave to Abraham" (Genesis 28:1-4).

What a change there was in Isaac. He came to his senses and discovered a man was a fool to go against the will of God because it cannot be done. God's will shall not be stopped by any of our plans. However, we can choose to refuse His will and go to hell, but God does not desire "for any to perish but for all to come to repentance" (2 Peter 3:9).

What is faith? A realization of the will of God, a resignation to the will of God, and a reliance upon the will of God.

God will let us have our share of our own free will, but under our free will is God's overriding will. We ought to take the will of God and stand on it and love it because God wants for us what we would want for ourselves if we had enough sense to want it. God's plan for Esau was rooted in His love as was God's plan for Jacob as well as God's plan for us. We need to respond by faith.

What is faith? A realization of the will of God, a resignation to the will of God, and a reliance upon the will of God. This is what Isaac did, and he is listed in the Hall of Fame.

---ᗉᗊᗉ---

Even though God is all-knowing,
He chooses not to leave us
in confusion and darkness.
He will alway provide us light.

8

The Dependence of Faith

"By faith Jacob, as he was dying, blessed each of the sons of Joseph, and worshipped, leaning on the top of his staff" (Hebrews 11:21).

In the previous chapter, we saw Jacob as a conniver, a man who was always trying to rig things and make things work for him. However, God had been working on him to make him what He wanted him to be. God is working on us that way also and will not be finished with us until our total and complete dependence is not on ourselves but on Him. With God's help, we are going to become something in the Lord Jesus Christ. "For I am confident of this very thing, that He who began a good work in you will perfect it until the day of Christ Jesus" (Philippians 1:6).

After Jacob stole the blessing from Esau, he had to flee because Esau had blood in his eyes. As the firstborn and Jacob's twin brother, Esau wanted to kill Jacob.

Jacob had been out in the wilderness, had used a rock for a pillow, and had seen a ladder with angels ascending and descending to and from heaven. He had an experience with God, and God had spoken to him. A lot of wonderful things had happened to him; but for 20 years, he had been in the school of hard knocks. Now he wanted to make it right with Esau because he could not really be right with God until he was right with Esau, the brother he tricked and cheated. Furthermore, he heard that Esau was coming to meet him. God was going to use this situation to cause Jacob to grow and cease to depend upon himself.

God is working on us that way also and will not be finished with us until our total and complete dependence is not on ourselves but on Him.

GOD WILL PROVIDE FOR US BUT HE WILL PUSH US

"Jacob . . . worshipped, leaning on the top of his staff" (Hebrews 11:21). Why would God tell us that Jacob worshipped leaning on the top of his staff? The first principle we are going to learn is that God will protect us, but He will not pamper us.

"Now as Jacob went on his way, the angels of God met him. Jacob said when he saw them, 'This is God's camp,' So he named that place Mahanaim" (Genesis 32:1-2).

Jacob was fleeing, and he suddenly saw angels. He realized that during his 20 years in the wilderness and various places, he had had an angel escort. The angels of God had been encamped round about him to protect him. At this point, Jacob was not totally right with God, but the angels were watching and protecting him. We should thank God for the angels that encamp around us to protect us when we do not deserve it. I have no doubt at all that

God's angel escort has protected me throughout my life. We all have angels watching over us.

Jacob said, "Look at that! Why, there are two hosts. There is the host of people who are with me and then there is the heavenly host encamping all about me." Even though God was protecting him, God did not pamper him. God allowed him to go through great need and difficulty.

With blood in his eyes and an army of 400 strong men, Esau was coming to where Jacob was. God could have kept Esau from coming against Jacob, but God engineered it. God was bringing trouble to Jacob.

Jacob's father-in-law, Laban, wanted to know how to deal with Jacob. "God came to Laban the Aramean in a dream of the night and said to him, 'Be careful that you do not speak to Jacob either good or bad'" (Genesis 31:24). Laban was not to hurt him nor help him; he was just to let him go. God will let us have our way until we come to the end of ourselves. Here was a man in danger, and God was protecting him with angels but not pampering him by removing him from difficulty.

God will let us have our way until we come to the end of ourselves. Here was a man in danger, and God was protecting him with angels but not pampering him by removing him from difficulty.

When Jacob learned that Esau was coming with 400 armed men, he began to plan and scheme. We can see his self-sufficiency.

Then Jacob sent messengers before him to his brother Esau in the land of Seir, the country of Edom. He also commanded them saying, "Thus you shall say to my lord Esau: 'Thus says your servant Jacob, "I have sojourned with Laban, and stayed until now; I have oxen and donkeys *and* flocks and male and female servants; and I have sent to tell my lord, that I may find favor in your sight"'" (Genesis 32:3-5).

Hear Jacob's flattering tongue calling Esau "my Lord," the brother he had connived against and scorned and cheated. No wonder he says this. Notice what else Jacob did:

The messengers returned to Jacob, saying, "We came to your brother Esau, and furthermore he is coming to meet you, and four hundred men are with him." Then Jacob was greatly afraid and distressed; and he divided the people who were with him, and the flocks and the herds and the camels, into two companies; for he said, "If Esau comes to the one company and attacks it, then the company which is left will escape" (Genesis 32:6-8).

Jacob was trying to cut his losses by dividing things up. He first used flattery and then strategy and finally prayer.

Jacob said, "O God of my father Abraham and God of my father Isaac, O Lord, who said to me, 'Return to your country and to your relatives, and I will prosper you,' I am unworthy of all the lovingkindness and of all the faithfulness which You have shown to Your servant; for with my staff only I crossed this Jordan, and now I have become two companies. Deliver me, I pray, from the hand of my brother, from the hand of Esau; for I fear him, that he will come and attack me and the mothers with the children. For You said, 'I will surely prosper you and make your descendants as the sand of the sea, which is too great to be numbered'" (Genesis 32:9-12).

Jacob was quoting the promises of God when God said He was going to bless him and protect him, but now he was saying, "O God, take care of me. I'm in trouble!" It was not wrong for Jacob to pray; he should have. However, prayer was not his first thought; it was his last resort.

After Jacob prayed, he returned to the use of public relations.

So he spent the night there. Then he selected from what he had with him a present for his brother Esau: two hundred female goats and twenty male goats, two hundred ewes and twenty rams, thirty milking camels and their colts, forty cows and ten bulls, twenty female donkeys and ten male donkeys. He delivered them into the hand of his servants, every drove by itself, and said to his servants, "Pass on before me, and put a space between droves" (Genesis 32:13-16).

He divided the 580 valuable animals into lots of five and "put a space" between them. Jacob was smart and knew how to rig things—how to make things happen. He was trying to appease his brother because he knew trouble was coming. He was saying, "Lord, I trust you, but . . . Lord, I don't trust You completely." Genesis 32:20 says, "And you shall say, 'Behold, your servant Jacob also is behind us.'" For he said, "I will appease him with the present that goes before me. Then afterward I will see his face; perhaps he will accept me."

Appeasement. Strategy. Flattery. Appeasement. All of these things in his mind were working together. God let him stew in his own juices. The angels were there.

God wants us to grow; God wants to deliver us from self-sufficiency. God will protect us, but He will not pamper us.

God wants us to grow; God wants to deliver us from self-sufficiency. God will protect us, but He will not pamper us.

GOD WILL CHASTISE US BUT HE WILL CARE FOR US

God will chastise us, but He will care for us. Genesis 32:24 says, "Then Jacob was left alone, and a man wrestled with him until daybreak."

God engineered circumstances where Jacob was left alone. We have a generation of people who cannot stand solitude, cannot stand to be alone with God. This is the reason that when most people walk into a hotel room or their home, they turn on the television automatically. We do not want to be alone with God because we cannot look God or ourselves in the face.

When Jacob was alone, he had a confrontation with God. "Then Jacob was left alone, and a man wrestled with him until daybreak" (v.24). He was alone in the dark when someone jumped on him, and he found himself in a wrestling match. It was the preincarnate Christ. Jesus Christ had come to wrestle with Jacob.

Many of us think Jacob was wrestling with an angel, but that is not the point. The angel started the wrestling match with Jacob. God was trying to do something with Jacob, to deliver him from his self-sufficiency.

All night long they wrestled. A mortal man in a wrestling match with Almighty God. When day was about to break, the angel did something very significant. "When he saw that he had not prevailed against him, he touched the socket of his thigh; so the socket of Jacob's thigh was dislocated while he wrestled with him. Then he said, 'Let me go, for the dawn is breaking.' But he said, 'I will not let you go unless you bless me'" (Genesis 32:25-26).

As they were wrestling back and forth, the angel could have thrown Jacob at any time; but the fight was fixed. Had it just been an ordinary angel, it would have been no wrestling match; however, he is wrestling with the preincarnate Christ. After wrestling all night long, it was as though the Lord said, "I hate to do this to you, Jacob," and then He reached under the hollow of his thigh and shriveled it up, and Jacob could wrestle no more.

The most important muscles to a wrestler are the thighs — the legs — for that is where the strength lies; consequently, the angel of the Lord crippled Jacob's thigh so he could wrestle no more. The angel said, "Let me go"; and Jacob responded, "I'm not letting you go, not until you bless me." If it was the Lord Jacob was wrestling with, why did He say, "Let me go"? Because the Lord did not want him to let go. That does not make sense, does it? Yes, it does.

If we study the Bible, we find many times that God would act as though He wanted to get away from us when He really wanted us to pursue Him with all our hearts. Consider when the two disciples were on the road to Emmaus after the resurrection, and Jesus appeared in His resurrected body. He was walking with them, and their hearts were burning within them. Jesus made as if He would go farther; and they said, "Oh, no, no, don't. Spend the night with us here," and He did (Luke 24:13-35).

The angel said, "Let me go, for the dawn is breaking" (Genesis 32:26). Jacob had come to the end of himself. He had even lost his secret weapon: "If my flattery doesn't help Esau, if he kills all my people on either side and I've sent him these gifts and they don't soften him up, if he finally comes, at least I can run. Now, I can't even run. I don't have any hope except you, O God, and I will not let you go."

God had brought this man to the place where he realized his only hope was God, not his scheming but his surrendering, not his bargaining nor his begging.

God had brought this man to the place where he realized his only hope was God, not his scheming but his surrendering, not his bargaining nor his begging. God hurt him, but God did not harm him.

God loves us too much to leave us self-sufficient. The grand story of the Bible is not men and women in the search for God, but rather, God constantly seeking men and women. From the very beginning, in the garden of Eden, the first question asked by God "Where are you Adam?" God will protect us, but He will not pamper us. God may hurt us, but He will not harm us. He never takes His eyes off us. "For whom the Lord loves, He reproves" (Proverbs 3:12). God will not harm us; we can trust Him. "All discipline for the moment seems not to be joyful, but sorrowful; yet to those who have been trained by it, afterwards it yields the peaceful fruit of righteousness" (Hebrews 12:11).

GOD WILL STRETCH US BUT HE WILL SAVE US

God will stretch us, but He will save us. What was the wrestling match all about? "So he said to him, 'What is your name?' And he said, 'Jacob'" (Genesis 32:27).

The word Jacob meant supplanter and conniver; however, the name Jacob had now been transformed. It was now an honorable name because of what God had done.

"So he said to him, 'What is your name?' And he said, 'Jacob.' He said, 'Your name shall no longer be Jacob, but Israel; for you have striven with God and with men and have prevailed'" (Genesis 32:27-28). The word Israel means prince. Jacob used to be named con artist, but now his name was prince because he had power with God and with men because he prevailed.

"Then Jacob asked him and said, 'Please tell me your name.' But he said, 'Why is it that you ask my name?' And he blessed him there. So Jacob named the place Peniel, for he said, 'I have seen God face to face, yet my life has been preserved.' Now the sun rose upon him just as he crossed over Penuel, and he was limping on his thigh" (Genesis 32:29-31).

He had had this encounter with God, and it was now sunrise. Jacob still had the limp and was halting upon his thigh. God broke him because He wanted to bless him. No longer was he Jacob; he was Israel, a prince. When the Lord asked Jacob, "What is your name?" He wanted him to admit to being a con artist, conniver, and schemer.

God is going to ask us the very same thing: "What is your name?" Then we must answer: "My name is lazy" or "my name is lustful" or "my name is doubter" or "my name is liar" or "my name is selfishness."

Jacob was crippled that he might be crowned. He was broken that he might be blessed. He went from a name of shame to the Hall of Fame. For the rest of his life he had to walk with a staff. When the time came to die, he worshipped, leaning upon his staff. Learning to lean, learning to lean, learning to trust in Jesus. Jacob was broken that he might be blessed.

Man throws broken things away, but God never really ever uses anything until He first breaks it.

Man throws broken things away, but God never really ever uses anything until He first breaks it. David said, "A broken and a contrite heart, O God, You will not despise" (Psalm 51:17). Most of us are not being used of God because we have never been broken; however, if God breaks us and we become broken bread and poured out wine, God can use us.

We may say, "I don't want to be broken." There is a sense that we do not have to be broken if we will break ourselves: "If we judged ourselves rightly, we would not be judged" (1 Corinthians 11:31).

We read earlier: "By faith Jacob, as he was dying, blessed each of the sons of Joseph, and worshiped, *leaning* on the top of his staff" (Hebrews 11:21). Jacob was now an old man and he was dying, but he was leaning upon his staff. All his life he had been limping; all his life he had to have that staff. Yet even when he was dying, he was worshipping God, leaning upon his staff. He was stronger crippled leaning upon his staff than he ever would have been standing on his own two feet. When we wrestle with God and prevail, we never walk like we used to walk!

Failure does not need to be final. Jacob was a man who was a failure, but God took him and used him. For those who have been a Jacob, running from God, conniving, self-sufficient, there is hope. If we are wise, we will save ourselves a wrestling match by making a full surrender now. If we judge ourselves, we will not have to be judged. If there is suffering in our lives, let it teach us to lean on the Lord Jesus Christ. When it is all done and all settled, it is our worship by faith that really matters.

How does God sum up Jacob's life? There were so many episodes, but God sums it up in a pithy little sentence: When he died, he worshipped leaning upon his staff. Jacob was 147 years old when he died. He was weak and weary, but he spent his last moments worshipping the Lord. What a way to go!

There is a story of a man who wanted to get right with God. He thought perhaps he could do that if he became a hermit, so he went and lived in a cave. One day someone came to him and said, "Are you still wrestling with the devil?" He responded, "Not any longer. Now I'm wrestling with God." The man said, "You are? You don't hope to win, do you?" He said, "No, I hope to lose; I hope to lose."

That is what I hope for all of us—that we will bow before Him and say, "I will not let You go unless you bless me."

When we have wrestled with the Lord and prevailed, we will not walk like we used to walk.

9

The Dreams of Faith

When we get where we are going, where will we be? We are going somewhere, but where are we headed? Are we satisfied with the direction of our lives? Are we living, or are we merely existing? People without a dream exist; people with a vision take hold of life with both hands and move into it.

People without a dream exist; people with a vision take hold of life with both hands and move into it.

What is our spiritual growth objective? What plan do we have? What kind of a Christian do we want to be? Do we want to be people with a working knowledge of the Word of God? If we do not have that as a goal or an objective, it will not happen by osmosis. We are not going to get it like a fungus in the air.

What is our physical health objective? We are all limited to a degree by our genes and chromosomes; however, there is much we could and should be doing physically if we would only act rather than react.

What is our professional objective? What do we see ourselves doing in our jobs ten years from now? What skills would we like to acquire? Do we simply say, "As long as I make enough money to subsist, that's all I want"?

What about our financial objective? What about retirement and savings? What about our ability to give? What about how much money we feel would be a right amount to be trusted with?

What about our family life objectives? Have we ever written them down? Do we think good families just happen by chance?

What are our ministry objectives? Do we want a ministry? If so, what kind of a ministry would we like to have? Would we like to be soul winners, Bible teachers, missionaries? Would we like to have a neighborhood influence? Would we like to minister to children or adults?

After we have these general objectives, we must begin to quantify, qualify, and stratify in order to turn these objectives into goals.

Perhaps our family life objective is a godly home. A popular adage often attributed to Benjamin Franklin, the father of time management, is that "failing to plan is planning to fail." Therefore, we must develop a strategy to win. Each of our goals needs a strategy to achieve it. In essence, our lives are made up of our future, faith, family, fitness, finance, and fun. We need objectives, goals, and strategies for each of these main areas of life.

We may ask what faith has to do with this or what kind of difference it makes to have faith for these goals. Unsaved people can no doubt develop objectives, describe goals, and deploy strategies. Even though this may be correct on the surface, we want our objectives to be God-given and our goals to come from the heart of God. We want our strategies to be implemented and blessed by God; consequently, we will need faith in order to be successful.

We have the vision, but the goals and strategies that come out of the vision—the objectives—are the middle part of this bridge that relates to faith because it is by faith that we will reach those goals and perform those strategies.

When we have a vision and believe the vision is from God, then we can exercise faith.

We may ask what the difference is between a vision and a daydream and what we can have faith for. We cannot have faith if we are not certain and do not feel in our hearts that it is what God wants. "This is the confidence which we have before Him, that, if we ask anything according to His will, He hears us" (1 John 5:14). Therefore, we must ask ourselves if this is just something we have cooked up or if it is a daydream or if it is a vision. We must determine if it is a whim or if God has said that this is the plan for us.

A vision starts with God: "I will pour forth of My Spirit on all mankind; and your sons and your daughters shall prophesy, and your young men shall see visions, and your old men shall dream dreams" (Acts 2:17). Dreams and visions are a result of God's pouring out His Spirit. The vision is not cooked up; it comes down.

A daydream begins with us; a vision comes from God. "Where there is no vision, the people perish" (Proverbs 29:18 KJV). When we have a vision and believe the vision is from God, then we can exercise faith. Faith comes from hearing from God. Faith is a response of the person who has heard from God.

The word and concept of vision are also related to the word provide or provision. One of the more commonly recognized biblical names of God is Jehovah Jireh, the Hebrew phrase for "The Lord will provide." The word provide means to "pre-see." It comes from the Latin prōvidēre meaning to foresee, provide for, equivalent to prō+vidēr to see. God is able to pro-vide because He is able to pre-see.

The problem with flawed finite humanity is our inability to see beyond the present. We are so limited in our vision, so nearsighted and shortsighted, that we cannot see beyond the now. Consequently, we are preoccupied and often so worried and anxious about the problems and challenges we see in the "right now" that our faith is often shaken and our trust in God is weakened. However, God is our provider who has a pro-video and is able to pre-see so that while we are struggling and wrestling with the problem in the "right now," God is far down the road and is seeing in the "not yet." By the time we get from the "right now" to the "not yet," He has moved the problem from the "not yet" into the "no longer," all because He has pre-vision and can pro-vide and truly is Jehovah Jireh, our Provider! Our lives are not snapshots or moments frozen in time; they are videos and ongoing revelations of God's ordained will for our lives, and the camera is still rolling! We are not where we are going, and it is not over until God says it is over. Our God shall supply all our needs because He sees the needs before we get there!

How do we see ourselves? The mind cannot distinguish between a mental image and an actual image in time. What the mind sees, it believes. If for some reason we have gotten stuck in the past image of our lives, we must begin today reframing that image by moving toward a video vision of from where we were to where we are. The way we see ourselves is in comparison to the way others will see us. If we take ourselves seriously, others around us will see us "seriously" in their eyes.

"By faith Joseph, when he was dying, made mention of the exodus of the sons of Israel, and gave orders concerning his bones" (Hebrews 11:22). It was there that God smiled upon Joseph's life because of the faith he demonstrated before the Lord. This story helps us fulfill what the Lord has called us to be, do, and go in this life. The vision of Joseph's youth came to pass through the corridor of time regardless of all the obstacles of the pit, prison, and palace.

WE NEED TO REMEMBER THE UNBREAKABLE PROMISES OF GOD

As faith leaders, *we need to remember the unbreakable promises of God*. Hundreds of years earlier, the Lord had given promises to Abraham as it related to his lineage throughout the earth and had spoken not only to Abraham but also to Isaac and Jacob as well as Joseph. When God spoke to Abraham centuries earlier, He shared with him that he was going to have a son, his son was going to become a nation, that nation would eventually be relocated in a distant land, and they would eventually be forced into slavery followed by an exodus when the people would come back to the land of Canaan. God told Abraham this would take at least four hundred years and was beyond the scope of his life on earth. The Lord was telling Abraham, "I'm making a promise to you, and the promise I am making is larger than you are and longer than your lifespan. By the time this promise is fulfilled, you will be at peace with your fathers."

Abraham understood what God had planned, so he sought a bride for Isaac. A bride was found, and the process began for the nation of Israel to be born and broadened throughout the earth. Even though there were times when Joseph was discouraged and possibly felt defeated, he did not let the dream die or the promises be removed from his life. He understood what the promise was; he understood what the plan was. Regardless of the pit, the prison, the palace, or Pharaoh, Joseph was going to be faithful to the assignment. We need to remember the unbreakable promises of God.

We can either be blessed by God's promises or broken by God's promises, but we will never bend the promises of God.

Some people try to break God's promises and end up being broken by them. We can either be blessed by God's promises or broken by God's promises, but we will never bend the promises of God.

Wise is the visionary leader who gets in synch with where God is going and asks God to bless and prosper the path. Joseph was one of those in his generation who understood it; and even though the promises of God were not first and foremost given to us, we have inherited them. As Joseph was getting ready to cross the finish line into glory, he pulled his family members together and reminded them of God's promise and where they were headed. Joseph understood that this needed to be placed in the hearts of his people.

What is amazing about this story is that 25 percent of the Book of Genesis is devoted to this one person named Joseph; yet in the Hall of Fame of Faith, he only gets one verse (Hebrews 11:22) that speaks of when Joseph made mention of the exodus of the sons of Israel and gave orders concerning his bones. I want to encourage us to remember the unbreakable promises of God because one day the glory of the Lord will cover the earth like the water covers the sea. There is not one dry spot on the bottom of the ocean, and one day there will not be a dry spot where the glory of the Lord has not kissed the earth.

In Revelation 7, we read that every tongue, tribe, and nation will one day stand at the throne of God. This is going to happen whether we get involved or not. The Lord will pass us by if we do not get in synch with where He is going. I want to encourage us to remember the unbreakable promises of God. There are more promises than there are problems, and the Holy Trinity never meets in an emergency session. God is not worried about providing for us. Most of the time we do not have a money problem; we have a vision problem. Oftentimes people say, "I wish I had enough money," but the question is whether we have enough vision because out of the vision comes the provision.

If we do not have a vision, it does not take much money to fund it; but if we do have a God-sized vision, we need a God-sized provision to fulfill it. We must remember the unbreakable promises of God. It is important that we understand that when Joseph was in the land of Egypt, he was not impressed with the pyramids nor the wealth of the Pharaoh; he understood that God had him on a divine assignment. He saw his role in God's goal and his part in God's heart; and he was faithful to see it through, all the way to placing the vision in the hearts of his children and grandchildren so they could continue the assignment long after he was gone. There are times when problems and stress and difficulties can discourage us, but we need to remember the unbreakable promises of God.

WE NEED TO REALIZE THE UNSHAKABLE POWER OF GOD

As faith leaders, *we need to realize the unshakeable power of God.* Companies start up and companies close down;

denominations are founded and sometimes fade out of existence; empires are raised up and later come crashing down. However, the kingdom of God has never experienced a recession; it continues to grow every year. Exponentially, the Church is growing faster today than ever before. We are living in the greatest times of evangelism, church planting, global networking, and the possibility of fulfilling the Great Commission in this century. We need to realize the unshakeable power of God.

The next time the devil reminds us of our past,
we need to remind him of his destined future.

Look at what Joseph chose to do—he pulled his family members together. No doubt there were concerns all around him as there are around us. Joseph understood that life was about to change for him and for those following behind him. How did Joseph handle it? When he pulled his family members together, he did not fill them with worry and anxiety, dread and doubt but reminded them of God's plan and mission—where they were headed. The next time the devil reminds us of our past, we need to remind him of his destined future. Joseph realized the unshakeable power of God and knew that God was going to see it through to the end. In fact, Joseph had demonstrated this many years earlier when his father passed away.

When Jacob, Joseph's father, passed away, Joseph stopped what he was doing and took Jacob back to the land of promise to a small village called Shechem which means a place of prosperity. He took his father back to prosperity, buried him there, and came back and stayed on his assignment. Joseph realized where his home would be, understood where the people were going, and went ahead and made a deposit by burying his father in the land of promise. When he pulled his family members together, he did not fill them full of worry and doubt and dread but renewed and encouraged them to let them know that everything was going to be great and wonderful down the road.

There be labor instead of favor, famine instead of feasting, and hardship and heartache; but God would see them through to the other side. It should not matter to us who the "Pharaoh" is or how many chariots he may have because when God says He is going to do something, we can count on it—He WILL do it.

No doubt there were concerns all around him as there are all around us. No doubt there are financial and family concerns and health and ministerial concerns. No doubt there are many different obstacles that we may be facing; however, the Lord, who started us on the journey, wants to help us finish what we started. He wants to give us enough financial resources, momentum, and people in our lives to be able to achieve what we can by working together.

Not only is there concern, but there is also change— radical and dramatic change that has impacted our lives. In the last 10-15 years specifically, this generation has experienced more change than any other generation since the beginning of time. In the last 20-30 years, more dramatic informational technological change has happened on the planet that has catapulted the nations of the earth forward in a way that no previous generation has ever known, yet we are not fearful of the change but welcome it.

Joseph knew that change was coming for him for he was dying and his time on earth was drawing to a close. What he had to do, he had to do quickly and decisively to make sure his family members were ready to continue what he had started. People often talk about their legacy—what they are leaving behind. I occasionally reflect not just on what I am leaving behind but also on what I started while on earth. My prayer is that I start more ripples than I will ever be able to see completed in my short tenure in the world.

No doubt there were concerns and change around Joseph as there are for us as well, but it is important to understand the chronology that is behind us. We have come a long way in a short period of time.

Joseph understood the chronology behind him because he knew the day was coming when God was going to fulfill the promise of the exodus. The prophet Habakkuk exhorts us to write the vision down plainly and concisely so that we might run with it. The vision God has put in our hearts needs to be clear. The history behind us is prologue, and the future is bright and brilliant before us. We need to realize the unshakeable power of God. It does not really matter what the armies of the world may say or do or what empires are raised up in the years ahead because God is going to keep His word and use people who desire to be used. God is the extra that turns the ordinary into the extraordinary. It is the extra things He does for us every day, the extra people He sends along our path, the extra thoughts He puts in our hearts, and the extra faith He puts in our lives. It is the extra abilities He gives us so we can do the extraordinary to be about the Lord's business and believe that it is possible to fulfill the Great Commission in our generation.

WE NEED TO REST IN THE UNMISTAKABLE PEACE OF GOD

As faith leaders, *we need to rest in the unmistakable peace of God.* We sometimes wonder if the Lord is going to come through, if the Lord is going to be on time; but the Lord is never late and always comes through with His plan for His people.

When we think of Joseph as he crossed the finish line, he smiled at death; and his family lay him to rest. Then one year goes by, five years, a hundred years; and one day Moses walks into Pharaoh's court and demands, "Let My people go" (Exodus 9:1). This is the day of the divine exodus, one of the big red-letter days on God's calendar. It is on this day that Moses, the great general, leads nearly two million people out of Egypt, the phenomenal exodus God had spoken to Abraham about centuries earlier. Moses gave the command to take the bones of Joseph with them (Exodus 13:17-19). I was taught in Sunday School that only two people who came out of Egypt crossed over into Canaan, but three people went into Canaan because Joseph also came out of Egypt and crossed over into Canaan.

The Lord is never late and always comes through with His plan for His people.

In my mind's eye, I can see them bringing Joseph out of Egypt at the front of the exodus. Though the Bible does not tell us where they positioned Joseph, I have a hard time believing they brought him out and put him at the back of two million people. I like to think they brought him to where Moses was. How long did they carry Joseph? The entire time of the wilderness wanderings: 40 years — through the Red Sea, by Mount Sinai, and by Mount Nebo where God buried Moses. However, Joseph did not stop there but continued right on into Canaan.

Israelites were buried every day during the travels through the wilderness, an entire generation of Israelites; but God raised up a new generation that would go into the land of Canaan. There was more faith in the bones of Joseph than in the feet of the Israelites. Joseph went through the Red Sea and by Gilgal and Jericho, and he was there the day the sun stood still (Joshua 10:12-13). It was in Shekem that they buried Joseph (Joshua 24:32), the same place that Joseph, more than a hundred years earlier when he was the Prime Minister of Egypt, had buried Jacob.

We need to remember the unbreakable promises of God and rest in the unshakeable power of God and the unmistakable peace of God.

What an amazing story is the life of Joseph. Sold into slavery, falsely accused and placed in prison, brought to Pharaoh's palace and made the second in command, buried in Egypt, his bones carried throughout the wilderness wanderings and through the years in Canaan and all the battles, and buried next to his father, Jacob, more than a hundred years later. What God starts, He finishes. We need to remember the unbreakable promises of God and rest in the unshakeable power of God and the unmistakable peace of God.

There are many change agents that come and go in this world, but only a few that can say at the end of life's journey, "Not only did I help to bring change, but I also helped to bring salvation."

As we end this chapter, there is one perplexing question I would like to ask: Why was Joseph discontent to be left in Egypt? Why did he not encourage his family to go on to the land of Canaan and one day they would all rendezvous in glory? Why was he so emphatic to say that "when God takes you out, you must take me with you"? The answer is simply that Joseph wanted to be involved in what God was doing whether he was dead or alive. He had a desire to be included in God's plan in establishing

118

the kingdom on the earth. If we will cultivate that kind of passion as visionary leaders, our reservoirs will never run dry, our fountainheads will never be dammed up, and we will never burn out or rust out!

I challenge us to become faith leaders in this generation and mobilize our churches, ministries, and organizations to be baptized into the God-sized vision that has been entrusted to us.

---❦---

We are not only called
to have life for the day,
but for life beyond the grave!

10

The Defiance of Faith

Hebrews 11 lists the heroes of the faith and includes two names that are possibly little known—Amram and Jochebed, the parents of Moses. However, their claim to fame was not that they were the parents of Moses but that they believed God and their faith pleased God. If we want to please God, we must learn how to believe God for "without faith it is impossible to please Him" (Hebrews 11:6).

Without faith, it is impossible to please God; and there is a process of growing our faith in God.

A frequent greeting in the church is often, "How are you feeling?" Perhaps a more important question should be, "How are you faithing?" for it is not according to our feelings but "it shall be done to you according to your faith" (Matthew 9:29 NASB); not according to our friends, but "according to your faith"; not according to our fame but "according to your faith"; not according to our fortune but "according to your faith."

Without faith, it is impossible to please God; and there is a process of growing our faith in God.

"By faith Moses, when he was born, was hidden for three months by his parents, because they saw he was a beautiful child; and they were not afraid of the king's edict" (Hebrews 11:23).

Amram and Jochebed were two slaves who got in touch with Almighty God by faith. They did something so marvelous and wonderful that it was recorded forever in the annals of God's Word in the Hall of Fame of Faith.

The Hebrews were slaves in the land of Egypt, and another Pharaoh came to power who had not known Joseph and was a cruel and hard taskmaster. It seemed as though there was a population explosion among the Hebrews as they were growing in strength, virility, and number. Pharaoh became apprehensive, so he sent out a decree that all the male babies were to be cast into the Nile and drowned.

Through prayer, Amram and Jochebed were led of the Lord to do something very unusual. They hid their baby boy for three months; however, there came a time when they could no longer hide him. Led by the Holy Spirit, they made a little ark of bulrushes, waterproofed it, took it down by the Nile, and placed it in the bulrushes. The daughter of Pharaoh "saw the basket among the reeds and sent her maid, and she brought it to her. When she opened it, she saw the child, and behold, the boy was crying" (Exodus 2:5-6), and her heart was moved with compassion. She took the baby into her home, and Moses' own mother became a nursemaid to her own child. In time, Moses became Mighty Moses who delivered the Hebrews from the land of bondage.

Amram and Jochebed are listed in God's Hall of Fame of Faith. They were common, ordinary slaves; but they had faith in God. They show us the process of growing in faith.

FAITH'S VISION: OUR LOVE

Through the vision of their faith, they saw that "he was a beautiful child" (Hebrews 11:23). They had insight that this child was a very special child, a unique child.

Faith is a response to the revealed will of God.

God had made a promise that the Israelites would stay in the land of bondage in Egypt for four hundred years; however, after four hundred years, God said, "They're coming out." Amram and Jochebed were praying people and attuned to the Word of God. They knew the time was getting short, and it would soon be time for God to keep His Word because almost four hundred years had passed.

They were in contact with God through the Holy Spirit, and the Holy Spirit said, "Moses is the proper child to get the job done."

By the providence of God, the life of Moses was spared. We think it was so mean, so hard, and so cruel that Pharaoh put all those babies to death but consider the millions of unborn babies who never had a chance to be what they could be, what they ought to be, what God intended for them to be because they were aborted.

Some years ago, a professor in a medical school said:

I want to give you a case, and I want you to decide what ought to be done with certain people. Here is the family history. The father has syphilis. The mother has tuberculosis. They have already had four children. The first one is blind. The second one died. The third is deaf. The fourth has tuberculosis. The mother is pregnant with her fifth child. The parents are willing to have an abortion if you decide they should. What do you think?

Most of the students in that class voted for the mother to have an abortion. The professor said, "Congratulations, you have just murdered Beethoven because that was the situation and the home of his birth."

We do not have the right to take a human life, whether born or unborn. We have no right to be a Pharaoh or a Herod and say, "The innocents should be slaughtered!" We live in a strange day when a person who destroys an eagle's egg can be fined $500, yet an abortionist can destroy a human embryo and be paid that much or more. Amram and Jochebed set about to see to it that baby Moses had a chance to become an adult Moses, that he had an opportunity to be God's man. They had a vision from the Lord; however, they could not have faith until God spoke: "Faith comes from hearing, and hearing by the word of Christ" (Romans 10:17).

God must speak to us either from the Bible or by the Holy Spirit. Most likely, it will be a combination of the two; but we must hear God speak. Faith is not just simply deciding we want something and then believing for it. Faith is not simply positive thinking or wishful thinking. Faith is a response to the revealed will of God. Faith is "the assurance of things hoped for" (Hebrews 11:1 NASB); but those things are there, and we have evidence they are there because we have faith in our hearts. Faith is placed in our hearts so the thing that God wants accomplished will be done!

"Now faith is the assurance of things hoped for, the conviction of things not seen" (Hebrews 11:1).

Moses' parents were in tune with God. The natural eye sees natural facts and reacts naturally. The spiritual eye sees spiritual facts and reacts supernaturally. Faith's vision is to walk by a sixth sense of faith for it was "by faith" that they saw that Moses was a beautiful child. God was speaking: "I have a special plan for this baby."

They exercised faith despite all the difficulties and circumstances that seemed to be to the contrary. They did not have their eyes on natural facts; they had their spiritual eyes on supernatural facts! That is faith, and it does not care about circumstances or appearances. We need to have a mighty faith in God's promises and look to God alone to fulfill those promises.

Moses' parents were seemingly hopeless, helpless slaves; but they believed the Word of God: "Faith comes from hearing, and hearing by the word of Christ" (Romans 10:17).

How can we know whether what we feel in our hearts is the prompting of the Holy Spirit or merely human desire? How can we tell whether we are just wishing for something or whether God is wanting us to believe for something?

It is nothing that can be explained but something that must be experienced. Praying in the Spirit is not an explanation but an experience. It is nontransferable. We must walk close to God, get into the Word of God, and abide in Christ and let Him abide in us until the Holy Spirit says, "This is the way; walk in it. This is the promise; believe it." There must be the vision of faith, and faith's vision was when Amram and Jochebed saw that "he was a beautiful child."

FAITH'S VENTURE: OUR LEAP

We must not only have faith's vision but also faith's venture. Moses' parents did something about it. Real faith is belief with legs on it. They did not just say, "Oh well, God's going to take care of little Moses. I'm trusting God." They put their faith into action: "By faith Moses, when he was born, was hidden for three months by his parents" (Hebrews 11:23). James tells us clearly and plainly that when we believe God, we do something about it: "Even so faith, if it has no works, is dead, being by itself" (2:17). Moses would have been dead had his parents not put some works with their faith.

When they believed God, they did something about it.

"Faith without works is dead" (James 2:26). When they believed God, they did something about it. They did not just practice fatalism and say, "What will be, will be." The opposite of fatalism is fanaticism. They did not take baby Moses and throw him to the crocodiles and say, "Let's see if he can swim. He's three months old." They did nothing irrational.

Some people try to prove their faith by handling snakes. That is not faith; that is foolishness. Faith does something. Faith acts. By faith, Moses was hidden. It was his parents' faith that propelled them to action.

We want our children to be delivered from the pharaohs of this world and grow up to be mighty men and women of God; therefore, we had best get busy and put legs to our faith by praying and witnessing, being a member of a Bible-believing church, and training others if God has given us the ability to do so. Our children must be under the care and instruction of born-again teachers who really care for their souls.

Bible faith gets busy; it does not sit around and twiddle its thumbs. "Train up a child in the way he should go, even when he is old he will not depart from it." (Proverbs 22:6). So many people are not training their children while many others train them the wrong way.

The Bible does not say to "teach a child the way that he should go" but to "train up a child in the way he should go." There is a difference in teaching a child what is right and training a child. Anything we teach a child, someone else can teach differently. The child may decide to believe what someone else teaches rather than what we teach. What does it mean to "train"? The dictionary gives the meaning as "to prepare for a contest." Consider those who train for a football game, a basketball game, or a track meet: to instruct by exercise, to drill, to form to a proper shape, to discipline for use. We must train our children in the way they should go.

"Even when he is old he will not depart from it (Proverbs 22:6). We may say, "Well, I'm giving him a good education." Theodore Roosevelt said, "When you educate a man in mind and not in morals, you create a menace to society." What are we doing? Are we rearing our children to know the Lord? Moses' parents did all they could; they believed God. Amram and Jochebed saw that Moses was "a beautiful child." They had vision, and then there was faith's venture: They hid Moses.

FAITH'S VALOR: OUR LEADERSHIP

"By faith Moses, when he was born, was hidden for three months by his parents, because they saw he was a beautiful child; *and they were not afraid of the king's edict*" (Hebrews 11:23 emphasis added).

127

"Then Pharaoh commanded all his people, saying, 'Every son who is born you are to cast into the Nile, and every daughter you are to keep alive'" (Exodus 1:22). All the boy babies were to be slain; but even though Amram and Jochebed were slaves, they were not afraid.

If I did not know the Lord, I would be afraid for myself and my children as these are dark days in which we live. In spite of the dark days in which Moses' parents also lived, they were not afraid of Pharaoh's command because they knew the King of kings.

When we get in step with God, He will go before us to make crooked paths straight so we can have victory.

Moses' parents were not successful because of an abundance of finances; they were poor and poverty-stricken. Nor were they successful because they had a lot of friends. There is no indication that anyone else was defying Pharaoh, but Amram and Jochebed were not filled with fear but with faith. When we get in step with God, He will go before us to make crooked paths straight so we can have victory. Moses' parents did all they could to be obedient before the Lord when they hid Moses for three months; but as the baby became older, it became more difficult to hide him.

What if another Hebrew slave family knew that Amram and Jochebed did not throw their baby boy in the Nile. Would that slave family keep quiet? Probably not. Though Amram and Jochebed did all they could to hide him, it was becoming harder and harder to do so. Their valor to disobey Pharaoh's command was moving them closer to victory with each passing day.

FAITH'S VICTORY: OUR LEGACY

God honored the faith of Moses' parents: "By faith Moses, when he had grown up, refused to be called the son of Pharaoh's daughter, choosing rather to endure ill-treatment with the people of God than to enjoy the passing pleasures of sin, considering the reproach of Christ greater riches than the treasures of Egypt; for he was looking to the reward. By faith he left Egypt, not fearing the wrath of the king; for he endured, as seeing Him who is unseen" (Hebrews 11:24-27).

How did Moses get all this faith? From Amram and Jochebed.

Now a man from the house of Levi went and married a daughter of Levi. The woman conceived and bore a son; and when she saw that he was beautiful, she hid him for three months. But when she could hide him no longer, she got him a wicker basket and covered it over with tar and pitch. Then she put the child into it and set it among the reeds by the bank of the Nile. His sister stood at a distance to find out what would happen to him.

The daughter of Pharaoh came down to bathe at the Nile, with her maidens walking alongside the Nile; and she saw the basket among the reeds and sent her maid, and she brought it to her. When she opened it, she saw the child, and behold, the boy was crying. And she had pity on him and said, "This is one of the Hebrews' children." Then his sister said to Pharaoh's daughter, "Shall I go and call a nurse for you from the Hebrew women that she may nurse the child for you?" Pharaoh's daughter said to her, "Go ahead." So the girl went and called the child's mother. Then Pharaoh's daughter said to her, "Take this child away and nurse him for me and I will give you your wages." So the woman took the child and nursed him" (Exodus 2:1-9).

Faith honors God; God honors faith. God began to move heaven and earth to honor the faith of these two helpless slaves. Imagine a royal princess bathing in the dirty Nile. She had her marbled, lavish tubs and perfumed soaps; but she doubtless remembered the old swimming hole where she used to play as a little girl. While walking alongside the Nile, she saw the basket by the providence of God.

Faith honors God; God honors faith.

Her maid fetched it out of the water; and at just the right time, little Moses cried. He was pinched by an angel at the right moment, and Pharaoh's daughter's heart melted within her. Miriam stepped forward and said, "Would you like me to go get one of the Hebrews to nurse the baby for you?" Imagine a royal princess taking a suggestion from a slave girl! However, she said, "That's a good idea"; and here came Jochebed.

Pharaoh's daughter said, "Would you take this child and raise him for me, and I'll pay you for it." I doubt Jochebed haggled over wages but instead said, "I'll be happy to do that." Baby Moses had everything he needed and even received a scholarship to the University of Egypt with Pharaoh paying for it—his room, his board, his lodging, and his education! This happened by the providence of God!

God saw to it that Jochebed had her baby because God wants mothers to raise their own children, and Jochebed was able to put something in Moses' heart that no Egyptian university could take out.

We must raise our children in their formative years by praying over them, loving them, training them, and putting something into them no pagan university can take out.

"Moses was educated in all the learning of the Egyptians, and he was a man of power in words and deeds" (Acts 7:22). Moses received a Ph.D. from the University of Egypt but came out clinging to the faith once and for all delivered to the saints because his mother had trained him up in the way he should go.

We must raise our children in their formative years by praying over them, loving them, training them, and putting something into them no pagan university can take out.

"By faith Moses, when he had grown up, refused to be called the son of Pharaoh's daughter" (Hebrews 11:24). He forsook Egypt, cared not for its treasures, and said, "I'm going to be a man of God." Why? Because of a dad and mom who had faith in God.

Faith's vision: They saw the will of God.

Faith's venture: They did the will of God.

Faith's valor: They were not afraid of Pharaoh.

Faith's victory: They raised a child that delivered a nation.

———∞∞∞———

We need to hear the voice
of God, have a vision
from Him, venture out by faith,
and obtain the victory!

11

The Discernment of Faith

We will learn from one of the greatest visionaries of all time, Moses, because he saw the invisible, valued the imperishable, did the impossible, and was a man with incredible vision.

Helen Keller, born blind, was asked, "What could be worse than being born blind?" Her response: "Having sight but no vision." Proverbs tell us that "where there is no vision, the people are unrestrained" (29:18).

Vision is hope with a blueprint, a star to steer by, and a bridge to the future.

We are not talking about daydreams but about **vision which is seeing the invisible and turning it into reality**. Vision is the dominant factor of our lives. It will determine our friendships, our relationships, and our choices. Our vision is what our prayers are about and what we are giving our influence, money, and energy toward.

Vision is hope with a blueprint, a star to steer by, and a bridge to the future. George Barna defined vision as "foresight with insight based on hindsight" (*Christian Educators Journal*, cejonline.com, posted April 30, 2013). In other words, seeing what has happened, seeing what ought to happen, and seeing it with insight.

There was a man, one of the brightest stars in the Hebrew heaven, named Moses who had a vision and built a bridge to the future.

> By faith Moses, when he had grown up, refused to be called the son of Pharaoh's daughter, choosing rather to endure ill-treatment with the people of God than to enjoy the passing pleasures of sin, considering the reproach of Christ greater riches than the treasures of Egypt; for he was looking to the reward. By faith he left Egypt, not fearing the wrath of the king; for he endured, as seeing Him who is unseen. By faith he kept the Passover and the sprinkling of the blood, so that he who destroyed the firstborn would not touch them. By faith they passed through the Red Sea as though they were passing through dry land; and the Egyptians, when they attempted it, were drowned. By faith the walls of Jericho fell down after they had been encircled for seven days (Hebrews 11:24-30).

The wonderful miracles of faith were rooted in a God-breathed, God-given vision. Without a vision, we are merely existing, not living. All we are doing is simply drawing our breath and our salaries and fighting to live while we live to fight but not going anywhere.

Christopher Wren, one of the greatest architects of the centuries, designed St. Paul's Cathedral in London, England. As the cathedral was being constructed, Sir

Christopher Wren disguised himself as an ordinary person and walked among the workmen. He asked one man, "What are you doing?" and the man said, "I am cutting stone." He asked another man, "And what are you doing?" whereby the man answered, "I am earning five shillings, two pence a day." He asked a third man, "What are you doing?" and the third man replied, "I am helping Christopher Wren build a great cathedral." Are we simply cutting stones and drawing our salaries, or is there something bigger, something larger? We need a vision, and our families need a family vision. Individuals, families, and churches all need a vision.

Moses saw the invisible, sought the imperishable, and did the impossible.

Moses saw the invisible, sought the imperishable, and did the impossible. He did it by a faith that was rooted in a vision. He had a discernment of the future, and faith in God helped him to bring it to reality.

As mentioned previously, we are not talking about a daydream or a carnal ambition. "Where there is no vision, the people are unrestrained" (Proverbs 29:18) is sometimes translated as "where there is no open revelation, the people perish." A vision is a revelation from God, not what we simply dream or our ambition. It is what we see by faith from God as an open revelation; therefore, we will not perish.

WE NEED TO FORESEE THE TREASURES

"By faith Moses, when he had grown up, refused to be called the son of Pharaoh's daughter, [that is, he could have been called the grandson of a king] choosing rather to endure ill-treatment with the people of God than to enjoy the passing pleasures of sin, considering the reproach of Christ greater riches than the treasures of Egypt; for he was looking to the reward" (Hebrews 11:24-26).

Why? Because of the treasures he foresaw: "Considering the reproach of Christ greater riches than the treasures of Egypt; for he was looking to the reward" (v.26). Moses was no fool; he did not live on the negative side of the ledger but on the positive side.

Most peoples' lives are not energized because there can be no power for the present if there is no faith for the future. It is a vision that energizes and infuses our lives.

In a vision, there is always a prize to possess. Why do we want to get to the other side of the bridge? Because of what is over there! Moses had been doing some estimations, and he saw the riches of Christ. Vision and values are always linked together.

Moses was calculating the present versus the future — spiritual "figuring." What he saw was that the reproaches of Christ were greater riches than the treasures of Egypt. Although the treasures of Egypt were incredible and were at his fingertips — position, power, prestige, and pleasure, he said, "I've got something greater than all of the riches of Egypt." He looked at it this way: He could be a grandson of Pharaoh or a son of God in a grand way.

He could have the pleasures of sin or the joys of Jesus, the riches of Egypt or the rewards of heaven. He could have that which was temporary or that which was eternal.

Most people need to stop, sit down, and think — which few of us rarely do. Instead, we go about the mundane things of life and never stop to ask ourselves where we are going, what we are doing, and what it is all about. Most of us spend more time planning a seven-day vacation than eighty years of our lives.

When we get where we are going, where will we be? Like it or not, we are on a journey. Moses saw the lean look and the long look and liked the long look better. We need a vision.

Most peoples' lives are not energized because there can be no power for the present if there is no faith for the future. It is a vision that energizes and infuses our lives.

Research shows that 95 percent of people have never written down their goals in life. Of the 5 percent who have, 95 percent achieved their goals.

A survey conducted at Yale University found that only 3 percent of the students who graduated had specific goals; that is, they had a vision. These 3 percent achieved more than the other 97 percent put together. That is the power of a vision.

It is much better to look ahead and prepare than to look back and regret.

It is much better to look ahead and prepare than to look back and regret. Many people are going to come to the end of their lives and look back and say, "Well, what did I do? I didn't make any preparation. I had no dreams for myself, my family, or my church."

A man aboard the Queen Mary asked the captain, "How long does it take to stop this ship?" The captain replied, "If I were to shut down all the engines, all of the power, it would take me a mile to bring this great ship to a dead stop. A good captain looks at least a mile ahead."

There are forces in our lives which are taking us somewhere. We need to look to the future. "It is not good for a person to be without knowledge, and he who hurries his footsteps errs" (Proverbs 19:2). If we do not consider where we are going and just keep on going there, we are living in sin.

"By wisdom a house is built, and by understanding it is established; and by knowledge the rooms are filled with all precious and pleasant riches" (Proverbs 24:3-4). Do we have understanding and knowledge? Do we have a vision, or is life just happening to us?

"A prudent man sees evil and hides himself, the naïve proceed and pay the penalty" (Proverbs 27:12). A prudent man looks to the future while the simple, the nonchalant, and the naïve just pass on.

Moses did all of this in the midst of a pagan and materialistic society. He had to be different and separate himself from the herd. We must learn to think for ourselves and not let our friends, secular society, fads, and pleasures dominate our lives. Moses had to sit down and do some calculating and honest thinking.

In the 1990s during a 10,000-meter NCAA race, in Riverside, California, 123 of the 128 runners missed a turn. However, one of the runners, Mike Decalvo, saw the right way and turned around and beckoned to the other runners to follow him. Only 4 runners followed him, and the rest of them laughed at him. They thought he had taken a wrong turn and gone the wrong way, but the reality was that only 5 out of 128 runners took the right way. There are people who will laugh at us if we set some standards and will say, "Hey, you'd better get with the crowd." Let them laugh. Take the long look.

WE NEED TO FORSAKE THE PLEASURES

The reason some people do not live by vision is because they are not willing to pay the price. Moses, however, was willing to make a choice and pay the price: "By faith Moses, when he had grown up, refused to be called the son of Pharaoh's daughter, choosing rather to endure ill-treatment with the people of God than to enjoy the passing pleasures of sin" (Hebrews 11:24-25). At any given moment, a vision will help us to forsake all that we are in order to gain all we can be.

In many ways, Moses had already arrived. After all, he was a big shot in Egypt and heir to the throne; but he turned his back on it all because he saw something greater. He had to figure the treasures and forsake the pleasures.

The problem with many people is they have never really gotten a vision of what they could be, what they ought to be, or what the treasures of Jesus are.

We may pay now or later, but we always pay. It is a principle of life. We can live in indolence, be a couch potato, eat everything we want, drink anything we want, do whatever we want, and sleep whenever we desire; but we will pay the price.

Suppose a dog has a nasty, smelly, stinky bone he wants to bring into the house. The dog's owner tries to get it away from him, but the dog will not let go. As a matter of fact, if the dog does not belong to us, he may bite us if we try to take that bone away. However, there is one way to get a bone away from a dog—by putting a steak on the ground. Why would he not drop the bone to get the steak? It is a matter of values.

There are certain things the Bible calls the pleasures of sin, and Moses said, "I don't want them." Why? Who would not give up a nasty bone for a steak? Vision and value are linked. The problem with many people is they have never really gotten a vision of what they could be, what they ought to be, or what the treasures of Jesus are.

WE NEED TO FIGURE THE MEASURES

A vision without a plan is a daydream. Notice the measures Moses followed: "By faith Moses, when he had grown up, refused to be called the son of Pharaoh's daughter, choosing rather to endure ill-treatment with the people of God" (Hebrews 11:24-25). In our own plans, there needs to be **cooperation** first. For us to be all that we can be, we need to help others be all they can be.

Moses chose to suffer affliction with the people of God. His vision was not selfish or self-centered. If we have a God-given vision, it will include our family, others, our church, and the world. If we have a vision that is egocentric and self-centered, it is not of God but of Satan.

Many years ago, Vincent Lombardi was asked, "What does it take to make a great team?" His response:

> There are a lot of coaches with good ball clubs who know the fundamentals. They have plenty of discipline, but they still don't win the game because the third ingredient is missing. If you're going to play together as a team, you have to care for one another and love one another. Each player has to be thinking about the next guy and saying to himself, "If I don't block that man, Paul is going to get his legs broken. I have to do my job well in order that he can do his." The difference in mediocrity and greatness is feeling that these guys love each other.

We do not often think of football players as loving each other, but they do for they are a team. How much more so with the Church of the Lord Jesus Christ. We must take seriously the command of Jesus to love one another — not because we are lovely but because He loves us.

Our visionary plan must also include **courage**. "By faith he left Egypt, not fearing the wrath of the king" (Hebrews 11:27). If we are looking for a cheap, easy, or lazy way to be all that we can be, we will not be. The devil is the sinister minister of fear, our Pharaoh, trying to keep us in the land of Egypt and in a life of mediocrity, enjoying the pleasures of sin rather than knowing the riches of Christ. It is our vision that will help us overcome this matter of fear.

It is one thing to have a vision and another thing to go beyond a vision and have faith. At the end, there must be obedience.

Our visionary plan must not only have cooperation and courage but also **continuance**. "By faith he left Egypt, not fearing the wrath of the king; for he endured, as seeing Him who is unseen" (Hebrews 11:27).

Many of us start and then fail. We lose the vision, the dream. We do not pursue the plan or endure. A vision was what kept Moses on track and enabled him to endure.

Moses was the greatest man in the Old Testament and Paul in the New Testament for they both had a vision. Though Paul suffered affliction, sorrow, heartache, tears, and trials, he knew triumph. As the greatest church builder, the greatest missionary, and the greatest Christian who ever lived, he gave us the secret: "So, King Agrippa, I did not prove disobedient to the heavenly vision" (Acts 26:19).

It is one thing to have a vision and another thing to go beyond a vision and have faith. At the end, there must be obedience.

Jesus was the center of Moses' vision: "He endured, as seeing Him who is unseen" (Hebrews 11:27). The riches of Christ.

12

The Dimensions of Faith

We are living in a time of plagues, promises, and the Passover.

> By faith he left Egypt, not fearing the wrath of the king; for he endured, as seeing Him who is unseen. By faith he kept the Passover and the sprinkling of the blood, so that he who destroyed the first-born would not touch them. By faith they passed through the Red Sea as though they were passing through dry land; and the Egyptians, when they attempted it, were drowned (Hebrews 11:27-29).

Life is short, death is sure, sin is the cause, and Christ is the cure. We need to understand that the malady of this world is indeed sin. We are all sinners by nature, by birth, and by practice. We may be rich sinners or poor sinners, educated sinners or ignorant sinners, religious sinners or irreligious sinners, or baptized sinners or nonbaptized sinners; but by birth, by nature, and by choice, we are sinners and need to be saved.

America needs more than a war on poverty or a war on COVID-19; the need is for a war on sin. The costliest thing around is sin which brings poverty. We certainly would not expect a senator to stand up in Congress and say, "Ladies and Gentlemen, the problem is sin," nor would we expect a military officer to stand up in the Pentagon and say, "Our enemy is sin." We would not expect a professor in one of our universities to stand up and say that it is the sin factor that has caused so much pain, moan, groan, woe, and heartache in the world. We have never dealt with the problem because mankind in general has never made the right diagnosis. We spend the time knocking down cobwebs rather than killing spiders. We must understand that the cobweb is the result of the spider; thus sin.

Life is short, death is sure, sin is the cause,
and Christ is the cure.

From where will the answer come? From the truth first taught thousands of years ago.

WE NEED FAITH THAT LEADS TO A DEFINITE DECISION

"By faith he [Moses] left Egypt" (Hebrews 11:27). In the Bible, Egypt is symbolic of the bondage of sin; and Pharaoh, the king of Egypt, is symbolic of Satan. Moses' forsaking Egypt symbolizes Moses' forsaking sin.

Pharaoh did not want to let them go. Satan never gives anyone or anything up without a fuss, a fight, or a struggle.

Pharaoh, representing Satan, offered Moses some clever compromises to keep him out of the promised land, calling for him and Aaron to "go, sacrifice to your God within the land" (Exodus 8:25). This is the compromise of **salvation**.

Pharaoh felt there was no need to break with Egypt. If Moses wanted to be religious, he could go right ahead; however, he had to do it in Egypt. What Satan was saying to Moses and Aaron was the same thing he will say to us. If we want to be religious, it is quite all right; all we need to do is just tack our religion onto our old, sinful life.

Satan tries to get us to be religious—and lost. He would rather we substitute education for regeneration and culture for Calvary. The devil had just as soon send us to hell from the pew as from the gutter. He does not mind if we are religious—just as long as we stay in Egypt.

However, Moses said, "Pharaoh, we're not going to stay in this place. We are coming out of the land of bondage."

"Pharaoh said, 'I will let you go, that you may sacrifice to the LORD your God in the wilderness; only you shall not go very far away'" (Exodus 8:28). If the devil cannot convince us to compromise our salvation, he will tempt us to compromise our **separation**. God had not called them to the wilderness but to the promised land. God had not called them to rocks and sand and rattlesnakes but to milk, honey, pomegranates, grapes, hills and valleys, and waterfalls and rivers. However, Pharaoh says "All right, if you're going, don't go very far."

If Satan cannot keep us from going, he will try to keep us from going all the way by making us wilderness Christians and carnal Christians. However, God wants us to be different. The Bible says we are to go all the way.

We learn that God made a difference between the Egyptians and the Israelites. We also ought to be different for a Christian should stand out in this world like a gardenia in a garbage can.

"Come out from their midst and be separate" (2 Corinthians 6:17). Are we separate and different, or have we taken the devil's compromise? Can the people who look at us tell the difference between us and a real child of God?

If the devil cannot convince us to compromise our salvation or separation, he will tempt us to compromise our soulwinning.

Moses said, "Look, Mr. Pharaoh, we're going and we're going all the way." Well, Pharaoh did not give up yet.

So Moses and Aaron were bought back to Pharaoh, and he said to them, "Go, serve the Lord your God! Who are the ones that are going?" Moses said, "We shall go with our young and our old; with our sons and our daughters, with our flocks and our herds we shall go, for we must hold a feast to the Lord." Then he said to them, "Thus may the Lord be with you, if ever I let you and your little ones go! Take heed, for evil is in your mind. Not so! Go now, the men among you, and serve the Lord, for that is what you desire" (Exodus 10:8-11).

Pharaoh said, "Moses, if you're going and you're going all the way, tell me who is going." Moses said, "We're all going." Pharaoh said, "Now wait a minute. Don't take your families with you; leave your children and wives behind. It might be dangerous out there." If the devil cannot convince us to compromise our salvation or separation, he will tempt us to compromise our soulwinning.

146

Moses said, "Look, we're going, we're going all the way and all of us are going." The devil hates family religion, yet the Bible teaches it. I do not understand how anyone could be content to go to heaven and leave their loved ones behind to go to hell. I know somehow God is going to make it all right, but I do not understand how I could be in heaven and my children go to hell. Moses told Pharaoh, "We're going and we're all going. We're not going to leave our children and wives behind."

Nevertheless, devil had not given up yet. Next comes the fourth compromise.

> Then Pharaoh called to Moses, and said, "Go, serve the LORD; only let your flocks and your herds be detained. Even your little ones may go with you." But Moses said, "You must also let us have sacrifices and burnt offerings, that we may sacrifice them to the LORD our God. Therefore, our livestock too shall go with us; not a hoof shall be left behind, for we shall take some of them to serve the LORD our God. And until we arrive there, we ourselves do not know with what we shall serve the LORD" (Exodus 10:24-26).

Moses was emphatic when he said, "Not a hoof shall be left behind" (Exodus 10:26). If the devil could not get them on the **salvation** compromise or on the **separation** compromise or on the **soulwinning** compromise, he tried to get them on the **stewardship** compromise.

Some of us are going to heaven, but the devil has our businesses. Some have never taken their substance, their business, and dedicated it to Jesus Christ; therefore, there is a dimension in their worship that is failing because Moses said, "Look, we need these things to serve God, to sacrifice to God. Our pocketbook, our bank account, belongs to the Lord Jesus."

Moses made a decision. He forsook Egypt and said, "Mr. Pharaoh, I want you to know we're going and we're going all the way. I want you to know we're all going and we're going with all we have. We are taking our flocks with us; and neither hide nor hair, nor hoof nor horn is going to be left behind." If we are going to get ready for the Passover, we need to understand there is a decision that needs to be made.

WE NEED FAITH THAT LEADS TO A DIVINE DELIVERANCE

"By faith he kept the Passover and the sprinkling of the blood, so that he who destroyed the firstborn would not touch them" (Hebrews 11:28).

It is one thing to repent, but that repentance must be towards God and faith towards our Lord Jesus Christ— faith in His shed blood as exemplified by the Passover.

It was not enough for Moses simply to decide that he was going to forsake Egypt. If that was all he had done, he would have been like so many of us and simply turned over a new leaf.

Moses determined to be and do better. With the decision, there must be a dynamic—the dynamic that delivers us from the power of Egypt. It is one thing to repent, but that repentance must be towards God and faith towards our Lord Jesus Christ—faith in His shed blood as exemplified by the Passover.

When God led the children of Israel out, He taught them to slay a Passover lamb which was a picture, a prophesy, of the Lord Jesus Christ. The New Testament tells us that Christ, our Passover, was sacrificed for us and the Old Testament lamb represented God's lamb.

> Now the LORD said to Moses and Aaron in the land of Egypt, "This month shall be the beginning of months for you; it is to be the first month of the year to you. Speak to all the congregation of Israel, saying, 'On the tenth of this month they are each one to take a lamb for themselves, according to their fathers' households, a lamb for each household. Now if the household is too small for a lamb, then he and his neighbor nearest to his house are to take one according to the number of persons in them; according to what each man should eat, you are to divide the lamb. Your lamb shall be an unblemished male a year old; you may take it from the sheep or from the goats. You shall keep it until the fourteenth day of the same month'" (Exodus 12:1-6).

A Righteous Lamb

This lamb was to be a **righteous lamb** — a male of the firstlings and without blemish — a pure and spotless lamb. This lamb was a picture of the Lord Jesus Christ.

They were to keep the lamb for three days, and it would be inspected extremely carefully. The Old Testament rabbis would even examine the eyelids of that little lamb. If even one blemish was detected, the lamb was disqualified. Why? Had Jesus Christ not been the perfect Lamb of God, absolutely sinlessly perfect, He would have been disqualified.

149

The rabbis raised special Passover lambs in the fields of Bethlehem, the fields of Boaz. When Passover was drawing near, the shepherds would bring those lambs into the city of Jerusalem by the sheep gate. On the same day those lambs were coming into the city of Jerusalem to be examined, Jesus Christ, God's lamb, was also coming into the city of Jerusalem for His triumphal entry.

Had Jesus Christ not been the perfect Lamb of God, absolutely sinlessly perfect, He would have been disqualified.

The Sadducees examined Him, the Pharisees examined Him, the priests examined Him, Pilate and the civil leaders examined Him. Jesus looked at them and said, "Which one of you convicts Me of sin?" (John 8:46). However, all of them knew in their heart of hearts that there was not one sin against God's sinless lamb. Even Pilate said, "I find no guilt in Him" (John 19:4).

A Required Lamb

Not only was He a sacred lamb, but He was also a **required lamb**. "You shall keep it until the fourteenth day of the same month, then the whole assembly of the congregation of Israel is to kill it at twilight" (Exodus 12:6).

There was a special time when this lamb was to be slain—the Jewish time that was spoken of was the fourteenth day of April. Jesus came in the fullness of time as God's slain lamb.

The father would take the spotless little lamb, pull the chin up, and take a razor-sharp knife to the throat of that lamb while the lamb made not a sound as its blood drained into a basin.

Imagine the scene at the Lord's crucifixion. Bethlehem's lambs are coming into the city; and Bethlehem's lamb, the Lord Jesus Christ, was also coming into the city. Those little lambs were examined as was Jesus. When Abraham was about to offer Isaac on Mount Moriah, he saw a ram caught in the thicket. The Bible says Abraham saw Jesus and was glad. (John 8:56)

The significance of the ram that Abraham saw caught in the thicket was that when Abraham and Isaac were getting ready to go up Mount Moriah, Isaac was supposed to have been the sacrifice. When Isaac asked, "Where is the lamb for the burnt offering?" (Genesis 22:7), Abraham responded, "God will provide for Himself the lamb for the burnt offering" (Genesis 22:8). Notice carefully: He did not say the Lord will provide a lamb for Himself, but the Lord will provide Himself as a lamb—"I will be that lamb." When John the Baptist saw Jesus coming by Jordan, he said, "Behold the Lamb of God" (John 1:29).

As the Levites were slitting the throats of those little lambs on that Passover day, Jesus was dying in agony and blood on the cross. As God's lamb was dying, He bowed His head and said, "It is finished!" (John 19:30.)

WE NEED FAITH THAT LEADS TO A DECLARED DEMONSTRATION

A Redemptive Lamb

The lamb that was a slain lamb became a **redemptive lamb**. "Moreover, they shall take some of the blood and put it on the two doorposts and on the lintel of the houses in which they eat it" (Exodus 12:7).

"The blood shall be a sign for you on the houses where you live; and when I see the blood I will pass over you" (Exodus 12:13). Judgment was deserved, but God said that when He saw the blood, He would pass over them. They were to take the blood and strike it on the two side posts. Imagine the father as he dipped his cup in the basin of blood and struck it on his doorposts—not just rubbed it on. He then took it and struck it on the lintel of the door.

We can see the cross of our Lord and Savior Jesus Christ as the blood dripped from the lintel upon the threshold. This is a picture of the blood of Jesus Christ which cleanses us from all sin.

Imagine a little Hebrew boy back in the time of the Exodus talking to his father: "Dad, Moses says we're to get a lamb and kill it and put the blood on the doorposts of our house; and if we don't do it, the firstborn in the family is going to die. Dad, since I happen to be the firstborn, do you mind if we check it out one more time?"

He was saying, "Dad, have we done it according to the Word of God?" and his dad responded, "Yes, son."

"Dad was our Lamb without spot, without blemish?"

"Yes, son."

"Father, did we put the blood on the side posts and the lintel of our house?"

"Yes son, we've done everything we are supposed to do."

"Thank you, Dad, and good night."

The son went to bed and slept soundly because he trusted the Word of God and the work of God.

Imagine another little Jewish boy who also had a fine dad. He said to his dad, "Since I'm the firstborn in our home, I just want to check...did we get us a spotless lamb?"

"Yes, we did, son."

"Did we kill it as God said?"

"Yes, we did."

"Did we apply the blood specifically the way God told us to apply it?"

"Yes, son, we did."

"Well, Dad, all of this sounds good; but if you don't mind, I'm just going to sit up and pray all night because I don't think I can sleep a wink."

The death angel came and passed over the first house and then came to the second house which he passed over also. That poor little boy worried all night for nothing.

Some people are going to heaven first class while others are going second class. The blood makes us safe, and the Word makes us sure. When we believe the Word of God, we rest in what God says; and since God cannot lie, we might as well rest in the finished work of the Lord Jesus.

When we believe the Word of God, we rest in what God says; and since God cannot lie, we might as well rest in the finished work of the Lord Jesus.

Imagine a third boy, Pharaoh's son, who said, "Dad, this guy, Moses, is making all kinds of predictions that are coming true. There have been all kinds of plagues, and now he's saying that the plague of all plagues is coming — that if we do not place the blood of a lamb upon the doorposts of our house, a death angel is going to come and destroy the firstborn; and I'm the firstborn!"

Pharaoh says, "Son, don't worry about it. I'm Pharaoh, and we've got many religions here in Egypt — good religions with the best priests that money can buy."

"But Dad, we've got lots of lambs."

Pharaoh says, "Moses is a religious fanatic; don't worry about that blood of the lamb stuff. Go to sleep. Daddy loves you."

At midnight, however, there was a flash and a gasp and a scream; and Pharaoh's son was cold and dead for the death angel had come.

God said, "When I see the blood I will pass over you" (Exodus 12:13). Had they taken a live lamb and tied it to the door, it would have done no good. Salvation does not come by learning lessons from the life of Christ but by receiving life from the death of Christ. Had they taken rubies and diamonds and gold and silver and adorned their lintels, it would have done no good for God said, "When I see the blood I will pass over you."

"Without shedding of blood there is no forgiveness" (Hebrews 9:22).

A Reciprocal Lamb

This lamb was a special lamb. It was not only a saving lamb but also a **reciprocal lamb**. The Old Testament predicted the coming of the Messiah. Jesus was an Old Testament shadow. Jesus Christ is our Passover for He sacrificed Himself for us.

Not only was it the lamb that was delivering them, but it was also the lamb that was energizing them.

That same night, the Israelites roasted the lamb with fire and ate unleavened bread with bitter herbs (Exodus 12:8-9).

We can hardly imagine what the Egyptians were thinking while a quarter of a million lambs were being barbequed in one night. The aroma must have filled the air.

What was happening was that a group of slaves were becoming a nation and a bunch of sinners began to fellowship with God and one another over the lamb. Not only was it the lamb that was delivering them, but it was also the lamb that was energizing them. Jesus Christ gave

Himself for us that He might give Himself to us. "Christ in you, the hope of glory" (Colossians 1:27).

The next morning, each family left Egypt by walking under the blood with a lamb on the inside. We ask how we get to heaven from this earth—under the blood with the Lamb of God on the inside.

In Genesis, when a person sinned, the sacrifice required was one lamb per person. In Exodus, it was one lamb per family. In Canaan, it was one lamb per nation each year. When John the Baptist came preaching, he said, "Behold, the Lamb of God who takes away the sin of the world!" (John 1:29).

If Satan cannot keep us
from going, he will try to keep
us from going all the way by
making us wilderness Christians
and carnal Christians.

13

The Difficulties of Faith

God wants us to live, learn and lead a grand life of faith. Membership is available to those who walk by faith and not by sight. When God comes to measure our lives, He will say, "According to your faith, be it unto you" (Matthew 9:29 KJV). We will be summed up not according to our fame, our fortune, our friends, our feelings, or our fate but according to our faith.

As people of God, we still face obstacles that need to be removed; and through the Lord Jesus Christ and by faith, we can be victorious.

"By faith the walls of Jericho fell down after they had been encircled for seven days" (Hebrews 11:30). Jericho lay before the children of Israel. God had promised them a land that flowed with milk and honey; but between them and the fulfillment of God's promise, God's plan, and God's provision for their lives was mighty Jericho.

As people of God, we still face obstacles that need to be removed; and through the Lord Jesus Christ and by faith, we can be victorious. However, Satan will see to it that there are great obstacles that loom large and impossible between us and the plan and will of God for our lives. The Jericho for each of us will be different. It may be a family or financial problem, an unhappy marriage, an unholy life, an unhealthy body, an unfulfilled dream, or unrecognized potential; but we will definitely face problems.

Perhaps in these key problems are strategic forces of evil that stand between us and all that God would have us to be; however, we can overcome these obstacles by faith: "By faith the walls of Jericho fell down" (Hebrews 11:30). No other way—simply by faith the walls of Jericho fell after they were encompassed about seven days. When God has a gigantic task to perform, it is a person of faith who gets the contract. Faith is the link that binds our nothingness to His almightiness. God's plan was to build the faith of His people one day at a time so they could see the walls of Jericho tumble down. That is what God does in our lives—builds our faith one step at a time so we can live in continuous victory over this world and know the power of God.

God has called us to conquer each Jericho in our lives. We can see the walls of sin come down if we will simply follow the three strategic stages in Joshua 6.

WE NEED AN OBSERVATION OF THE CITY

A City of Antiquity

"Now Jericho was tightly shut because of the sons of Israel; no one went out and no one came in" (Joshua 6:1).

Jericho was a city of antiquity, one of the oldest cities in the ancient world; however, it was not only a city of antiquity but also a city of iniquity.

A City of Iniquity

The people of Jericho were vile, wicked, sinful, and idolatrous. They had turned their hearts and lives from the principles of Jehovah God.

A City of Enormity

Not only was Jericho a city of antiquity and iniquity but also a city of enormity—a massive, mighty, and powerful city. God has called us to reach our cities; however, it will not be done through finances but through faith alone—faith in Almighty God.

Like Jericho, our cities are filled with crime, corruption, and carnality as well as with sin, idolatry, and vile and wicked imaginations. Satan and his demonic spirits are stalking our streets for they are out to steal, kill, and destroy.

If we are going to reach our cities with the gospel and tell men, women, boys, and girls about Jesus, we will need faith to pull down the strongholds of the enemy and spread the Good News that Jesus Christ is still the Savior of the world.

It is not someone else's responsibility to observe our cities; it is our responsibility. When was the last time we took a long, hard look at our cities and asked, "God, what can I do to reach my city?"

In 1987 little Jessica McClure fell into a well. Scenes of her were broadcast continually on television and photos published in newspapers. Following her rescue, little Jessica met with the president of the United States. No one cried out and said we had spent too much to save this little girl for everyone was convinced that we somehow had to rescue her. However, some things are more tragic than a child's falling into a well, such as many people falling into hell. May God help us not only to observe our cities but also to get a burden for the lost. When was the last time we asked God to awaken us to the urgency and emergency of reaching dying men and women on their way to hell?

Joshua 6:1 tells us that Jericho's doors were closed. The enemy had literally shut every door. Why is it so hard for us to penetrate our schools and cities for God? The enemy is doing everything he can to lock the doors so no one will hear the good news of the gospel. However, if we have faith, it does not matter what the devil does because faith can accomplish mighty exploits in the name of the Lord Jesus Christ.

If we have faith, it does not matter what the devil does because faith can accomplish mighty exploits in the name of the Lord Jesus Christ.

Each Jericho in our lives represents the obstacles that are keeping us from entering God's rest and experiencing God's best. Even though it may appear that all doors are shut, our God has a plan for success.

WE NEED AN ORIENTATION OF CHRIST

We need to know God's plan. After observation, we need orientation. After pinpointing the problem, we need to perceive God's plan.

There Is Divine Intervention

"The Lord said to Joshua…" This phrase is repeated numerous times. May we come back to the place where we hear the voice of God in our hearts, come back to the place of divine intervention where we are able to listen and do what God calls us to do.

Now it came about when Joshua was by Jericho, that he lifted up his eyes and looked, and behold, a man was standing opposite him with his sword drawn in his hand, and Joshua went to him and said to him, "Are you for us or for our adversaries?" He said, "No; rather I indeed come now as captain of the host of the LORD." And Joshua fell on his face to the earth, and bowed down, and said to him, "What has my lord to say to his servant?" The captain of the LORD's host said to Joshua, "Remove your sandals from your feet, for the place where you are standing is holy." And Joshua did so (Joshua 5:13-15).

While Joshua was looking at his problem, he became aware of a presence. There was someone near him, and he knew not who it was. He pulled his sword instinctively and wheeled around only to come face-to-face with a man with a drawn sword. Joshua had never seen him before and asked the question, "Are you for us or for our adversaries?"

The man said, "No." Imagine how frustrating that would be. "Are you for us or are you for our adversaries?" "No." In effect, he said, "I'm not for you and I'm not for them. I'm the captain of the Lord's host. I have not come to take sides; I have come to take over."

Who was this whom Joshua met? The preincarnate Christ! Before His incarnation, the Lord Jesus frequently visited earth. He appeared as the angel of Jehovah and as the captain of the Lord's host. Joshua came face-to-face with the Lord Jesus; and when he saw this, he put down his sword, fell in the dust, and worshiped his Lord.

When Joshua surrendered and prostrated himself before this person and worshiped Him, his faith began to grow and build. Our faith will also grow and be built as we worship the Lord. The writer of Hebrews (12:1-3) tells us that to have faith, we must look to Jesus, the author and finisher of our faith. Joshua was doing just that — looking to Jesus; and his faith began to increase in his heart and life.

Many of us are problem-conscious and see Jericho; however, we all need to take our eyes off Jericho and fix "our eyes on Jesus, the author and perfecter of faith" (v.2). When we catch a vision of Him, worship Him, and bow before Him, we will find our faith growing. We must learn to glance at our problems and to gaze at our Lord.

When we catch a vision of Him, worship Him, and bow before Him, we will find our faith growing. We must learn to glance at our problems and to gaze at our Lord.

Faith never grows in the heart of a rebel. Rebellion and faith cannot be in the same heart and life. We will never, never, never have faith until we bow before Him and say what Joshua said to the captain of the Lord's host: "What has my lord to say to his servant?" (Joshua 5:14).

Each of us must say, "Lord, what do you want me to do? I'll do what You want me to do, I'll be what You want me to be, I'll say what You want me to say, I'll give what You want me to give." Faith begins with bowing before the Lord, taking the shoes off our feet, and recognizing His holiness.

It is far more important to be on God's side than to have God on our side. God is not going to get on our side. We may say, "Well, I want the Lord on my side." Well, forget it. Joshua asked, "Are you for us or for them?" to which the Lord responded, "No, I've come to take over." We must realize that God wants to take over.

There Is Direct Inspiration

"The LORD said to Joshua, 'See, I have given Jericho into your hand, with its king and the valiant warriors'" (Joshua 6:2).

God told Joshua that He had given him the merchants, the king, and the mighty men of valor. It is God's plan that we take back every facet of our cities to include the political and social arenas. He wants us to march into the center of our cities with faith to do mighty exploits in the name of the Lord Jesus Christ.

There Is Definite Instruction

You shall march around the city, all the men of war circling the city once. You shall do so for six days. Also seven priests shall carry seven trumpets of rams' horns before the ark; then on the seventh day you shall march around the city seven times, and the priests shall blow the trumpets. It shall be that when they make a long blast with the ram's horn, and when you hear the sound of the trumpet, all the people shall shout with a great shout; and the wall of the city will fall down flat, and the people will go up every man straight ahead (Joshua 6:3-5).

If a man in a church business meeting were to stand and suggest that God had revealed to him that everyone in the congregation should march around the city for a certain number of days and at the right moment they should blow trumpets and shout loudly and that the plan would work for winning the city for God, most churches would excommunicate him. However, that was exactly God's plan for taking the city of Jericho. God taught us that we do not take a city by force but by faith.

In the gold rush days of 1849, wagon trains heading west from Saint Joseph, Missouri, passed a sign which read, "Choose your rut carefully for you will be in it for a long time."

We need to make sure we do not get into a rut of forms and rituals, that we do not just go to church and forget about our cities and the people who need the Lord. Good churches and good preachers can get into ruts. We must keep a fresh touch of God's Spirit in our hearts, families, and churches. We need to observe our cities, and we need to have the orientation from Christ.

After pinpointing the problem and perceiving God's plan, we must then practice God's procedure.

WE NEED THE OPERATION FOR CONQUEST

After pinpointing the problem and perceiving God's plan, we must then practice God's procedure. After God gives the Gilgal of revelation, He wants to give the Jericho of rejuvenation. After we have seen Jesus and laid our swords at His feet, we can then go and take a city with the Captain of the Lord of Hosts. We will see God's plan for this operation of conquest so we must make it our plan, heartbeat, and mindset.

The Devotion of Faith

> So Joshua the son of Nun called the priests and said to them, "Take up the ark of the covenant, and let seven priests carry seven trumpets of rams' horns before the ark of the Lord." Then he said to the people, "Go forward, and march around the

city, and let the armed men go on before the ark of the LORD." And it was so, that when Joshua had spoken to the people, the seven priests carrying the seven trumpets of rams' horns before the LORD went forward and blew the trumpets; and the ark of the covenant of the LORD followed them. The armed men went before the priests who blew the trumpets, and the rear guard came after the ark, while they continued to blow the trumpets. But Joshua commanded the people, saying, "You shall not shout nor let your voice be heard nor let a word proceed out of your mouth, until the day I tell you, 'Shout!' Then you shall shout!" (Joshua 6:6-10).

Joshua's compliance. Joshua did what God told him to do (vv.6-7). He had heard from God and heeded and responded to the voice of God. Likewise, we need to obey what we hear from God and do what God has called us to do. If we want victory, if we want to reach our cities, we must obey the Word of God.

The Jews' cooperation. For the first time in forty years, the Jews worked together without bickering, complaining, moaning, or groaning. When God's people live in Canaan, they learn to work, serve, worship, and obey Him together. We can always tell whether someone is in Canaan or not by what comes from their lips. Joshua said to all the people, "You shall not shout nor let your voice be heard nor let a word proceed out of your mouth, until the day I tell you, 'Shout!' Then you shall shout!" (v.10).

He told them that because he wanted to restrict their handicap. God was tired of their complaints and said,

"Quit murmuring and start marching; quit talking and start walking." God wants His people to work, serve, worship, and witness together. Stopping the unnecessary talking was one of the hardest things for these people to do, but God recognized their helplessness in bringing down the walls of Jericho; they had to depend on Him.

It is not enough to say one time that we are going to serve God. Every morning we should get up with a renewed commitment to serve the Lord the best we know how.

A story has been told of a group of monks in a particular monastery. The qualification for serving was the restriction of being permitted to speak only two words every five years. After the first long period, everyone wondered what the newest monk would say. In a tempered tone they finally heard him say, "Food's bad." After five more years of silence, his two words were, "Work's hard." Before long, five more years had passed. Again, a crowd gathered to hear his next two words. The now not-so-young monk said in a determined voice, "I quit."

Do we complain about doing work for Jesus, saying the work is too hard or the costs are too great? I am so thankful a preacher was bringing forth the gospel when the Holy Spirit pricked my heart. I responded by going to the altar and giving my life to Christ. This is not the time to complain but to go in the name of Jesus and, by faith, take our cities for Christ.

The Determination of Faith

"So he had the ark of the LORD taken around the city, circling it once; then they came into the camp and spent the night in the camp" (Joshua 6:11).

This is step one in our determination to take our cities for God.

> We **confirm our pledge.** The first time we go out, we are saying to the Lord we have heard His call and are confirming our pledge to Him. When we come to the altar, we are saying we are pledging to do what He has called us to do. They confirmed their pledge, but they also continued their plan.

> We **continue our plan.**

> Now Joshua rose early in the morning, and the priests took up the ark of the LORD. The seven priests carrying the seven trumpets of rams' horns before the ark of the LORD went on continually, and blew the trumpets; and the armed men went before them and the rear guard came after the ark of the LORD, while they continued to blow the trumpets. Thus the second day they marched around the city once and returned to the camp; they did so for six days (Joshua 6:12-14).

> It is not enough to say one time that we are going to serve God. Every morning we should get up with a renewed commitment to serve the Lord the best we know how. Every day we should be telling the people of our cities about Jesus. They confirmed their pledge, continued their plan, and completed their project.

We **complete our project.** "Then on the seventh day they rose early at the dawning of the day and marched around the city in the same manner seven times; only on that day they marched around the city seven times" (Joshua 6:15).

They kept doing what God told them to do until the job was finished. Our problem is that we go six times and then quit. It does not matter how we add it up — if we have been out there six days, we have not fully obeyed God's Word. God tells us to continue until our work is finished — we are not to stop nor to quit too early.

There will be bad days, there will be obstacles, and there will be tough times; but if we have faith in our hearts, we will keep on keeping on until our task is completed.

One week before my wedding, my mother underwent major surgery. I told her not to even think of making the long journey. Of course, we all know how mothers feel about these kinds of things; and she insisted she would be present. The next Saturday morning, she boarded an airplane from a wheelchair for the flight to our wedding. We insisted on pushing her down the aisle in the wheelchair, but she would have none of that and walked to her place in the second row. We told her she could be seated for the receiving line. Again, she was determined to stand throughout and was there for the pictures and the reception as well. Nothing could keep her from attending and participating in our wedding.

We need to have that same kind of determination when taking our cities for the Lord Jesus Christ. There will be bad days, there will be obstacles, and there will be tough times; but if we have faith in our hearts, we will keep on keeping on until our task is completed. The Bible tells us about the devotion of faith and the determination of faith and also about the declaration of faith.

The Declaration of Faith

"At the seventh time, when the priests blew the trumpets, Joshua said to the people, 'Shout! For the LORD has given you the city'" (Joshua 6:16).

The **anticipation of God's performance.** When they began to shout that day, the walls were still standing. It was a shout of victory, and they shouted because of the anticipation of God's performance and the association of God's presence.

The **association of God's presence.** Every time they circled the city, the ark went around with them. God walked with His people. When we know God is there, we can be assured that the victory is ours; and when God is on our side, we have every reason to shout for even though the walls may still be standing, we know God will give us the cities we want to win. Even though there may be thousands in the area who do not know Christ as Savior and all kinds of sin, iniquity, crime, immorality, and perversion abound, God is still able to give us our cities.

The **acclamation of God's power.** They shouted to the people of Jericho that the city would soon be theirs. Some may have mocked them from atop the walls, but the Jews did not let the jeers of Jericho rob them of the victory. The victory was an acclamation of God's power. Their confession brought their possession! May we learn to confess that God's Word said it and that settles it. We will take our cities in the name of the Lord Jesus Christ. Joshua was not being presumptuous when he told the people to shout while the walls were still standing for God had already given them the city; he only repeated what God had already said.

This principle is illustrated in Hebrews 13:5, "For He Himself has said, 'I will never desert you, nor will I ever forsake you.'" In other words, God has said the cities are ours and we can reach them in the name of the Lord Jesus Christ so we should be willing to say it also.

The Jews shouted victory because they knew that even though the walls still stood, God had already given them the victory. That is faith, and confession is faith turned inside out. It is when we take God literally at His Word. God had told Joshua, "The city is yours," so Joshua stood in front of the multitude and repeated, "The city is ours. Go ahead and shout because the city is ours." If God has promised it, we can say it. If God has said victory is ours, we can say victory is ours.

The Demonstration of Faith

"So the people shouted, and priests blew the trumpets; and when the people heard the sound of the trumpet, the people shouted with a great shout and the wall fell down flat, so that the people went up into the city, every man straight ahead, and they took the city" (Joshua 6:20).

When the trumpet sounded and the Israelites shouted, the walls collapsed; and they marched into the city and did a mighty work in the name of Jehovah God. Our faith will also be increased as we walk into the cities of our world. When we experience the demonstration of faith in our own personal lives, our faith will be increased and we will say what God has said. We will then see the walls of sin and evil crumble and fall. God has said we are to reach our world, so we must take God at His Word.

The world was amazed to see the walls of communism fall in Eastern Europe on November 9, 1989. The communists had sealed off East Berlin with a concrete wall along the east/west boundary in 1961. The city of West Berlin had become the main escape route from bondage to freedom. During those days, the East German police had orders to kill anyone who tried to go over the wall. For nearly thirty years, the Berlin Wall divided the west from the east, freedom from oppression.

God specializes in tearing down walls of sin and separation. The walls around our cities are not physical but spiritual, and mighty is He who is able to pull down all the strongholds of the enemy of our souls. When we have faith, it will be demonstrated and the walls will be pulled down. We will see victory in our churches and in our lives.

The Delegation of Faith

After the walls of Jericho fell, there was a faithful commission given to the two men who had spied out the city before its fall.

> There was a **faithful commission.** "Joshua said to the two men who had spied out the land, 'Go into the harlot's house and bring the woman and all she has out of there, as you have sworn to her'" (Joshua 6:22).

> These men found Rahab and her family, and theirs was a faithful commission amid all that happened in the battle. The Lord has

commissioned us to go into our world — into our cities — to save the lost, the perishing, and the dying in the midst of pain and judgment. We are called to go into this world and reap people who need to know Christ as Savior and Lord.

There was a **fiery consumption.** "They burned the city with fire, and all that was in it. Only the silver and gold, and articles of bronze and iron, they put into the treasury of the house of the LORD" (Joshua 6:24).

The entire city was destroyed. Not one stone was left on top of another. Likewise, judgment is coming, and we must reach the people of our communities before it is too late. We must tell people about Christ before they are lost for eternity.

There was a **family conversion.** "However, Rahab the harlot and her father's household and all she had, Joshua spared; and she has lived in the midst of Israel to this day, for she hid the messengers whom Joshua sent to spy out Jericho" (Joshua 6:25).

Rahab the prostitute went from the house of shame to the Hall of Fame. She became the great-great-grandmother of King David, a member of the lineage of Christ the Lord. Just as God reached down and saved Rahab, so He can also save our families, friends, and the people of our cities.

It is not through force but through faith that we will see all our family members come to know Christ as Savior and Lord and see walls torn down in the hearts of people so they can come to know Jesus as Savior.

Some years ago, a prostitute lay dying in a hospital in Brazil from the diseases of her lifestyle. Though weak and near death, she looked up from her bed and prayed, "Jesus, if you can forgive my sins and heal my body, I will do my best to tell others about You." In that moment of faith and repentance, a very sinful woman was suddenly forgiven and healed. After leaving the hospital, she kept her promise by telling others what Jesus had done for her. In time, she led more than 300 people to Jesus, and they gathered regularly to hear more from this woman about God. She soon met the leaders of the Assemblies of God in her area and asked for a pastor to be sent to minister to her group of converts. That congregation grew very large and started many other churches in an effort to reach the people of their cities for Christ.

It is not through force but through faith that we will see all our family members come to know Christ as Savior and Lord and see walls torn down in the hearts of people so they can come to know Jesus as Savior.

Like the Jews did in Jericho, this former prostitute moved into the city and claimed lives for the kingdom. At Jericho, a trumpet sounded followed by a shout that ushered in judgment. It may not be much longer before we hear another trumpet and a shout — not of people but of an angel from Heaven — and then the judgment. The Church hopes that Jesus will come soon; but until He does, we must be believers of faith who are about the business of trying to reach the people of our cities for God.

When the Lord comes, He does not choose sides; He comes to take over. Our goal is not to get the Lord on our side, but to get on His side.

14

The Decision of Faith

"By faith Rahab the harlot did not perish along with those who were disobedient, after she had welcomed the spies in peace" (Hebrews 11:31). This is the story of the transformation of a harlot whose name was Rahab and what the gospel did for her.

The transforming power of the life of faith! Nature forms us, sin deforms us, the world conforms us, education informs us; but faith transforms us.

Nature forms us, sin deforms us, the world conforms us, education informs us; but faith transforms us.

Rahab was a pagan living in spiritual darkness and degradation, a Canaanite destined for sure destruction; yet this woman found grace through faith and was so transformed that she married a prince of Israel, became the great-great grandmother of King David, and was in the bloodline of our Lord and Savior Jesus Christ!

In the genealogy of Jesus, we read that Rahab went from the house of shame to the Hall of Fame, from being a child of hell to being a citizen of heaven, and from being a shady lady to being a shining star transformed by the grace of God.

Joshua 2 tells of the Israelites who had just come into Canaan to take the land that flowed with milk and honey, the Promised Land; but between them and the Promised Land was the city of Jericho.

We talked about that story in Chapter 13—how the walls fell down by the faith of Joshua and the Israelites. Then God said He wanted the city destroyed. Joshua, God's general and commander-in-chief, selected two men to go into Jericho where they met Rahab. Through their witness, she was transformed and converted. There are several faith qualities that took place in the life of Rahab.

WE NEED TO BE CONVICTED BY THE SPIRIT

Rahab was convicted by the Spirit. The spies came to her house which was on the walls of Jericho and engaged her in conversation. She put them on the roof to hide them; but before they lay down to go to sleep, she said to them:

> I know that the LORD has given you the land, and that the terror of you has fallen on us, and that all the inhabitants of the land have melted away before you. For we have heard how the LORD dried up the water of the Red Sea before you when you came out of Egypt, and what you did to the two kings of the Amorites who were beyond the Jordan, to Sihon and Og, whom you utterly destroyed. When we heard it, our hearts melted and no courage remained in any man any longer because of you;

for the LORD your God, He is God in heaven above
and on earth beneath (Joshua 2:8-11).

Imagine a Canaanite talking that way! Imagine a
sinful, fallen, depraved woman making such a glorious,
marvelous statement of faith! The Holy Spirit of God had
been speaking to Rahab, and it was remarkable that she
had such conviction.

God has an assignment for each of us.
If we get right with God, stay right with God,
and walk in the Spirit, we would almost have
to backslide to keep from winning souls.

The Holy Spirit searched the city of Jericho, saw a
woman with a predisposition towards spiritual things — a
woman with a heart open to the things of God, and brought
her under deep conviction. The Holy Spirit still works in
the same manner, searching throughout cities to find those
who are open to spiritual things and bringing someone to
them so they can receive the gospel.

There were many people in the great city of Jericho so
it was not by chance that the spies happened to go the
house of Rahab; it was the providence of God. These men
were in the stream of the Spirit and, like a guided missile,
God brought them right to the heart and to the home of
the woman He had been preparing.

There are numerous examples of this divine providence in Scripture — the Ethiopian eunuch and Philp's
being led to Samaria (Acts 8), Peter's going to Cornelius's
house (Acts 10), Jesus's meeting the woman at the well
(John 4), and Barnabas's going to Saul (Acts 9). The Holy

Spirit is constantly working on the hearts of people who want to know Christ while leading God's people to them.

God has an assignment for each of us. If we get right with God, stay right with God, and walk in the Spirit, we would almost have to backslide to keep from winning souls. On the one hand, God and His Holy Spirit are preparing a lost person while on the other hand, God wants to use us and guide us to that person. It was not by chance that these men went to the one house in the entire city of Jericho where a woman was already under deep conviction.

What brought Rahab under the conviction of the Holy Spirit was what she had heard God had done for His people: "For we have heard how the Lord dried up the water of the Red Sea before you when you came out of Egypt, and what you did to the two kings of the Amorites who were beyond the Jordan, to Sihon and Og, whom you utterly destroyed" (Joshua 6:10). There is a twofold responsibility in regard to soulwinning. We are to be witnesses as a part of the evidence!

What God is doing in our lives, our churches, and our ministries ought to bring our towns, cities, and world under conviction. They ought to look at us and see there is something different and supernatural about the way we live. In order to bring conviction, the Holy Spirit uses His own people, their lives and their victories, to bring conviction to the unsaved.

Rahab had seen the exploits of the people of God — something so marvelous, so wonderful, so inexplicable that it brought her under conviction. The reason more people are not saved is not because they are so hard-hearted; instead, we must look at our churches, ourselves, and our friends. When we begin to live victoriously and walk in the stream of the Spirit, God the Holy Spirit is going to bring that unsaved individual and that soulwinner together. He will be working both sides of the fence.

WE NEED TO BE CONVINCED BY THE SCRIPTURE

> Now therefore, please swear to me by the Lord, since I have dealt kindly with you, that you also will deal kindly with my father's household, and give me a pledge of truth, and spare my father and my mother and my brothers and my sisters, with all who belong to them, and deliver our lives from death (Joshua 2:12-13).

The sentence of death and judgment was upon them as it is upon every person outside of Christ. The men answered her, "Our life for yours" (Joshua 2:14). From this, we see a pre-figuring of the cross. "We will lay down our life for you if you will enter into a covenant with us."

> "Our life for yours if you do not tell this business of ours; and it shall come about when the Lord gives us the land that we will deal kindly and faithfully with you." Then she let them down by a rope through the window, for her house was on the city wall, so that she was living on the wall. She said to them, "Go to the hill country, so that the pursuers will not happen upon you, and hide yourselves there for three days until the pursuers return. Then afterward you may go on your way." The men said to her, "We shall be free from this oath to you which you have made us swear, unless, when we come into the land, you tie this cord of scarlet thread in the window through which you let us down, and gather to yourself into the house your father and your mother and your brothers and all your father's

179

household. It shall come about that anyone who goes out of the doors of your house into the street, his blood shall be on his own head, and we shall be free; but anyone who is with you in the house, his blood shall be on our head if a hand is laid on him. But if you tell this business of ours, then we shall be free from the oath which you have made us swear" (Joshua 6:14-20).

Rahab's response: "According to your words, so be it" (Joshua 6:21). She was convicted by the Spirit and convinced by the Word of God she received, not by the words of the spies. James calls the two men "messengers" (2:25) for they were more than spies; they were spokesmen of Almighty God. They had heard the Word of God and gave the Word to Rahab. We know she had faith because she said, "According to your words, so be it." Real faith, biblical faith is not believing we can do certain things nor is it self-confidence, positive thinking, or "wishing on a star." It is not believing that makes it so but taking God at His Word.

It is vital that we listen to the voice of God and be attuned to the Word of God. It is vital that we get alone with God and spend quiet time with Him, getting into the Word of God and saturating our souls with scripture.

We cannot have faith until God gives us a word. Faith is our response to the Word of God. It is vital that we listen to the voice of God and be attuned to the Word of God. It is vital that we get alone with God and spend quiet time with Him, getting into the Word of God and saturating our souls with scripture for "faith cometh by hearing, and hearing by the word of God" (Romans 10:17 KJV). We will never, never, never have faith until we begin to listen to God. We do not just decide what we want and think that believing will make it so. We cannot believe it until it is so. We might just as well try to ice skate on water as to have faith without a word from God first. That word might come from scripture, from the Spirit, or from someone else; but God will always speak.

WE NEED TO BE CONVERTED BY THE SAVIOR

> She said, "According to your words, so be it." So she sent them away, and they departed; and she tied the scarlet cord in the window. They departed and came to the hill country, and remained there for three days until the pursuers returned. Now the pursuers had sought them all along the road, but had not found them (Joshua 2:21-22).

It was not just happenstance that she let them down by a scarlet cord for they told her to tie a scarlet cord in her window and when they saw it, they would pass over her house and no judgment would come to it.

This reminds us of when God told the people to take the blood of a perfect lamb, one without spot or blemish, and put the blood of that lamb on the doorposts of their houses for He had said, "When I see the blood, I will pass over you" (Exodus 12:13).

The spies told Rahab to put a scarlet cord in the window as a symbol, a token, a sign that she was coming into the covenant of those who had been redeemed by the blood. Of course, the Lord Jesus Christ had not yet died; but all these Old Testament symbols and types and figures were merely shadows that pointed toward the blood redemption of our Lord and Savior Jesus Christ. That scarlet line runs all the way through the Bible. When God made coats of skin for

Adam and Eve in the Garden of Eden, He had to shed the blood of an innocent animal in order to do so. When Abel offered his lamb, there was shed blood yet none in Cain's offering of the fruit of the ground. When Abraham was to offer Isaac on Mount Moriah, a ram caught in the thicket became a blood substitute. When Noah came out of the ark, he offered a blood sacrifice. Thousands of smoking altars in the tabernacle and the temple tell us blood was shed. Over and over, God said that "without shedding of blood there is no forgiveness" (Hebrews 9:22). We are all guilty before God for "all have sinned" (Romans 3:23). Rahab had sinned, but so has each of us. "What can wash away my sin? Nothing but the blood of Jesus" (Robert Lowry, 1876).

The important factor is not that Rahab escaped death because she eventually died nor is the most important thing for us to live two or three years longer but to live for eternity. It is not the sparing of our physical lives but the cleansing of our souls.

Rahab had far more happen to her than simply escaping the sword; she was justified (James 2:25) and made right in the sight of God, a filthy harlot made whiter than the driven snow.

"'Come now, and let us reason together,' says the LORD, 'Though your sins are as scarlet, they will be white as snow; though they are red like crimson, they will be like wool'" (Isaiah 1:18).

Jesus Christ worked a miracle in Rahab's heart, and she was made pure, was transformed, and is listed in the genealogy of our Savior and in God's Hall of Fame. This is what the Savior can do.

"All have sinned and fall short of the glory of God" (Romans 3:23). It is not the amount of sin that condemns us; it is the fact of sin. One unforgiven sin is enough to send us to hell "for whoever keeps the whole law and yet stumbles in one point, he has become guilty of all" (James 2:10). Many say, "I don't need to be saved; I live a good life"; but not one of us can live a good life until we get saved — not really a good life. The worse form of badness is human goodness when that human goodness becomes a substitute for the new birth.

If we are saved, it will be because we have been convicted by the Spirit, convinced by the Word, and converted by the blood.

Jesus told the chief priests and the Pharisees that "tax collectors and prostitutes will get into the kingdom of God before you" (Matthew 21:31). He was addressing their self-righteousness for they did not see their need of salvation but instead boasted of their own goodness. Conversely, Rahab knew she needed the Lord.

The greatest tragedy is that "He came to His own, and those who were His own did not receive Him" (John 1:11). The greatest transaction was that "as many as received Him, to them He gave the right to become children of God, even to those who believe in His name, who were born, not of blood nor of the will of the flesh nor of the will of man, but of God" (John 1:12-13). The greatest tragedy is when people refuse Him; the greatest transaction is when people receive Him; and the greatest transformation is when people become children of God.

There is no one who is too bad to be saved for if Rahab could be saved, anyone can be saved. There is no one without Christ who is so good that they do not need to be saved. Whosoever will may come. If we are saved, it will be because we have been convicted by the Spirit, convinced by the Word, and converted by the blood.

We cannot have faith until God
gives us a word. Faith is our
response to the Word of God.

15

The Design of Faith

And what more shall I say? For time will fail me if I tell of Gideon, Barak, Samson, Jephthah, of David and Samuel and the prophets, who by faith conquered kingdoms, performed acts of righteousness, obtained promises, shut the mouths of lions, quenched the power of fire, escaped the edge of the sword, from weakness were made strong, became mighty in war, put foreign armies to flight (Hebrews 11:32-34).

Gideon was one of the judges who ruled over Israel during a period when they were without a king. The Israelites had sinned and gone after false gods—one god in particular: a fertility god named Baal.

They worshipped Baal with licentiousness, sexuality, and sensuality; and the judgment of God fell upon them. God sent a fearsome, warlike people named the Midianites to press Israel on every side. It was a terrible and horrible time for Israel.

However, there was a man named Gideon, a farmer, an ordinary man, who had a heart for God. While he was beating out wheat in the wine press to save it from the Midianites, the angel of the Lord appeared to him and said, "The LORD is with you, O valiant warrior" (Judges 6:12). When the Lord said that to Gideon, I imagine he looked over his shoulder to see to whom the Lord was speaking for he was certain He was not speaking to him; however, the Lord said, "Gideon! You're the man I'm going to use to deliver my people from the oppressive heel of the Midianites." Gideon then began to argue with the Lord and tell Him that he was not worthy for this leadership role; but God revealed to Gideon that through His power and strength, he would be able to fight the good fight of faith.

Gideon then began to argue with the Lord and tell Him that he was not worthy for this leadership role; but God revealed to Gideon that through His power and strength, he would be able to fight the good fight of faith.

There is a spiritual war being fought—the unseen war between darkness and light, good and evil, and heaven and hell. The stakes are high, and our enemy is Satan who is letting loose all the artillery of the pit. He is fighting like a cornered animal because he can see the signs of the times and knows he has but a little while.

We are going to be drawn into this battle, and there is no way of escape. If we are children of God, we are also soldiers of the cross—and if soldiers, then also warriors. We must learn to fight the many enemies that are marshaled against us. We are not called to a playground but to a battleground. This thing called the church is not a showboat; it is a battleship, and we are called to fight the good fight of faith (1 Timothy 6:12).

What God told Gideon to do so long ago is mentioned in the New Testament as an illustration to Christians. There are steps in the life of overcomers, the steps of conquest.

WE NEED TO BE A PEOPLE OF COURAGE

We read the story of Gideon in Judges 7. God had called and commissioned Gideon and told him, "I want you to call an army," so Gideon sent out the call and gathered 32,000 soldiers.

> Then Jerubbaal (that is, Gideon) and all the people who were with him, rose early and camped beside the spring of Harod; and the camp of Midian was on the north side of them by the hill of Moreh in the valley. The Lord said to Gideon, "The people who are with you are too many for Me to give Midian into their hands, for Israel would become boastful, saying, 'My own power has delivered me.' Now therefore come, proclaim in the hearing of the people, saying, 'Whoever is afraid and trembling, let him return and depart from Mount Gilead.'" So 22,000 people returned, but 10,000 remained (Judges 7:1-3).

Gideon told them, "We're going into battle! All of you men of war listen to me! If anybody is afraid, he should go home!" Consequently, a herd of people left him; 22,000 in all packed their bags and left.

Through this, God showed that the first principle of conquest was courage. God cannot use cowards for being a coward and afraid fits us for failure, not for fighting. We are not to be afraid "for God hath not given us the spirit of fear; but of power, and of love, and of a sound mind" (2 Timothy 1:7 KJV).

One of the worst things about fear is that it is infectious. We have the ability to make others afraid when we are afraid. "Then the officers shall speak further to the people and say, 'Who is the man that is afraid and fainthearted? Let him depart and return to his house, so that he might not make his brothers' hearts melt like his heart'" (Deuteronomy 20:8).

Moses faced the same thing when he sent out twelve spies, and ten of them came back with an evil report. Although they said it was a beautiful land with milk and honey, they also reported there were giants there, the sons of Anak, and they were like grasshoppers in their eyes.

I have tried to lead people for a long time and have found it is wonderful to propose a vision to God's people when they respond by saying, "By faith we can do it." However, it is a terrible thing when there are those who are not walking closely enough to the Lord to hear the voice of God, and they take counsel with their fears and respond by saying, "It can't be done." Those kinds of people are infectious and hinder God's people from entering into the blessings they ought to have.

There is a principle I call the scarecrow principle; that is, whenever we see a scarecrow, we know there is something good nearby—perhaps grain or strawberries or tomatoes. A farmer puts a scarecrow in the middle of his field to scare the crows off. He does not put the scarecrow in a pasture nor on a highway or in a vacant lot but where there is something good. The devil puts up his scarecrows to scare us off because God has some blessings for us; but if we are walking in the Spirit, Satan cannot harm us. We need not let the devil scare us away from a blessing.

There are three kinds of fears that keep us from serving the Lord as our God. First, there are believers who are afraid of God the **Father**—not the reverential fear of God for "the fear of the LORD is the beginning of wisdom"

(Proverbs 9:10) but because their lives are not right and they are not walking in faith.

When Adam and Eve hid in the Garden of Eden, God called to Adam, "Where are you?" (Genesis 3:9). Adam responded, "I heard the sound of You in the garden, and I was afraid" (Genesis 3:10). The first words man uttered after his sin were "I was afraid." The deeper people go into sin, the more they are enwrapped in their fears.

In the parable of the talents (Matthew 25:14-30), the man who was going on a journey gave his possessions to his servants: five talents to one man, two talents to another, and one talent to the third man. The man with the five talents took it and invested it and gained five more talents. The man with the two talents also invested it and gained two more talents. However, the third man with only one talent took it and buried it in the ground. When the master came and asked for an accounting of that talent, the servant said, "'Master, I knew you to be a hard man, reaping where you did not sow and gathering where you scattered no seed. And I was afraid, and went away and hid your talent in the ground" (Matthew 25:24-25). The master said to him, "You wicked, lazy slave" (Matthew 25:26).

There are some who are hiding their talents in the ground because they are afraid of God — fearful that He does not love them enough, fearful to give their hearts to the Lord Jesus Christ because of what they think God would do to them. They believe they are safer in the devil's camp than under God's provision. They fear that if they confess their sin to the Lord, He will scold them; however, it is the unconfessed sin that will get them in trouble.

God does not love us because we are lovely, but "God demonstrates His own love toward us, in that while we were yet sinners, Christ died for us" (Romans 5:8). God loves us, and "we need have no fear of someone who loves us perfectly" (1 John 4:18 TLB).

The second kind of fear that keeps us from serving is the fear of **failure**. There are those who can sing but will not try, those who can preach but will not try, and those who can teach but will not try for they are all afraid of failure. I have often driven behind people who approach every traffic light like it is going to turn red; and sure enough, it does. There are churches like that also that are so afraid they are going to make a mistake that they never do anything.

The future has two handles: fear and faith.
We can take hold of either handle. Let us take hold
of the handle of faith and not let fear of the Father,
fear of failure, fear of the future, or any other kind
of fear be the devil's scarecrow that will keep us
from fighting the good fight of faith!

The third kind of fear that keeps us from serving is the fear of the **future**. There are those who are afraid of tomorrow—what is going to happen. They are afraid to build a house because it might not turn out great; they are afraid to buy something or sell something for fear of what might happen. "He who watches the wind will not sow and he who looks at the clouds will not reap" (Ecclesiastes 11:4). A farmer would never have a crop if he said, "Well, we might have a drought or we might have a rain or we might have this or we might have that."

The future has two handles: fear and faith. We can take hold of either handle. Let us take hold of the handle of faith and not let fear of the Father, fear of failure, fear of the future, or any other kind of fear be the devil's scarecrow that will keep us from fighting the good fight of faith!

Now it came about when the sons of Israel cried to the LORD on account of Midian, that the LORD sent a prophet to the sons of Israel, and he said to them, "Thus says the LORD, the God of Israel, 'It was I who brought you up from Egypt and brought you out from the house of slavery. I delivered you from the hands of the Egyptians and from the hands of all your oppressors, and dispossessed them before you and gave you their land, and I said to you, "I am the LORD your God; you shall not fear" (Judges 6:7-10).

God said, "Fear not," at least 365 times in the Bible, one for every day of the year. There are three classes of people in the world: those who are afraid; those who do not know enough to be afraid; and those who know their Bibles. The Word of God challenges us not to be afraid.

WE NEED A PRIORITY OF COMMITMENT

Then the LORD said to Gideon, "The people are still too many; bring them down to the water and I will test them for you there. Therefore it shall be that he of whom I say to you, 'This one shall go with you,' he shall go with you; but everyone of whom I say to you, 'This one shall not go with you,' he shall not go." So he brought the people down to the water. And the LORD said to Gideon, "You shall separate everyone who laps the water with his tongue as a dog laps, as well as everyone who kneels to drink." Now the number of those who lapped, putting their hand to their mouth, was 300 men; but all the rest of the people kneeled to drink water. The LORD said to Gideon, "I will deliver you with the 300 men who lapped and will give the Midianites into your hands; so let all the other people go, each man to his home." So the 300 men took the people's provisions and their trumpets into their hands. And Gideon sent all the other men of Israel, each to his tent, but retained the 300 men; and the camp of Midian was below him in the valley. (Judges 7:4-8).

The Word of God reveals the second test where God separated the men from the boys. "You shall separate everyone who laps the water with his tongue as a dog laps, as well as everyone who kneels to drink" (Judges 7:5).

Of the 10,000 men who were left, 9,700 of them put their faces in the water and began to lap up the water just as an animal would. That left 300 valiant men who knelt down — perhaps on one knee — with their heads and shoulders erect, looking around and watching for the enemy.

They would have lapped the water with their hands, getting a little water in their palms and drinking it. These I call "the committed" — the ones who meant business. The others were careless so God could not use them. When they put their heads into the water, the enemy could have attacked and all of them would have been slaughtered. Consequently, the Lord said, "This one shall not go with you" (Judges 7:4) for they were more interested in satiating their thirst than in the battle.

God knows we need a drink of water just as He knows we need clothing, food, shelter, rest, recreation, and fellowship; however, these things cannot come first. The men who got down on their hands and knees were putting their sensual, selfish desires first. Both groups of men got a drink of water; but the 300 were saying, "Yes, I know I have needs; but the Lord has called me to be a soldier first." When we are called to be soldiers, we must endure hardship as a good soldier of the Lord Jesus Christ. If we are not committed enough to put Jesus Christ and the battle of faith first, we will be defeated.

Some talk about getting their lives in order but say, "Well, I don't have to worry about this because I'm trusting God." If we are trusting God, we will keep our lives in order and "be of sober spirit, be on the alert. Your adversary, the devil, prowls around like a roaring lion, seeking someone to devour" (1 Peter 5:8).

If we are not committed enough to put Jesus Christ and the battle of faith first, we will be defeated.

On the one hand, faith is not being afraid; however, on the other hand, faith is also not being foolish. God cannot use the fearful or the foolish, the cowards or the careless. Those who were fearful were sent home and those who did not have enough sense to be afraid were sent home as well leaving only 300 men who were committed. God said, "I can use them."

Satan wants to harm our homes, our families, and our children. We must learn to be sober and so committed to Christ that we serve Him and His cause first.

WE NEED A PROCESS OF CONFIDENCE

Now the same night it came about that the LORD said to him, "Arise, go down against the camp, for I have given it into your hands. But if you are afraid to go down, go with Purah your servant down to the camp, and you will hear what they say; and afterward your hands will be strengthened that you may go down against the camp." So he went with Purah his servant down to the outposts of the army that was in the camp. Now the Midianites and the Amalekites and all the sons of the east were lying in the valley as numerous as locusts; and their camels were without number, as numerous as the sand on the seashore. When Gideon came, behold, a man was relating a dream to his friend. And he said, "Behold, I had a dream; a loaf of barley bread was tumbling into the camp of Midian, and it came to the tent and struck it so that it fell, and turned it upside down so that the tent lay flat." His friend replied, "This is nothing less than the sword of Gideon the son of Joash, a man of Israel; God has given Midian and all the camp into his hand." When Gideon heard the account of the dream and its interpretation, he bowed in worship. He returned to the camp of Israel and said, "Arise, for the LORD has given the camp of Midian into your hands" (Judges 7:9-15).

Under the inspiration of the Lord, Gideon went on a spy mission to find out what was happening and infiltrated the enemy's camp where he heard two of the Midianites talking. One of them said, "I really had a weird dream last night. I want to see if you know what it means. I dreamed that a loaf of barley came tumbling into the camp, and it went right through the armies and hit a tent. It went down into that tent, and the whole tent just collapsed and fell flat on the ground! What on earth do you think that means?" The other fellow said, "I know what it means. That loaf of barley was a man named Gideon, and God is going to use him to defeat our army!" When Gideon heard this, he was so excited that he worshipped the Lord and went back and told his 300 men, "Hallelujah! God has given us the victory!"

Hearing this changed Gideon. The principle was that barley bread was the poorest, coarsest and cheapest of all of the bread. If a man could not get anything else to eat, he would eat barley bread. In the dream, a barley bread loaf rolled through this mighty army and destroyed a tent. God told Gideon, "You are that loaf of barley bread."

God showed Gideon a great secret that it is not our ability but our availability, not our fame but our faith, not our scholarship but our relationship, and not whom we know but who are that counts with God.

When the Lord said to Gideon, "The Lord is with you, O valiant warrior" (Judges 6:12) and Gideon's response was, "O Lord, how shall I deliver Israel? Behold, my family is the least in Manasseh, and I am the youngest in my father's house" (Judges 6:15), Gideon was saying, "Of all the tribes in Israel, Manasseh is the worst; of all the families in Manasseh, my family is the poorest; and of all the kids in the family, I am the runt of the litter. You reached the very bottom of the barrel when you got me, Lord. Surely, you don't want me!" However, the Lord was saying to Gideon, "You may be like a loaf of barley bread — very poor, unrefined, and coarse; but I want to use you!"

"So the Spirit of the Lord came upon Gideon" (Judges 6:34). How we all would like for God to wear us like a suit of clothes! Paul said, "It is no longer I who live, but Christ lives in me; and the life which I now live in the flesh I live by faith in the Son of God, who loved me and gave Himself up for me" (Galatians 2:20). What a difference it makes when God is in the man!

God showed Gideon a great secret that it is not our ability but our availability, not our fame but our faith, not our scholarship but our relationship, and not whom we know but who are that counts with God. "But God has chosen the foolish things of the world to shame the wise" (1 Corinthians 1:27). God uses ordinary people. If we were to take the time to read the entire story of Gideon, we would find that he was not a very sharp guy. He messed up on a number of occasions and failed in many ways. Some bad things are written about Gideon, but thank God that when He writes the record, He does not write the bad things because He remembers our sins no more but He never forgets our faith. It was faith that made Gideon the man that he was. Gideon was an ordinary man—loaf of barley bread; and if God can use Gideon, He can use us!

God does not want us to serve Him in a poor little weak way! He wants us to serve Him in His mighty, dynamic way because God takes ordinary people and gives them extraordinary power.

Some people say, "Well, I just serve God in my poor little weak way." God does not want us to serve Him in a poor little weak way! He wants us to serve Him in His mighty, dynamic way because God takes ordinary people and gives them extraordinary power.

We insult God by saying that He cannot use us. Before Gideon even got there, the Midianites were afraid they were going to die. The Kingdom of Darkness—Satan and all his dominions—is fearful that Christians will awaken to their power and authority in Christ over all the powers of darkness.

WE NEED A PURPOSE OF CONQUEST

When Gideon heard the account of the dream and its interpretation, he bowed in worship. He returned to the camp of Israel and said, "Arise, for the LORD has given the camp of Midian into your hands." He divided the 300 men into three companies, and he put trumpets and empty pitchers into the hands of all of them, with torches inside the pitchers. He said to them, "Look at me and do likewise. And behold, when I come to the outskirts of the camp, do as I do. When I and all who are with me blow the trumpet, then you also blow the trumpets all around the camp and say, 'For the LORD and for Gideon.'" So Gideon and the hundred men who were with him came to the outskirts of the camp at the beginning of the middle watch, when they had just posted the watch; and they blew the trumpets and smashed the pitchers that were in their hands. When the three companies blew the trumpets and broke the pitchers, they held the torches in their left hands and the trumpets in their right hands for blowing, and cried, "A sword for the LORD and for Gideon!" (Judges 7:15-20).

Imagine an army of 300 hundred men armed with only clay pitchers, oil lamps, and trumpets. This was all Gideon had against the gigantic army of the Midianites, but "the weapons of our warfare are not of the flesh, but divinely powerful for the destruction of fortresses" (2 Corinthians 2:4).

If the Midianites had seen them coming and had known they only had clay pitchers, oil lamps, and trumpets for weapons, they would have laughed them to scorn;

but Gideon had 300 men he could count on who did not question God but simply obeyed.

There must be compliance of faith. Even when God's plan does not make sense to us, it does not mean it does not make sense. The world has one way and God has another, and we are to live our lives trusting the Lord.

Most people would love to have a promotion on their jobs. "For not from the east, nor from the west, nor from the desert comes exaltation; but God is the Judge" (Psalm 75:6). What does it mean that promotion does not come from the east nor from the west nor from the south but God is the judge? What direction is left? The north. In Leviticus 1:11, the north side of the altar was the place of sacrifice where the blood was poured out. I believe God is saying that promotion comes to those who are willing to obey and sacrifice. The Lord Jesus went out of Jerusalem to Calvary through the north gate of sacrifice.

There can be no conquest without compliance. We might say, "I want to live a life of faith! I want God to be real to me!" If so, we must take our Bibles and start obeying. God will not give us faith if we do not obey His Word for "faith comes from hearing, and hearing by the word of Christ" (Romans 10:17).

WE NEED THE POWER OF CONFESSION

When I and all who are with me blow the trumpet, then you also blow the trumpets all around the camp and say, "For the LORD and for Gideon." So Gideon and the hundred men who were with him came to the outskirts of the camp at the beginning of the middle watch, when they had just posted the watch; and they blew the trumpets and smashed the pitchers that were in their hands. When the three companies blew the trumpets and broke the pitchers, they held the torches in their left hands and the trumpets in their right hands for blowing, and cried, "A sword for the LORD and for Gideon!" (Judges 7:18-20).

Three hundred men circled the camp of the Midianites. It was pitch-black as the light burning inside the earthen pitchers could not have been seen. At just the right moment, Gideon smacked his pitcher which broke and crumbled, and the light was lofted high. He put a trumpet to his lips and gave a mighty blast followed by 300 men who broke their pitchers, held high their torches, blasted with their trumpets, and then gave a great shout: "A sword for the LORD and for Gideon!" Imagine what happened in the camp of the Midianites. All of a sudden, the camp was ablaze with light and the ecstatic sounds of the trumpets and shouts of victory! Suddenly, great terror went through the camp of the Midianites. Gideon and his 300 men had obeyed the Lord.

God directed it be done in that specific manner in order to teach a great spiritual lesson. In the Bible, trumpets always speak of testimony: "For if the bugle produces an indistinct sound, who will prepare himself for battle?" (1 Corinthians 14:8). The blast of the trumpet speaks of a sure testimony — not an uncertain sound. Light also speaks of testimony: "Let your light shine before men" (Matthew 5:16). There are two kinds of testimony: what we say — the trumpet, and what we do — the light. Both must be sounded in battle.

Every Christian is to be a light and sound production — what we say and what we do. It was easy to blow the trumpet, but the light would not shine until the pitcher was broken. The pitcher stands for our lives. "For God, who said, 'Light shall shine out of darkness,' is the One who has shone in our hearts to give the Light of the knowledge of the glory of God in the face of Christ. But we have this treasure in earthen vessels" (2 Corinthians 4:6-7).

We all have the light of God in us — Jesus! As the light of the world, He lights up our lives and lives within us. However, we will never see that light until our earthen vessel is broken.

We all have the light of God in us — Jesus! As the light of the world, He lights up our lives and lives within us. However, we will never see that light until our earthen vessel is broken.

Churches and Christians need a spirit of brokenness. We do not have revival because we are unbent, unbroken, unbowed, and unbloodied. "A broken and a contrite heart, O God, You will not despise" (Psalm 51:17).

"Each stood in his place around the camp" (Judges 7:21). There was a **sure** testimony because it was like a trumpet; there was a **sacrificial** testimony because of the broken pitchers; and there was a **steadfast** testimony for they stood every man in his own place. What would happen in our cities if all Christians would live broken lives, let their lights shine, sound the clarity and call of the trumpet of the Lord Jesus Christ…and **STAND** regardless of what the enemy might do.

16

The Distance of Faith

When Mikhail Gorbachev was president of the former Soviet Union in 1990-1991, a good friend of his became an astronaut and was sent into space on a short, routine mission. The trip was supposed to last for only a few days; but while he was away, the government of his country began to fall apart and Gorbachev was relieved of his national duties. Because of all the incidents, it was decided that the astronaut should stay in orbit for several months. By the time he returned home, his world was very different. He had a new country, a new president, and a new system of law. His world had completely changed in a very short time.

We too are living in a rapidly changing world. The world we have known in the past is not going to be the world of the future. Overnight, time and distance have collapsed; and we are living in a technologically sophisticated society. If we are to be invincible, we have to see the invisible. If we are to be practical and powerful, we have to understand the principles behind the dark side.

Using his imaginative mind, executive producer George Lucas created the Star Wars films in 1977; and throughout the decades since its first edition, people have been impacted and influenced.

If we are to be invincible, we have to see the invisible. If we are to be practical and powerful, we have to understand the principles behind the dark side.

When Theodore Roosevelt was the president of the United States, he had a confidant with whom he shared the pressures, problems, and perplexities of the day. After such discussions, they would often take a walk at night and cast their eyes on the stars above in a race to find the Andromeda Galaxy. The one who found it first would utter the words, "That speck of light is the Andromeda Galaxy. It is bigger than our Milky Way and contains more than 100 billion suns, each bigger than our own sun. It is only one galaxy of more than a hundred million such galaxies." After that statement was uttered, they would look at each other and say in unison, "Now, since we have gained a better and broader perspective of life, let us retire to bed for the evening."

We can get a bigger perspective simply by looking at the stars at night. Some of the greatest promises are never seen until after sunset for God put the stars in the heavens to paint pictures and give us promises for our lives. Without exception, everyone is either in league with the stars or will stumble over the stars. Everyone is in the battle of their lives, the battle of Star Wars.

Our Star Wars battle is not about a fictional battle played out on a silver screen between the Sith Lords and the Jedi Knights or between Obi-Wan Kanobi and Luke Skywalker and Darth Vader and his master. It is not a battle conjured up in the imagination of George Lucas, but it is the battle of our lives—the battle of Star Wars—the original version.

Israel was in a deplorable condition. Their political system was corrupt, and immorality and idolatry were rampant. The people had rebelled against God, and God had allowed them to be taken into captivity. Under the authority of an unkind commander named Sisera, they were oppressed for twenty years in slavery. Their cities had become their prisons.

WE NEED TO REALIZE THE SOURCE OF FAITH

Deborah, a prophet and judge of Israel, had received a word from God for her nation and culture. "Faith comes from hearing, and hearing by the word of Christ" (Romans 10:17). It is not about having faith in faith—that is positive thinking. Faith in God, however, is salvation; and there is a world of difference. It is not mind power, motivational power, or muscle power but the mighty power of the King of kings and the Lord of lords. Many people want to put their faith in faith, but our faith must be in God.

God inspired Deborah to give a word to a young man named Barak. Deborah knew how to pass her faith on to someone else. We like to hear the Word of God but often do not act on what we hear. Faith is belief with legs on. Deborah had faith, and Barak had feet—an army. Deborah could not lead the army, but Barak could so they took Deborah's faith and Barak's "feet" and put them together to win the battle of Star Wars. If we as God's people would put our faith and our feet together, there is no telling what we could accomplish for the glory of God. We often go to the house of God and hear His Word but then return home and never apply it to our lives. We must take the faith God has put into our hearts, stand upon His Word, and then do the work of God.

Many people think it takes great faith to win big battles, but the opposite is true. It is not great faith in God but faith in a great God that makes the difference. If the object of our faith is ourselves, our families, or our vocations, then the size of our faith will be no bigger than the object of our faith. However, if we put our faith in God, He will move the stars so we can win the battle for our good and His glory.

If we as God's people would put our faith and our feet together, there is no telling what we could accomplish for the glory of God.

The smallest amount of faith is still bigger than the largest amount of difficulty. Jesus taught His disciples about having faith the size of a mustard seed, which is similar in size to a fleck of pepper, so they could move mountains. If we will take whatever we are facing and put our faith in a big God, He will move the stars so we can win the battle of Star Wars.

The source of true faith is the Word of God. If we are going to know the God of the Word, we have to know the Word of God. It must take root in our hearts in order to grow.

It would be interesting to see all of God's people in church dressed according to their spiritual maturity. Some would be wearing diapers and carrying rattles because they are still babies in the faith. It is one thing for our faith to start small, but God wants our faith to grow for faith is taught and then caught. Barak chose to spend time with those who would teach him how to grow in his faith in

God; consequently, we must choose our friends wisely for the people we spend time with will be type of person we will become.

How we spend our spare time is extremely important. Some choose to skip church to watch their favorite sport, athlete, or television program; however, much to the surprise of many, the river of God's Spirit does not flow between the banks of the sofa and the television set. These things will not build our faith. When the game or program is over, the athlete or television personality will not call to thank us for watching nor will we receive a Christmas card from them. They will not be around to help when the bottom falls out of our lives. The problem is often that we have wrapped our lives around the world rather than the cross.

Barak spent time with people who challenged his faith to grow. We must make up our minds to be in God's house with God's people. Religion is hanging around the cross while Christianity is getting on the cross. It is time for God's people to pick up the cross and become followers of Jesus Christ. The Word of God is the source of all faith; and when we are together, our faith can grow.

WE NEED TO REVIEW THE COURSE OF FAITH

The course of Barak's faith brought him into battle with Sisera, commander of the Canaanite army of King Jabin of Hazor (Judges 4-5), who had 900 iron chariots. That would be like having 900 stealth bombers or 900 battleships carrying cruise missiles in our time. With his mighty army, he looked invincible. I can almost hear Sisera's thoughts questioning this unknown Barak and what he thought he could accomplish in battle. Someone should have passed a note to Sisera containing Psalm 20:7: "Some boast in chariots and some in horses, but we will boast in the name of the

LORD, our God." That is a good verse for us today for some trust in their financial resources or their Internet connections, but we will remember the name of the Lord our God.

God is both our greatest hope and our greatest threat. If He does not save us, we are finished. It is time to get on God's side and say, "God, help us to win the battle of Star Wars for the glory of God Almighty." Once God puts faith in our hearts, we must do something with it. God told Barak that he was about to get into the battle of his life. We should not be as concerned about the enemies around us as we are with the God above us. We can have the greatest arsenal of weapons; but if God is against us, the battle is already over.

We should not be as concerned about the enemies around us as we are with the God above us. We can have the greatest arsenal of weapons; but if God is against us, the battle is already over.

Many Christians never show up for the real battle because they spend their lives fighting with one another or fighting the wrong battle. An idea cannot be destroyed by a nuclear weapon or shot down by a cruise missile. We are in a battle of ideas; Hinduism, Buddhism, and New Ageism are all ideas. The only way to conquer these ideas is to replace them with a better idea, and the best idea is found wrapped up in the Lord Jesus Christ. Many of God's people are fighting on their own battlefronts when it is really a spiritual battle; and spiritual battles can only be won with spiritual weapons.

Barak went into battle against Sisera with only 10,000 troops, and the heavens dropped and the rains fell (Judges 5:4-5). It was not a thundershower but a downpour; and it was not a coincidence for when Barak stepped onto the battlefield by faith, God began to move in a supernatural way and the rains began to fall. Josephus, the historian of 2,000 years ago, wrote about this exact battle stating it rained on the backside of the Israelites and in the faces of the Canaanites so that the Canaanites could not see the Israelites coming. That enabled the Israelites to jump on the Canaanites like a spider after its next meal and eliminate every one of them.

All 900 iron chariots got stuck in the mud, and the horses began to flounder and fall. The nation of Israel won a supernatural battle that day. When Sisera saw which way the battle was going, he got off his horse and ran for his life — being the courageous man that he was. While running, he came upon the tent of a woman named Jael. Little did he realize that the name Jael rhymed with nail. She invited him inside to rest, and he was soon fast asleep on the floor. While Sisera slept, Jael drove a large spike through his temple and he died.

Barak's faith brought the rains, and his faith also brought down Sisera. It gets even better though because Barak's faith moved the stars in their courses. Not only is there the source of faith and the course of faith, but there is also the force of faith.

WE NEED TO RECOMMIT TO THE FORCE OF FAITH

Even the stars fought against Sisera and his army. The battle was over before it ever began. Barak had already won and Sisera had already lost. When Barak put his foot of faith onto the battlefield, God ordered the stars to fight against Sisera and his men. How much better to be a worm on God's side than to be the captain of a great army fighting against God. The person, family, organization, or religious group that fights against God has the whole universe fighting against them. Sin never wins; faith never fails. It is futile to fight against God.

The highest form of wisdom is simply to find which direction God is going and follow Him. Foolishness is opposing God. Those who think they can fight against God will find they will stumble over the stars. Every grain of sand and every stellar body will fight against the person who fights against God. Following are eight examples.

The highest form of wisdom is simply to find which direction God is going and follow Him.

Noah. God asked Noah to build an ark because He planned to flood the earth as judgment for the sins of the people. Though men mocked and ridiculed him day after day, Noah faithfully preached and worked on the ark for 120 years. The world aligned itself against God and Noah, but God aligned the whole universe against the world. Noah and his family marched into the ark as the minority but came out as the majority. Sin never wins; faith never fails. It is futile to fight against God.

Moses. God asked Moses to lead His people out of Egyptian bondage. Instead of cooperating and escorting the people of Israel out of Egypt and into Canaan, Pharaoh chose to fight against Moses and God. God aligned the whole universe against the nation of Egypt and left the bleached bones and rusted chariot wheels of their armies cluttering the Red Sea. Sin never wins; faith never fails. It is futile to fight against God.

Joshua. God was with Joshua at Jericho as he fought against three armies at the same time. When Joshua told the sun to stand still, "the sun stood still, and the moon stopped, until the nation avenged themselves of their enemies" (Joshua 10:13). God shut down the whole universe, stopping every stellar body, every galaxy, and every planet in its rotational track because one man on planet earth needed more time to win a battle for the glory of God. Sin never wins; faith never fails. It is futile to fight against God.

Elijah and the Hebrews. God was with Elijah when he stood against Ahab and Jezebel; with Shadrach, Meshach, and Abednego when they stood against Nebuchadnezzar; and with Daniel throughout his service in the wicked Babylonian empire. Sin never wins; faith never fails. It is futile to fight against God.

The New Testament Church. God put all the stars behind the New Testament Church as the apostles and faithful believers stood firm in their faith against the onslaught of pagan Rome. We read about the rise and fall of the Roman Empire while we sing about the Church triumphant. Sin never wins; faith never fails. It is futile to fight against God.

Napoleon. It was mentioned to Napoleon that he needed to find out if it was the will of God before marching his men into Russia. His response: "God is on the side of the best artillery." He was half right. God's will is not with the best artillery on earth because the best artillery is in the heavens. At first, there were only a few flakes of snow; however, that soon turned into a blizzard that left Napoleon's troops and animals lying on the frozen plains of Russia in defeat. Sin never wins; faith never fails. It is futile to fight against God.

The Nation of Israel. In the not-too-distant-future, the Battle of Armageddon will occur. With clenched fists, the people of the "New World Army" will make their way to the borders of Israel to pick a fight against God. This time, God's chosen people will be aligned with God. At that moment, God will put the whole universe behind the nation of Israel. The blood of the attacking armies will flow to the horse's bridles, and the sounds of battle will echo through every corridor of heaven and earth. All will know that the whole universe is fighting against those who fight against God. Sin never wins; faith never fails. It is futile to fight against God.

All of us. We are so significant to God that if we submit to the lordship of Jesus Christ, God will align the entire universe up behind us. Conversely, God is so serious about sin that if we allow it to reign in our lives, God will align the entire universe up against us. Sin never wins; faith never fails. It is futile to fight against God.

Sin never wins; faith never fails. It is futile to fight against God.

Imagine that we are on a beach and pick up a handful of sand. We gently blow on it until there is just one grain of sand left. That one grain of sand represents earth, a speck of dust, while all the other grains of sand represent the vastness of this universe.

Astrophysicists say the universe continues to expand at a rate of 35,000 miles per second — more than 2.5 billion miles every day — and that there are at least 100 billion galaxies the size of our Milky Way with each of those galaxies containing more than 100 billion stars each. That means 500 billion times 100 billion stars are in their courses!

God is so serious about sin that people who harbor sin in their hearts have 500 billion times 100 billion stars aligned against them. However, when people give their hearts and lives to Jesus Christ, God aligns all of those stars up behind them. Sin never wins; faith never fails. It is futile to fight against God.

God is telling us that we are in the battle of Star Wars. It is time for us to apply the highest form of wisdom to find which direction God is going and follow Him. If we do not, we will be like Sisera, thinking we can pick a fight with God and win. Sin never wins; faith never fails. It is futile to fight against God. God is looking for some Baraks who will put their faith and feet together and believe that God will order the stars in their courses for their good and for His glory. We will win the battle of Star Wars!

The people who are on the Lord's side have the entire universe behind them.

17

The Deliverance of Faith

"Now faith is the assurance of things hoped for, the conviction of things not seen. For by it the men of old gained approval" (Hebrews 11:1-2).

If God were to grade us, what would our report cards show as far as faith is concerned? Would we have earned an A? A+? C-? A young man came to his professor and said, "Professor, I don't believe I deserve this F," to which the professor responded, "Neither do I, but it was the lowest grade I could give." Hopefully, that is not the kind of faith we have.

By faith, the elders gained approval which is extremely important because "without faith it is impossible to please Him, for he who comes to God must believe that He is and that He is a rewarder of those who seek Him" (Hebrews 11:6).

"And what more shall I say? For time will fail me if I tell of Gideon, Barak, Samson, Jephthah, of David and Samuel and the prophets" (Hebrews 11:32). Following is the story of Samson who was also one of the great men of faith.

All of us at one time or another have not only felt like failures but have actually failed the Lord and believed we did not deserve a second chance. "Then the woman gave birth to a son and named him Samson; and the child grew up and the LORD blessed him. And the Spirit of the LORD began to stir him" (Judges 13:24-25).

All of us at one time or another have not only felt like failures but have actually failed the Lord and believed we did not deserve a second chance.

In the Hebrew, the name Samson means "sun," and what sunshine this little boy brought into the life of his mother. He was a very unusual child for the Spirit of the Lord God was upon him and began to move through him. He performed mighty, tremendous feats of strength — perhaps being the strongest man who ever lived. There was the time when a young lion came roaring toward him, and the Spirit of the Lord came mightily upon him and he tore the lion apart with his bare hands (Judges 14:5-6). Entire armies trembled at the sight of him. With the jawbone of a donkey, he slew a thousand Philistines (Judges 15:16). While spending time with a prostitute, he arose at midnight and took hold of the doors of the city gate and the two posts and pulled them up along with the bars and put them on his shoulders and carried them up to the top of a mountain (Judges 16:3). What a man of strength was this man Samson!

It would be tempting to think of Samson as the Incredible Hulk of the Old Testament with mountains of muscles and bulging biceps; however, the secret of his strength was not his physique which is one reason Delilah kept asking, "Please tell me where your great strength is" (Judges 16:6,10,13,15-16).

Some may say that the secret of his strength was in his long hair because he was a Nazirite; and in his day, a symbol of his Nazirite vow was that no razor would ever touch his head. However, his long hair was only a symbol of his submission to God.

The secret of Samson's strength was when "the Spirit of the LORD began to stir him" (Judges 13:25). God through the Holy Spirit gave him supernatural strength; and in the Old Testament, Samson's physical strength is meant to be illustration to us of the spiritual strength we can have through Holy Spirit in our day. Jesus said, "You will receive power when the Holy Spirit has come upon you; and you shall be My witnesses" (Acts 1:8).

To what great heights Samson had soared. He was the judge over all Israel for twenty years so not only was he a man of physical strength but also a man of great wisdom. He was the hero of his day, and his name was on everyone's lips. However, just as he soared to great heights, he also fell to great depths. Samson went from hero to zero, from victor to victim, and from overcomer to being overcome. How the mighty had fallen!

One of the saddest stories in the Bible is the story of the blighting, awful power of sin in the life of Samson. He went from disobedience to defeat to disgrace to disappointment and, finally, to destruction.

WE NEED TO RECOGNIZE THE ROOT OF SIN

God blessed Samson for "the Spirit of the LORD began to stir him" (Judges 13:25). If the Spirit of the Lord began to stir in Samson, where did the sin in his life come from? His "old nature" — no matter that he loved God, knew God, and believed in God. "That which is born of the flesh is flesh" (John 3:6). Samson took his eyes off the Lord and allowed himself to follow after certain temptations.

James tells us how temptation happens: "Let no one say when he is tempted, 'I am being tempted by God'; for God cannot be tempted by evil, and He Himself does not tempt anyone" (1:13). We cannot say, "God made me do it," or "The devil made me do it" because "each one is tempted when he is carried away and enticed by his own lust. Then when lust has conceived, it gives birth to sin; and when sin is accomplished, it brings forth death" (James 1:14-15).

There are three persons sitting in every seat in the local church. First is the *self* that is currently sitting there. Next is the *saint* we could be if we would just let go of this world and by faith take hold of the Lord saying, "Sink or swim, live or die, once and for all, now and forever, I'm going for God." There is no limit as to what God could do through us. The third person in the seat is the sinner we could become.

Most of us have no realization of the potential for evil in our lives. We often think that nothing bad could ever happen to us, but we are no better than Samson or Simon Peter or King David. Many of God's choicest vessels have sinned and fallen. "Let him who thinks he stands take heed that he does not fall" (1 Corinthians 10:12). There is no sin of the flesh that children of God are not capable of committing if they take their eyes off the Lord Jesus Christ. The source of sin is that "each one is tempted when he is carried away and enticed by his own lust. Then when lust has conceived, it gives birth to sin" (James 1:14-15).

WE NEED TO REMEMBER THE ROAD OF SIN

The course that sin took in Samson's life was first of all because of his **indifference of a careless life**.

Then Samson went down to Timnah and saw a woman in Timnah, one of the daughters of the Philistines. So he came back and told his father and mother, "I saw a woman in Timnah, one of the daughters of the Philistines; now therefore, get her for me as a wife." Then his father and his mother said to him, "Is there no woman among the daughters of your relatives, or among all our people, that you go to take a wife from the uncircumcised Philistines?" But Samson said to his father, "Get her for me, for she looks good to me" (Judges 14:1-3).

He was not thinking about pleasing God but only about pleasing himself; however, "without faith it is impossible to please Him" (Hebrews 1:6). Samson was not acting in faith but in the flesh. As mentioned previously, if we please God, it does not matter whom we displease; but if we displease God, it does not matter whom we please.

If we please God, it does not matter whom we displease; but if we displease God, it does not matter whom we please.

Samson had no business even being among the Philistines, no business looking at the unsaved girls, and certainly no business marrying one of them. Scripture is clear that a Christian is not to marry an unsaved person: "Do not be bound together with unbelievers" (2 Corinthians 6:14). Unfortunately, many young people who love the Lord with all their hearts often become unequally yoked with an unbeliever. Samson married a Philistine girl, a child of the devil from a demonic and wicked people.

Those who marry a child of the devil will reap the devil for a father-in-law. This is where Samson's problems began—marrying an unsaved girl and being out of the will of God. He had compromised his life with his **indifference of a careless life**.

Sin generally begins small. Very few go roaring off into sin. It often starts with being in the wrong company, and Samson was among the Philistines where he should not have been. He was not practicing biblical separation. The crowd we run with will tell the kind of person we are or will soon become. Before long, Samson was living in sin and acting like the Philistines. "The companion of fools will suffer harm" (Proverbs 13:20).

Samson also lived **the indulgence of a carnal life**.

Then Samson went down to Timnah with his father and mother, and came as far as the vineyards of Timnah; and behold, a young lion came roaring toward him. The Spirit of the LORD came upon him mightily, so that he tore him as one tears a young goat though he had nothing in his hand; but he did not tell his father or mother what he had done. So he went down and talked to the woman; and she looked good to Samson, When he returned later to take her, he turned aside to look at the carcass of the lion; and behold, a swarm of bees and honey were in the body of the lion. So he scraped the honey into his hands and went on, eating as he went. When he came to his father and mother, he gave some to them and they ate it; but he did not tell them that he had scraped the honey out of the body of the lion. Then his father went down to the woman; and Samson made a feast there, for the young men customarily did this. When they saw him, they brought thirty companions to be with him. Then

Samson said to them, "Let me now propound a riddle to you; if you will indeed tell it to me within the seven days of the feast, and find it out, then I will give you thirty linen wraps and thirty changes of clothes. But if you are unable to tell me, then you shall give me thirty linen wraps and thirty changes of clothes." And they said to him, "Propound your riddle, that we may hear it." So he said to them, "Out of the eater came something to eat, And out of the strong came something sweet." But they could not tell the riddle in three days (Judges 14:5-14).

Samson was walking along when a young lion came roaring toward him, thinking he would have a Samson steakburger; but the lion had made a mistake because Samson got hold of it and tore it from limb to limb. Samson went on to the feast and proposed a riddle to thirty young Philistines, telling them that if they could figure out the riddle within seven days, he would give them thirty brand new suits; but if they could not figure it out, they would have to give him thirty brand new suits. He proceeded to tell the riddle that "out of the eater came something to eat, and out of the strong came something sweet." Judges 14:18 tells us the lion was the eater, the meat was the honey, the lion was strong, and the honey was sweet.

When they could not figure out the riddle after three days, they went to Samson's new wife and said, "Entice your husband, so that he will tell us the riddle, or we will burn you and your father's house with fire" (Judges 14:15), so she asked Samson to tell her answer to the riddle. Samson responded, "Behold, I have not told it to my father or mother; so should I tell you?" (Judges 14:16). Perhaps that was not the wisest thing to tell a young bride so she turned on the waterworks and cried for seven days. On the seventh day, Samson "told her because she pressed him so hard" (Judges 14:17); and she in turn "told the riddle to the sons of her people" (Judges 14:17). When they told Samson the answer to the riddle, he was infuriated. "If you had not plowed with my heifer, you would not have found out my riddle" (Judges 14:18). While a wife should never double-cross her husband, neither is it wise for a husband to call his new bride a heifer.

Nevertheless, Samson paid off his debt. "He went down to Ashkelon and killed thirty of them [Philistines] and took their spoil and gave the changes of clothes to those who told the riddle" (Judges 14:19).

Samson began to go down, down, down due to gambling, fighting, and arguing and was already in a broken relationship with his wife who "was given to his companion who had been his friend" (Judges 14:20). Their home had not been built on Almighty God, and Samson's life began to come apart.

Samson took another step down and began to live **the iniquity of a callous life**. He "loved a woman in the valley of Sorek, whose name was Delilah" (Judges 16:4). He had lost his first wife and then had had an affair with another woman. Now he began keeping company with a harlot whose name was Delilah, also a Philistine.

It is so hard to believe that Samson, the man of God, was doing such a thing; however, the devil is very clever. He never told Samson this was the way he wanted him to end up nor does he come to us and say, "See that drunkard lying in the gutter covered with vomit and flies buzzing around his face, crawling in and out of his mouth? That's the way I want your end to be." No, instead he says, "If you drink, you will be a person of distinction"; however, it is the finished product that counts.

Sin starts small but does not end small. The devil does not say to a young woman, "See that woman over there with a child out of wedlock? See her filthy body that is ridden with disease? Do you hear her coarse laughter that is covering up her broken heart? I am going to make you just like that disgraced and broken woman!" No, the devil never does that; and Samson certainly never dreamed he would end up in the arms of a harlot named Delilah.

WE NEED TO RESIST THE RESULT OF SIN

The consequences of Samson's sin could not be escaped for "be sure your sin will find you out" (Numbers 32:23).

In a letter to Jean-Baptiste Le Roy in 1789, Benjamin Franklin wrote, "In this world nothing can be said to be certain except death and taxes," but we know that death is not certain "for the Lord himself will come down from heaven with a loud command, with the voice of the arch-angel and with the trumpet call of God, and the dead in Christ will rise first (1 Thessalonians 4:16).

There are many things we cannot be sure of but one thing we can know beyond a shadow of any doubt or peradventure: "Be sure your sin will find you out."

It has also been said that "the sun will rise and set regardless," but we know there was a day "when the sun stood still, and the moon stopped" (Joshua 10:13). There are many things we cannot be sure of but one thing we can know beyond a shadow of any doubt or peradventure: "Be sure your sin will find you out." Notice the deadly force of Samson's sin.

There was **the blinding force of sin**. Samson was keeping company with Delilah, and the Philistines hated him. "The lords of the Philistines came up to her and said to her, 'Entice him, and see where his great strength lies and how we may overpower him that we may bind him to afflict him. Then we will each give you eleven hundred pieces of silver'" (Judges 16:5).

Eleven hundred pieces of silver equates to about $3,000; consequently, Delilah began to entice him. "Sammy boy, would you tell me what makes you so strong?"

Samson said, "I can't tell you that."

She said, "Would you tell me how you could be tied up if someone wanted to hurt you? Just tell me. Just between you and me, Sammy boy."

He responded, "Well, if you were to tie me with seven green vines, I wouldn't be able to break them."

The Philistines brought her seven green vines and she bound Samson with them and said, "Samson! The Philistines!" He jumped up and broke those vines right away.

Delilah said, "Samson, you've lied to me. Now, tell me how you can be tied up and the secret of your strength," so Samson said, "If you tie me with seven new ropes, I wouldn't be able to move at all."

Delilah took seven brand new ropes and tied him up, and the same thing happened again: "Samson! The Philistines are here!" He jumped up and "snapped the ropes from his arms like a thread" (Judges 16:12). Delilah said, "You have deceived me and told me lies; tell me how you may be bound." What a shame that Samson did not hear God saying the same thing to him.

Next Samson told her to "weave my hair in the web of the loom; then I won't be able to move." He was getting closer to the truth now although he still was not telling her the truth. After weaving his hair in the loom, Delila said, "The Philistines are upon you, Samson!" But he awoke from his sleep and pulled out the pin of the loom and the web.

Delilah was quite upset and said, "How can you say, 'I love you,' when your heart is not with me? You have deceived me these three times and have not told me where your great strength is" (Judges 16:15).

Then Delilah "pressed him daily with her words . . . so that his soul was vexed unto death" (Judges 16:16 KJV). Then "he told her all that was in his heart and said to her, 'A razor has never come on my head, for I have been a Nazirite to God from my mother's womb. If I am shaved, then my strength will leave me and I will become weak and be like any other man'" (Judges 16:17).

Delilah called the lords of the Philistines, saying, "Come up once more, for he has told me all that is in his heart" (Judges 16:18), so the lords of the Philistines came to her and brought her the "blood" money. She made Samson sleep on her knees, called for a man to shave off the seven locks of his hair, and Samson's strength left him. As before, Delilah called out, "The Philistines are upon you, Samson!" (Judges 16:20). As he awoke from his sleep, he said, 'I will go out as at other times and shake myself free,' but he did not know that the LORD had departed from him'" (Judges 16:20).

A key verse is Judges 16:21: "Then the Philistines seized him and gouged out his eyes; and they brought him down to Gaza and bound him with bronze chains, and he was a grinder in the prison."

Consider the deadly force of his sin and what it did to him. Samson's punishment could have been inflicted in various ways such as by scooping out the eyeballs, piercing the eyes, or destroying the sight by holding a red-hot iron before his eyes. However it happened, Samson would never see the sun again. The blinding power of sin.

In truth though, long before the Philistines gouged out Samson's eyes, he was already blind. Delilah asked him numerous times, "Samson, what's the secret of your strength? How may you be bound to afflict you?" Most of us would feel like saying, "Samson, you nincompoop! Don't you see what she is trying to do to you? How can you be so blind? How can you be so stupid?" Unfortunately, there are none so blind as those who will not see.

People tell us we need to experience sin a little; we need to be part of the avant-garde—part of the sophisticated generation. They say, "Don't knock it until you've tried it!" That is what the devil told Eve in the Garden of Eden: "Live it up! Experience it! Don't be a babe in the woods!" We find, however, that the deeper a person goes in sin, the less that person understands about sin.

We find, however, that the deeper a person goes in sin, the less that person understands about sin.

How blind Samson was, and his physical blindness was only a graphic illustration of his greater spiritual blindness. "The god of this world has blinded the minds of the unbelieving" (2 Corinthians 4:4). Samson was blinded in his mind before he was blinded with his eyes.

In addition to the blinding force of sin is **the binding force of sin**. "They brought him down to Gaza and bound him with bronze chains" (Judges 16:2).

Here was mighty Samson, bound in fetters of bronze; however, before that, he was already shackled by his sin. The physical binding was only illustrative of the fact that he had already been bound by his sin.

There is no one so shackled as the one shackled by sin. People talk about being free and say, "I don't want to be a Christian; I want to be free"; yet those in the world who are the most deeply enslaved are those who are slaves to their own sins. When Satan says, "Jump," they say, "How high?" all the while talking about being free. "If the Son makes you free, you will be free indeed" (John 8:36).

Mighty Samson was bound. People say, "I want to be free to drink my whiskey or my wine." Unfortunately, it may be not long before they will be bound by that bottle of whiskey or that bottle of wine. A Japanese proverb says: "First the man takes a drink. Then the drink takes a drink. Then the drink takes the man." At first the man drank happily; then he drank heavily and habitually. At first the man drank delicately; then he drank daringly. At first the man drank proudly; then he drank ploddingly. At first the man was carefree about drinking; then he was crushed by it.

One of the Greek tyrants of Syracuse in Sicily was regarded by the ancients as an example of the worst kind of despot—cruel, suspicious, and vindictive. Once he was angry with the blacksmith, but the blacksmith did not know it. The tyrant called the blacksmith in before the throne said, "I want you to show me how you would forge a chain." The blacksmith got his molten metal, his anvil, and his hammer and began to make a chain of the finest steel. When he had finished, he held the chain out to the Tyrant of Syracuse and said, "This, Sire, is an example of my work! It's the finest chain in all of the kingdom! You could put a team of horses on either end, and they would not be able to part this chain." Then the Tyrant of Syracuse said, "Guards! Take him and bind him in that chain and cast him in the dungeon!" The blacksmith was forging the chain that would bind him.

That is exactly what Samson did. Samson was the one who forged the chains that bound him. There is the binding force of sin. Many today are slaves of sin rather than servants of the Lord Jesus Christ!

Not only was there the blinding force of sin and the binding force of sin, but there was also **the grinding force**

of sin. The Philistines "seized him and gouged out his eyes; and they brought him down to Gaza and bound him with bronze chains, and he was a grinder in the prison" (Judges 16:21). When they would grind out the corn and wheat, they would have a long pole with an animal tied to the pole—an ox or donkey. Using a goad, they would make the animal go round and round and round and round. Samson was being used like an ox or a donkey! The man who was meant to be a judge in Israel was grinding in the prison house!

Samson learned three things about sin:

1. *It will take us farther than we want to go.*
2. *It will keep us longer than we want to stay.*
3. *It will cost us more than we want to pay.*

If Samson could write his autobiography, he would have to say, "The devil lied to me and told me this was the way of joy, happiness, fun, and fulfillment." The devil will lie to us. It has been said that "the devil offers high wages but always pays off in counterfeit money." Dr. R. G. Lee said, "Sin promises substance, but it gives shadow. Sin promises velvet, but it gives a shroud. Sin promises nectar, but it gives gall. Sin promises sleep, and it gives sins' nightmares. It promises rest, and it gives sins' weariness."

The grinding power of sin. There is nothing good about sin for there is nothing good that sin can do for us, and we had best treat sin like sin will treat us! There is the blinding power of sin, the binding power of sin, and the grinding power of sin. This was the force of Samson's sin.

WE NEED TO REALIZE THE REMORSE OF SIN

However, the hair of his head began to grow again after it was shaved off. Now the lords of the Philistines assembled to offer a great sacrifice to Dagon their god, and to rejoice, for they said, "Our god has given Samson our enemy into our hands." When the people saw him, they praised their god, for they said, "Our god has given our enemy into our hands, even the destroyer of our country, who has slain many of us." It so happened when they were in high spirits, that they said, "Call for Samson, that he may amuse us." So they called for Samson from the prison, and he entertained them (Judges 16:22-25).

They made fun of him and ridiculed him like a big, overgrown buffoon. They jeered and mocked and laughed at the man of God — a judge in Israel, a man in whom the Spirit of God had rested Now he was bringing disgrace and contempt upon the name of Jehovah God. The remorse that Samson must have felt.

Samson learned three things about sin:

1. It will take us farther than we want to go.
2. It will keep us longer than we want to stay.
3. It will cost us more than we want to pay.

Never had there been a greater failure than Samson; but in his remorse, he began to think of the great God who loved him, of the mercies of God, and of the fact that God is always willing to forgive.

Then Samson said to the boy who was holding his hand, "Let me feel the pillars on which the house rests, that I may lean against them." Now the house was full of men and women, and all the lords of the Philistines were there. And about 3,000 men and women were on the roof looking on while Samson was amusing them. Then Samson called to the LORD and said, "O Lord GOD, please remember me and please strengthen me just this time, O God" (Judges 16:26-28).

How much better off Samson would have been had he prayed that prayer before he ever got into sin—when he was first tempted. Samson now wanted to be avenged of the Philistines for the loss of his two eyes.

Samson grasped the two middle pillars on which the house rested, and braced himself against them, the one with his right hand and the other with his left. And Samson said, "Let me die with the Philistines!" And he bent with all his might so that the house fell on the lords and all the people who were in it. So the dead whom he killed at his death were more than those whom he killed in his life (Judges 19:29-30).

In spite of what Samson had done and in spite of the terrible tragedy, God is the God of second chances. Samson is one of the great heroes of the faith because he had great faith. Though we may wonder where his great faith was, Samson had enough faith to know that even though he was a failure and a disgrace and had shamed God, God still loved him and would remember him when he came in repentance and faith. Faith is our acceptance of God's acceptance of us when we trust Him.

When we have failed and failed terribly, God still loves us; and the same God who blessed Samson chose him as an illustration of faith when he learned to face his failure with faith.

Faith is our acceptance of God's acceptance of us when we trust Him.

Samson died prematurely and lost so many of the blessings he could have had; however, when he overcame his defeat through faith, God moved in his life one more time. God will move in our lives also for He loves us very much.

—❧—

Sin will take us further than we want to go, stay longer than we want it to stay, and cost us more than we want to pay.

18

The Distinction of Faith

No greater lesson needs to be learned than how to stand alone for the Lord Jesus Christ because we are twice-born people in a world of once-born people and are going to be going against the tide most of the time.

The noose is tightening; the war is getting hotter. We must learn to stand alone and also teach our children to stand alone because if the Lord tarries His return, they are going to face a world even more difficult than the one in which we live.

We must not stand alone out of stubbornness or arrogance or narrow-mindedness, but we must be willing to stand alone for Jesus and the principles of His Word and for the things that are true and righteous and just and will last throughout time and eternity.

Athanasius was a bold, strong Christian in ancient times who would take a stand. Other people would say he was arrogant or stubborn or narrow-minded. Theodosius was the emperor at that time and told Athanasius that the whole world was against him to which Athanasius responded, "Then Athanasius is against the whole world."

It takes courage to stand alone in our offices and schools, on teams, and in our neighborhoods; but if it is necessary now, how much more necessary will it be for our children as the days get darker. We must not stand alone out of stubbornness or arrogance or narrow-mindedness, but we must be willing to stand alone for Jesus and the principles of His Word and for the things that are true and righteous and just and will last throughout time and eternity.

> Nebuchadnezzar the king made an image of gold, the height of which was sixty cubits and its width six cubits; he set it up on the plain of Dura in the province of Babylon. Then Nebuchadnezzar the king sent word to assemble the satraps, the prefects and the governors, the counselors, the treasurers, the judges, the magistrates and all the rulers of the provinces to come to the dedication of the image that Nebuchadnezzar the king had set up. Then the satraps, the prefects and the governors, the counselors, the treasurers, the judges, the magistrates and all the rulers of the provinces were assembled for the dedication of the image that Nebuchadnezzar the king had set up; and they stood before the image that Nebuchadnezzar had set up. Then the herald loudly proclaimed: "To you the command is given, O peoples, nations and men of every language, that at the moment you hear the sound of the horn, flute, lyre, trigon, psaltery, bagpipe and all kinds of music, you are to fall down and worship the golden image that Nebuchadnezzar the king has set up. But whoever does not fall down and worship shall

immediately be cast into the midst of a furnace of blazing fire." Therefore at that time, when all the peoples heard the sound of the horn, flute, lyre, trigon, psaltery, bagpipe and all kinds of music, all the peoples, nations and men of every language fell down and worshiped the golden image that Nebuchadnezzar the king had set up (Daniel 3:1-7).

The story of the three young Hebrew men and the fiery furnace is not just simply a record of what was done and said but also a record of what God is doing and is saying. Very soon we may find ourselves in a fiery furnace — some incendiary circumstance. When that happens, we will find that our faith will also be in the fire and it will be necessary for us, like these young men of old, to stand alone.

Nebuchadnezzar was an egomaniac — a megalomaniac — who was full of a sense of his own importance. So great was his ego and self-worship that he had an image made of himself and demanded that everyone bow down and worship his image or be thrown into a fiery furnace. This gigantic image which was 90 feet tall and 9 feet wide stood out on the plains of Dura like a missile on a pad waiting to be launched. When the band struck up, there were thousands who hit the dust and fell down in obedience before that golden image. However, not ALL bowed before Nebuchadnezzar's image for were three young men who stood alone and refused to bow. Consequently, they were thrown into the fiery furnace.

This story has great relevance in the age in which we live. Daniel is a book of prophecy; and Nebuchadnezzar was a type, a picture, an illustration of the Antichrist, the man who is coming to rule the world as Babylon was ruled by Nebuchadnezzar. He will be the devil's messiah. In Scripture, he is called *the Beast, the man of sin, the lawless one, the wicked one, the Antichrist.* All of these are different appellations, names, and descriptions of one incredibly wicked human being who may now be living and will one day rule the world during the period of the Great Tribulation.

The more we see antichrists, the spirit of antichrist that is in the world, we realize that we are living in the last days.

Evolutionists believe that man evolved from a beast, but we are headed to THE beast—the Antichrist. Some may ask, "Well, what does that have to do with me? I do not have to worry about the Antichrist. I understand the Scriptures to say that when the Christians are taken out of the world, the Antichrist will come," which is true.

"Children, it is the last hour; and just as you heard that Antichrist is coming, even now many antichrists have appeared; from this we know that it is the last hour" (1 John 2:18). The more we see antichrists, the spirit of antichrist that is in the world, we realize that we are living in the last days.

THE FURY WE WILL FACE

We see the story of these three young men, Shadrach, Meshach, and Abednego, who refused to bow down to the king's image. They stood alone but also faced fury.

As mentioned earlier, Nebuchadnezzar was a type of the Antichrist as spoken of in the Book of Revelation.

He performs great signs, so that he even makes fire come down out of heaven to the earth in the presence of men. And he deceives those who dwell on the earth because of the signs which it was given him to perform in the presence of the beast, telling those who dwell on the earth to make an image to the beast who had the wound of the sword and has come to life. And it was given to him to give breath to the image of the beast, so that the image of the beast would even speak and cause as many as do not worship the image of the beast to be killed (13:13-15).

Nebuchadnezzar told the people that if they did not worship his image, they would be killed. The Antichrist is coming and will make an image more incredible than the one Nebuchadnezzar made; and if the people living during that period of time refuse to worship the image, they will be killed.

There is an interesting use of the number 6 in Daniel 3:1: "Nebuchadnezzar the king made an image of gold, the height of which was sixty cubits and its width six cubits." Daniel 3:5 tells us there were 6 instruments of orchestration: the horn, the flute, the lyre, the trigon, the psaltery, and the bagpipe. All through this, we find 666 — the number of the beast, the Antichrist, that is to come. "Here is wisdom. Let him who has understanding calculate the number of the beast, for the number is that of a man; and his number is six hundred and sixty-six" — 666 (Revelation 13:18). The Antichrist will use the number 666 to cause universal worship.

What Nebuchadnezzar did so long ago to try to get people to conform, people in the last days will also face.

Emotional Enticement

"At the moment you hear the sound of the horn, flute, lyre, trigon, psaltery, bagpipe and all kinds of music, you are to fall down and worship the golden image that

Nebuchadnezzar the king has set up" (Daniel 3:5). The Babylonian orchestra began to play incredible music. Music touches the emotions and is a gift of God, but the devil also knows the power of music. Satan is using music as never before to enforce his diabolical plans upon the world as he is a master musician. Ezekiel 28:13 (KJV) even speaks of Satan as having tabrets of pipes in him. When he speaks, it is like majestic music which can be hideously beautiful or have a demonic beat; but it is a tool Satan is using as never before.

Social Inducement

There is not only emotional enticement but also social inducement. Daniel 3:2-3 tells us that everybody was doing it; and in Daniel 3:4, the herald proclaimed, "to you the command is given, O peoples, nations and men of every language." In the last days, everybody will be doing it, and anyone who does not do as they are told will face the consequences. We are quickly moving to a one-world government, and the America that we have known is being diluted and absorbed into a generation and a globalism spurred on by the global gullibility of those who will not stand alone and for what is right.

Governmental Enforcement

Next is governmental enforcement. "Whoever does not fall down and worship shall immediately be cast into the midst of a furnace of blazing fire" (Daniel 3:6). The government in that day was trying to squeeze everyone into a mold where they would not be allowed to stand for or against anything they believed in. We face similar things in our day with threats of being arrested for contempt of court for standing up for our Christian values or threats to take away churches' tax-exempt status. Christians are felt to be in the way of the progress of peace. Jesus said, "An hour is coming for everyone who kills you to think that he is offering service to God" (John 16:2).

Spiritual Defilement

Not only was there governmental enforcement but also spiritual defilement, and the devil was behind it all. "But whoever does not fall down and worship..." (Daniel 3:6). The devil does not want casualties; he wants converts. He wants to be worshiped as will the Antichrist when he comes.

> It was also given to him [the Antichrist] to make war with the saints and to overcome them [governmental enforcement] and authority over every tribe and people and tongue and nation was given to him. All who dwell on the earth will worship him, everyone whose name has not been written from the foundation of the world in the book of life of the Lamb who has been slain (Revelation 13:7-8).

These are the powers we are up against: emotional enticement, social inducement, governmental enforcement, and spiritual defilement.

The devil does not want casualties; he wants converts.

THE FAITH WE WILL HAVE TO FOLLOW

There were three things that helped Shadrach, Meshach, and Abednego to stand alone; and these are the things we and our children must have in order to stand alone as well.

Then Nebuchadnezzar in rage and anger gave
orders to bring Shadrach, Meshach and Abednego;
then these men were brought before the king.
Nebuchadnezzar responded and said to them, "Is
it true, Shadrach, Meshach and Abednego, that
you do not serve my gods or worship the golden
image that I have set up? Now if you are ready, at
the moment you hear the sound of the horn, flute,
lyre, trigon, psaltery and bagpipe and all kinds of
music, to fall down and worship the image that I
have made, very well. But if you do not worship,
you will immediately be cast into the midst of a
furnace of blazing fire;" [Notice the spirit of antichrist and the contempt he had for God.] "and what
god is there who can deliver you out of my hands?"
Shadrach, Meshach, and Abednego replied to the
king, "O Nebuchadnezzar, we do not need to give
you an answer concerning this matter." [They meant
they did not have to hesitate in giving an answer or
study about it or worry about it.] "If it be so, our
God whom we serve is able to deliver us from the
furnace of blazing fire; and He will deliver us out
of your hand, O king. But even if He does not, let it
be known to you, O king, that we are not going to
serve your gods or worship the golden image that
you have set up" (Daniel 3:13-18).

Imagine the average, carnal Christian speaking to
Shadrach, Meshach, and Abednego: "Now, boys, let me
give you some advice. You're all in a tough spot, and your
faith is about to be tossed in the fire. When in Babylon, do
as the Babylonians do. Go along to get along. After all, it
would be a whole lot better for you to compromise a little
bit in order to live longer so you can do more good. After
all, Christians are supposed to get along with everybody, so

don't stand alone." However, these young men would not bow and were able to stand because they had a settled faith.

A Settled Faith

They had a settled faith. In the vernacular, they said, "We do not have to think about the answer to give you, O king. We do not have to get in a huddle and talk it over or ponder it or ask for a night to sleep on it." These young men had already been in a revival meeting; there had been a revival in the preaching of Jeremiah. They had God's Word hidden down in their hearts and already knew what was right and what was wrong. There are too many Christians spending too much time trying to make up their minds about situations that arise in their lives. One of the greatest things I have learned in life is one right decision will keep us from a lot of wrong ones.

One of the greatest things I have learned in life is one right decision will keep us from a lot of wrong ones.

A Strong Faith

They had a strong faith: "Our God whom we serve is able" (Daniel 3:17). They knew the God who said, "Call upon Me in the day of trouble; I shall rescue you" (Psalm 50:15). If God does not deliver us from the fire, He will deliver us through the fire.

Have faith in God, He's on His throne,
Have faith in God, He watches over His own;
He cannot fail, He must prevail,
Have faith in God, Have faith in God.
("Have Faith in God,"
The Baptist Hymnal, B. B. McKinney)

A Steadfast Faith

These three young men had a settled faith—"O Nebuchadnezzar, we do not need to give you an answer concerning this matter" (Daniel 3:16) and a strong faith—"Our God whom we serve is able" (Daniel 3:17). Furthermore, they had a steadfast faith. "But even if He does not, let it be known to you, O king, that we are not going to serve your gods or worship the golden image that you have set up" (Daniel 3:18).

They had no doubt that God was able to deliver them; but if He did not, they still were not going to serve Nebuchadnezzar's gods. Does our faith have an "if not" clause in it? If God in His sovereignty does not deliver us, will we still serve Him?

> And what more shall I say? For time will fail me if I tell of Gideon, Barak, Samson, Jephthah, of David and Samuel and the prophets, who by faith conquered kingdoms, performed acts of righteousness, obtained promises, shut the mouths of lions, quenched the power of fire, escaped the edge of the sword, from weakness were made strong, became mighty in war, put foreign armies to flight. Women received back their dead by resurrection; and others were tortured, not accepting their release, so that they might obtain a better resurrection; and others experienced mockings and scourgings, yes, also chains and imprisonment. They were stoned, they were sawn in two, they were tempted, they were put to death with the sword; they went about in sheepskins, in goatskins, being destitute, afflicted, ill-treated (men of whom the world was not worthy), wandering in deserts and mountains and caves and holes in the ground. And all these,

having gained approval through their faith, did not receive what was promised (Hebrews 11:32-39).

Some would be tempted to say if Shadrach, Meshach, and Abednego had just had enough faith, they would have been delivered "from" the fire; however, they got an "A" on their report card of faith even though they were not delivered in a way that we would call deliverance for they did have to go "through" the fire.

It is one thing to have faith to escape while it is another thing to have faith to endure.

It is one thing to have faith to escape while it is another thing to have faith to endure. It is one thing to be sick and have faith to be healed and yet another thing to be sick, not be healed, and still praise God. The latter takes greater faith. It is one thing to be delivered and another thing to die—all by faith.

Faith is not, primarily, receiving from God what we want; it is accepting from God what He gives, and Shadrach, Meshach, and Abednego had a settled faith, a strong faith, and a steadfast faith—"Even if He doesn't deliver us, we're not going to bow; we're not going to budge; we're not going to bend. We may burn, but our God will deliver us out of your hand, Nebuchadnezzar."

THE FELLOWSHIP WE WILL FIND

They were indeed bound and thrown into the fiery furnace which had been heated seven times hotter than ever before. Even the men who threw them into the fire did not survive. Nebuchadnezzar was astounded and said, "Was it not three men we cast bound into the midst of the fire They replied to the king, 'Certainly, O king.' He said, 'Look! I see four men loosed and walking about in the midst of the fire without harm, and the appearance of the fourth is like a son of the gods!'" (Daniel 3:24-25). What happened in the fire?

The Cleansing of the Saints

The bonds—the ropes—that were put on them were "loosed" (Daniel 3:25), and the fire "had no effect on the bodies of these men nor was the hair of their head singed, nor were their trousers damaged, nor had the smell of fire even come upon them" (Daniel 3:27). The only thing the fire burned off of them was what the world had put on them. When we go through the fire, God cleanses us. We grow the most when our faith is put through the fire.

When we go through the fire, God cleanses us. We grow the most when our faith is put through the fire.

The Companionship of the Savior

Next was the companionship of the Savior. Jesus will never ever, ever, ever, ever be closer to us than when we take a stand for Him and say, "No matter what anyone else is going to do, Jesus, I'm going to please You even if it costs. If I'm cast in the fire or if I'm hated, castigated, refused, spurned, ignored, or killed—Jesus, I'm going to stand for You." Jesus will move in and lock arms with us and walk through that fire with us. If we want Jesus Christ to be real, we must stop being a candle-legged Christian, a Sunday morning benchwarmer. If we stand up for the Lord Jesus Christ, there will be the companionship of the Savior.

The Conviction of the Sinner

Last, there will be the conviction of the sinner. Nebuchadnezzar looked down and said, "What's happening here? Why aren't they burned up? Because their God delivered them?" The Babylonians worshiped the fire god Gibil, but Gibil was not like Jehovah. Nebuchadnezzar had to admit there was no God like our God (Daniel 3:29). The world is going to start having respect for the Lord Jesus Christ when each of us, by the grace of God, stands alone. We must also teach our children because the spirit of antichrist is already in the world (1 John 4:3).

Never make the mistake of saying that if we were God, we would do this and that for "blessed are all they that wait for Him" (Isaiah 30:18 KJV). To be blessed, we must wait on the Lord for "they that wait upon the LORD shall renew their strength" (Isaiah 40:31). God is waiting for us to wait on Him. We must not lose heart in doing good "for in due time we will reap if we do not grow weary" (Galatians 6:9). "For you have need of endurance, so that when you have done the will of God, you may receive what was promised" (Hebrews 10:36). May God help us to trust in Him, obey Him, and keep on keeping on.

—❀❀❀—

We must not bow, bend,
and burn in this world if
we are truly going to make
an eternal difference.

19

The Durability of Faith

There is a huge need today for men—real men—men of character, integrity, and strength. Our world is in trouble because our homes are in trouble, and our homes are in trouble because men have failed to be the men of God they ought to be.

A man named Jephthah is listed as one of the great heroes of faith. Though little is said about him in Hebrews 11:32, we read the following in Judges 11:1-3:

> Now Jephthah the Gileadite was a valiant warrior, but he was the son of a harlot. And Gilead was the father of Jephthah. Gilead's wife bore him sons; and when his wife's sons grew up, they drove Jephthah out and said to him, "You shall not have an inheritance in our father's house, for you are the son of another woman." So Jephthah fled from his brothers and lived in the land of Tob; and worthless fellows gathered themselves about Jephthah, and they went out with him.

There are several durable qualities of strong faith, and our Lord desires that these powerful qualities help us endure the tests and trials that will come our way.

———— ∞ ————

There are several durable qualities of strong faith, and our Lord desires that these powerful qualities help us endure the tests and trials that will come our way.

———— ∞ ————

WE NEED CHARACTER IN THE FACE OF DIFFICULTIES

If anyone ever had a background that he could use for an excuse, it was Jephthah. We need to learn to be unshackled by the past, quit making excuses for our background, stop blaming our circumstances, and forget the psychobabble that says, "What is wrong with you now is someone else's fault and something that happened to you some time ago."

Jephthah was the son of a harlot, hence an illegitimate child. In reality, there are no illegitimate children in the truest sense of the word—only illegitimate parents. Every child has a right to live, and we should be thankful Jephthah was not aborted. Nevertheless, he was looked down on by his half-brothers who disowned him and told him he would not be allowed to share in the inheritance. He was exiled—driven out. Jephthah had a bad environment and had known failure, rejection, and poverty.

Psychologists and sociologists today would say that they would not have expected much of Jephthah because he had an excuse if he turned out badly and was not to blamed because he was a product of his environment.

There is a war on guilt in our current culture. No one is to be held responsible anymore for what they do wrong for it is always someone else's fault. Guilt is considered unproductive making the word practically obsolete. It is an affront to our dignity and our self-esteem in this day where *me-ology* has taken over from *theology*.

Jephthah could have said: "Hey, don't blame me. I am not a perpetrator; I am a victim." We have a generation of victims today—no one is responsible; all are casualties. Furthermore, sin is not sin; it is a sickness, a disease; a dependency. We are not an alcoholic or a drug addict; we have a chemical dependency. We are not a glutton; we have an eating disorder. We are not a sex fiend; we are sexually challenged. Everything is all someone else's fault. Guilt is out-of-date.

Guilt is real and we are responsible, but grace is wonderful and forgiveness is free.

The therapy industry is booming as people spend millions to be told they are not sinful but rather they are sick and not responsible for their addictions—be it sex, gambling, nicotine, anger, physical abuse, child molestation, overspending, or overeating. The problem with this theory is that if someone receives the wrong diagnosis, they will never find the cure. Jesus did not die for mistakes; He died for sin. We must stop blaming our past and saying our problems are someone else's fault; otherwise, we will never become what we ought to be.

Guilt is real and we are responsible, but grace is wonderful and forgiveness is free. Jephthah was a man with a bad birth and a bad background; but the Bible teaches that if we are born wrong the first time, we can be born again and become a royal blueblood, a child of the King. Any rough background can become the black velvet on which the diamond of God's grace is displayed.

Think of Joseph who came out of great difficulty to great power. He also was disowned by his brothers and then sold as a slave, lied about, slandered, and almost rotted in prison; but his abasement was God's plan for his advancement and the saving of many lives. If the devil is against us, God will often use the sword that Satan sharpened to cut off Satan's own head just like David cut off Goliath's head with Goliath's own sword. The power of God is greater than all the odds stacked against us, and the grace of God is greater than all our sins. We must stop making alibis and excuses.

Jephthah was a man with a terrible background, but he is listed in the Hall of Fame of Faith. We must have character in the face of our difficulties and disentangle ourselves from our past and stop saying we are victims or have bad genes. We can be what we ought to be by the grace of God.

WE NEED CONFIDENCE IN THE FACE OF DANGER

We not only need character in the face of our difficulties but also confidence in the face of danger.

We Are Not Bound By the Past

"It came about after a while that the sons of Ammon fought against Israel. When the sons of Ammon fought against Israel, the elders of Gilead went to get Jephthah from the land of Tob" (Judges 11:4-5). The King James Version says, "It came to pass" (v.4). A man used to keep this phrase on his desk and would say, "When I look at that verse, I know if I am having a good time, it is going to pass; however, when trouble comes, it will pass also."

Jephthah must have already had a reputation for being an honorable and strong man because they sent for the man they had previously cast out, saying:

> "Come and be our chief that we may fight against the sons of Ammon." Then Jephthah said to the elders of Gilead, "Did you not hate me and drive me from my father's house? So why have you come to me now when you are in trouble?" The elders of Gilead said to Jephthah, "For this reason we have now returned to you, that you may go with us and fight with the sons of Ammon and become head over all the inhabitants of Gilead." So Jephthah said to the elders of Gilead, "If you take me back to fight against the sons of Ammon and the LORD gives them up to me, will I become your head?" The elders of Gilead said to Jephthah, "The LORD is witness between us; surely we will do as you have said." Then Jephthah went with the elders of Gilead, and the people made him head and chief over them; and Jephthah spoke all his words before the LORD at Mizpah (Judges 11:6-11).

We Are Not Bound By the Problem

Jephthah had great confidence in God and was a great man of faith; if not, he would not have been listed in Hebrews 11. From a bleak background with people hating and despising him—even his own flesh and blood, he had somehow seen God and had insight into the things of God. Jephthah had character in spite of difficulties and confidence in spite of danger. The foe did not faze him nor was he fettered by fear. Fear is a dark room where negatives are developed.

"And what more shall I say? For time will fail me if I tell of Gideon, Barak, Samson, Jephthah, of David and

Samuel and the prophets" (Hebrews 11:32). Jephthah is in the middle of an amazing list of names.

He had been cast out by his brothers; but when trouble came, they ran to him. Jephthah said, "You have sent for me because you need me, but I know it is not I that you need—it is God." However, he had a stipulation: "If I deliver you, will you then follow me? Will I be your head? Will I be your leader?"

We must never claim to be a person of strength if we are not a person of faith, and we must never claim to be a person of faith if we are not a person of prayer.

I see a glimmer of the Lord Jesus Christ in this story. Jesus was despised and rejected; however, when we are convinced of our sin and our difficulty, we say, "Lord God, come and help me." Jesus will then ask us the same question: "If I deliver you, will I rule over you? Will I be your head?" He is the head of the Church; and unless He is our Sovereign, He will never be our Savior unless we say, "Lord Jesus, deliver me; and You will be my head."

How much like our Lord was Jephthah! Those who despised him, rejected him, hurt him, and cast him out were the ones he came to save. Before the battle ever began, he went to God in prayer and asked for strength: "Then Jephthah went with the elders of Gilead, and the people made him head and chief over them; and Jephthah spoke all his words before the Lord" (Judges 11:11). Prayer was not his last resort; it was his first thought. We must never claim to be a person of strength if we are not a person of faith, and we must never claim to be a person of faith if we are not a person of prayer.

Jephthah unshackled himself from his past and refused to let present dangers intimidate him. Whatever dangers are we facing, we must get on our faces before God. It is crucial to remember that "greater is He who is in you than he who is in the world" (1 John 4:4).

WE NEED COMMITMENT IN THE FACE OF DISAPPOINTMENT

> Now the Spirit of the LORD came upon Jephthah, so that he passed through Gilead and Manasseh; then he passed through Mizpah of Gilead, and from Mizpah of Gilead he went on to the sons of Ammon. Jephthah made a vow to the LORD and said, "If You will indeed give the sons of Ammon into my hand, then it shall be that whatever comes out of the doors of my house to meet me when I return in peace from the sons of Ammon, it shall be the LORD'S, and I will offer it up as a burnt offering" (Judges 11:29-31).

In essence, Jephthah said, "God, these Ammonites are wicked, cruel, and fierce. I need Your help so I'm going to make You a solemn promise. If You will give me the victory, the first thing that comes out of my house to meet me when I get back—whatever it is—will be offered up to You."

> So Jephthah crossed over to the sons of Ammon to fight against them; and the LORD gave them into his hand. He struck them with a very great slaughter from Aroer to the entrance of Minnith, twenty cities, and as far as Abel-keramim. So the sons of Ammon were subdued before the sons of Israel. When Jephthah came to his house at Mizpah,

behold, his daughter was coming out to meet him with tambourines and with dancing. Now she was his one and only child; besides her he had no son or daughter. When he saw her, he tore his clothes and said, "Alas, my daughter! You have brought me very low, and you are among those who trouble me; for I have given my word to the LORD, and I cannot take it back." So she said to him, "My father, you have given your word to the LORD; do to me as you have said, since the LORD has avenged you of your enemies, the sons of Ammon." (Judges 11:32-36).

Jephthah had made a vow to God, and God had given him the victory. Imagine Jephthah's shock and devastation when his only daughter came out of the house, dancing and leaping with joy.

The first thing that comes to our minds is human sacrifice, but Jephthah did not kill his daughter. No man of God would have made a vow of human sacrifice.

If we go back to Judges 11:29-30, we see that "the Spirit of the LORD came upon Jephthah . . . and [he] made a vow to the LORD." Whatever Jephthah said, he said under the anointing of the Spirit of God as he was a man of faith and led by the Spirit.

The Bible expressly condemns human sacrifice: "You shall not behave thus toward the LORD your God, for every abominable act which the LORD hates they have done for their gods;" [talking about the Canaanites] "for they even burn their sons and daughters in the fire to their gods" (Deuteronomy 12:31).

Had Jephthah been an ungodly man and had this been a thoughtless promise and not a promise made under the anointing of the Spirit, then we could say, "Perhaps he carelessly and thoughtlessly promised to sacrifice a burnt offering, and now he had to kill his daughter." But God had already said, "Don't do that." We know Jephthah was led of the Spirit of God, and the Spirit of God would never lead Jephthah to contradict the Word of God.

A clue to the answer is found in Judges 11:31. "Then it shall be that whatever comes out of the doors of my house to meet me when I return in peace from the sons of Ammon, it shall be the LORD's, and I will offer it up as a burnt offering." The word *and* may also be translated as *or*, so the sentence would read, "When I return in peace from the children of Ammon, it shall be the LORD's, **OR** [emphasis added] I will offer it up for a burnt offering." Jephthah was saying that it was going to be consecrated to the Lord for His service, or it would be a burnt offering because he did not know what was going to come out of the door. He was simply saying, "Lord, the choice is Yours, and I can trust You. What comes out of the door will be consecrated to You or it will be a burnt offering. God, I can trust You to do the right thing." The Spirit of God was upon him; and when his beautiful daughter came out of the door, he kept his vow and consecrated her to the Lord.

This whole event was such a tremendous disappointment to him because Jephthah was a family man who had never really known the joys of family as a child. Like every Hebrew, he hoped that he would be a part of the line of Messiah — that the Savior would be in his descendancy, and young girls in biblical times truly valued becoming wives and mothers. Nevertheless, Jephthah gave his daughter over to being a perpetual virgin for her entire life; she was to be separated — never to marry but to serve the Lord, and Jephthah knew he would have no grandchildren.

> She said to her father, "Let this thing be done for me; let me alone two months, that I may go to the mountains and weep because of my virginity, I and my companions." Then he said, "Go." So he sent

her away for two months; and she left with her companions, [she would never know the joys of a home and children] and wept on the mountains because of her virginity. At the end of two months she returned to her father, who did to her according to the vow which he had made; and she had no relations with a man. Thus it became a custom in Israel, that the daughters of Israel went yearly to commemorate the daughter of Jephthah the Gileadite four days in the year (Judges 11:37-40).

What became a custom in Israel when a young woman set aside her virginity to serve the Lord could be counterpart today to those whom we call *nuns*. "The daughters of Israel went yearly to commemorate the daughter of Jephthah" (v.40). They do not speak of her as dead but as living. The word *commemorate* may also be translated *as to talk with*. They went yearly to see her — to talk with her.

We need character in the face of difficulty, confidence in the face of danger, and commitment in the face of disappointment.

Jephthah was a man of strength, a man of steel, who refused to be shackled by his past or bound by his enemies but was a man bound by his word. We need character in the face of difficulty, confidence in the face of danger, and commitment in the face of disappointment.

20

The Divineness of Faith

Throughout Hebrews 11, all the champions of faith had a particular promise from God in common; and though at times they acted imperfectly, they nevertheless trusted in that promise faithfully and saw God prove Himself to them. In doing so, they all proved what the writer of Hebrews said, "Now faith is the substance of things hoped for, the evidence of things not seen" (v.1 KJV).

In Hebrews 11:32, David and Samuel are linked together because their lives of faith are built upon two great promises from God that David would be king of Israel and that from him a king would be born who would have an everlasting kingdom. They lived the whole of their lives in light of these two great promises from God.

We can learn many divine faith lessons that can be applied to our lives and those of our families.

WE NEED TO BE CONVINCED OF OUR CALLING OF FAITH

David entered the scene at a time of great distress for Israel. The people had chosen a king for themselves; and in the process of doing so, they had rebelled against God as their true King. They had chosen Saul; but Saul was a fickle and disobedient man prone toward rebellion against God's good way for him. Consequently, God had already begun to seek for Himself "a man after His own heart" (1 Samuel 13:14).

After a particular occasion when Saul had grievously disobeyed God, God told His prophet Samuel, "I regret that I have made Saul king, for he has turned back from following Me and has not carried out My commands" (1 Samuel 15:11). Samuel wept bitterly at this news, but God had a plan.

> Now the LORD said to Samuel, "How long will you grieve over Saul, since I have rejected him from being king over Israel? Fill your horn with oil and go; I will send you to Jesse the Bethlehemite, for I have selected a king for Myself among his sons" (1 Samuel 16:1).

Samuel did as the Lord commanded; and he examined carefully all of the fine, outwardly-excellent sons that Jesse brought to him. However, the Lord made it clear to Samuel that He had chosen none of them.

> And Samuel said to Jesse, "Are these all the children?" And he said, "There remains yet the youngest, and behold, he is tending the sheep." Then Samuel said to Jesse, "Send and bring him; for we will not sit down until he comes here." So he sent and brought him in. Now he was ruddy, with beautiful eyes and a handsome appearance. And the LORD said, "Arise, anoint him; for this is he." Then Samuel took the horn of oil and anointed him in the midst of his brothers; and the Spirit of

the LORD came mightily upon David from that day forward. And Samuel arose and went to Ramah (1 Samuel 16:11-13).

David would never forget this anointed moment and always kept in mind that he had been chosen by God to be king of his people—anointed to that role by God's outstanding prophet Samuel.

WE NEED TO COMMUNICATE OUR CONFIDENCE OF FAITH

God had chosen David as king, but God's clear calling took time to be realized and for David to be accepted by God's people. Even as the chosen king, David continued to work the sheepfolds of his father, Jesse. However, the occasion for his confidence in his calling came through the oppression of the Philistines against the people of Israel and particularly through the threats of their giant champion, Goliath, who would come out daily and defy and terrify the armies of Israel and blaspheme the God of Israel. After having been sent by his father to the battle-field to bring food to his brothers, David heard this giant's taunts and of the reward Saul promised to whoever would defeat him.

The humble shepherd boy David responded to the call and said that he would defeat the giant.

When the words which David spoke were heard, they told them to Saul, and he sent for him. David said to Saul, "Let no man's heart fail on account of him; your servant will go and fight with this Philistine." Then Saul said to David, "You are not able to go against this Philistine to fight with him; for you are but a youth while he has been a warrior from his youth." But David said to Saul, "Your servant was tending his father's sheep. When a lion or a bear came and took a lamb from the flock, I went out after him and attacked him, and rescued it from his mouth; and when he rose up against me, I seized him by his beard and struck him and killed him. Your servant has killed both the lion and the bear; and this uncircumcised Philistine will be like one of them, since he has taunted the armies of the living God." And David said, "The LORD who delivered me from the paw of the lion and from the paw of the bear, He will deliver me from the hand of this Philistine" (1 Samuel 17:31-37).

He was confident in God's call on his life and knew that as long as God had appointed him to be king, he need never fear fighting the Lord's battles.

It may have seemed as though David was being youthfully reckless, but he was confident in God's call on his life and knew that as long as God had appointed him to be king, he need never fear fighting the Lord's battles. He even had some past experiences that helped him to appreciate that God did indeed have His hand on him. In the sense of God's call on his life, David was invincible.

Perhaps out of a sense of desperation, Saul sent this young, God-trusting shepherd to fight against Goliath. We need to note the confidence with which David went for he ignored the threats of Goliath.

You come to me with a sword, a spear, and a javelin, but I come to you in the name of the LORD of hosts, the God of the armies of Israel, whom you have taunted. This day the LORD will deliver you up into my hands, and I will strike you down and remove your head from you. And I will give the dead bodies of the army of the Philistines this day to the birds of the sky and the wild beasts of the earth, that all the earth may know that there is a God in Israel, and that all this assembly may know that the LORD does not deliver by sword or by spear; for the battle is the LORD's and He will give you into our hands (1 Samuel 17:45-47).

With the defeat of Goliath, David now stood out as God's appointed man. Saul became very paranoid in the days ahead, but David did not act toward Saul with the same kind of defiance that he had shown toward Goliath. David could afford to wait respectfully and had no need to make himself king before God's time. We see David's faith in God's promise demonstrated as he waited for it to be fulfilled.

WE NEED TO BE CONVICTED OF CALMNESS IN FAITH

David could be useful to Saul and "went out wherever Saul sent him, and prospered; and Saul set him over the men of war. And it was pleasing in the sight of all the people and also in the sight of Saul's servants" (1 Samuel 18:5).
Then the trouble began.

It happened as they were coming, when David returned from killing the Philistine, that the women came out of all the cities of Israel, singing and dancing, to meet King Saul, with tambourines, with joy and with musical instruments. The women sang as they played, and said,

"Saul has slain his thousands,

And David his ten thousands."

Then Saul became very angry, for this saying displeased him; and he said, "They have ascribed to David ten thousands, but to me they have ascribed thousands. Now what more can he have but the kingdom?" (1 Samuel 18:6-8).

If we are in God's will, we never need
to run ahead of Him.

Saul kept a suspicious eye on David from that day forward. David could very easily have taken advantage of the situation, but he did not. With full faith in God's promise that he would be king in God's time, he "behaved himself wisely" (v.14 KJV).

Now Saul was afraid of David, for the LORD was with him but had departed from Saul. Therefore Saul removed him from his presence and appointed him as his commander of a thousand; and he went out and came in before the people. David was prospering in all his ways for the LORD was with him. When Saul saw that he was prospering greatly, he dreaded him. But all Israel and Judah loved David, and he went out and came in before them (1 Samuel 18:12-16).

David did not take advantage of his favor in the sight of the people for he knew God would give him the promised kingship in His time and in His way without the use of unrighteous manipulation or wrongdoing. What a great example to us of how to truly live a life of confident faithfulness in the light of God's promises. If we are in God's will, we never need to run ahead of Him. In light of David's calmness and confident faith in God's promise, it is interesting to note how God responded by giving assurances to him.

WE NEED TO CONSIDER OUR CONFIRMATION OF FAITH

Consider the confirmation David received from Saul's own son, Jonathan, who knew that God had appointed David to be king over his father. Even though Saul hated David and sought to kill him, Jonathan requested that David show favor to him when he came to the throne: "If I am still alive, will you not show me the lovingkindness of the LORD, that I may not die? You shall not cut off your lovingkindness from my house forever, not even when the LORD cuts off every one of the enemies of David from the face of the earth" (1 Samuel 20:14-15).

When David was on the run for his life from Saul, Jonathan found him and brought comfort to him stating: "Do not be afraid, because the hand of Saul my father will not find you, and you will be king over Israel and I will be next to you; and Saul my father knows that also" (1 Samuel 23:17).

When Saul found out that Jonathan had made a covenant with David, he screamed at him in a fit of rage and said:

"You son of a perverse, rebellious woman! Do I not know that you are choosing the son of Jesse to your own shame and to the shame of your mother's nakedness? For as long as the son of Jesse lives on the earth, neither you nor your kingdom will be established. Therefore now, send and bring him to me, for he must surely die" (1 Samuel 20:30-31).

Saul not only recognized what God had planned for David, but the enemies of God's people did also. David fled from Saul and hid out among the people of Gath where he went to Achish, the king of Gath. However, Achish's servants strongly objected: "Is this not David the king of the land? Did they not sing of this one as they danced, saying, 'Saul has slain his thousands, And David his ten thousands?'" (1 Samuel 21:10-11).

The godly people of Israel themselves also seemed to recognize God's plan for David. Once when David and his band of men were treated very badly by a sheep rancher they had protected, David was prepared to destroy the man in a fit of rage; but the man's wife met him and stopped him from committing a rash act that would have been a great sin.

Please forgive the transgression of your maidservant; for the LORD will certainly make for my lord an enduring house, because my lord is fighting the battles of the LORD, and evil will not be found in you all your days. Should anyone rise up to pursue you and to seek your life, then the life of my lord shall be bound in the bundle of the living with the LORD your God; but the lives of your enemies He will sling out as from the hollow of a sling. And when the LORD does for my lord according to all the good that He has spoken concerning you, and appoints you ruler over Israel, this will not cause grief or a troubled heart to my lord, both by having shed blood without cause and by my lord having avenged himself. When the

LORD deals well with my lord, then remember your maidservant (1 Samuel 25:28-31).

In a most remarkable circumstance, even Samuel gave voice to affirm David after he had died. In the strange "séance" story in which Saul sought to use occult practices to contact Samuel, God allowed Samuel to appear and tell him news he did not want to hear: "Why then do you ask me, since the LORD has departed from you and has become your adversary? The LORD has done accordingly as He spoke through me; for the LORD has torn the kingdom out of your hand and given it to your neighbor, to David" (1 Samuel 28:16-17).

WE NEED TO COMMIT TO OUR CONQUEST OF FAITH

On the day after Saul's encounter with the witch, Saul and his son Jonathan were killed in battle.

Then it came about afterwards that David inquired of the LORD, saying, "Shall I go up to one of the cities of Judah?" And the LORD said to him, "Go up." So David said, "Where shall I go up?" And He said, "To Hebron." So David went up there, and his two wives also, Ahinoam the Jezreelitess and Abigail the widow of Nabal the Carmelite. And David brought up his men who were with him, each with his household; and they lived in the cities of Hebron. Then the men of Judah came and there anointed David king over the house of Judah (2 Samuel 2:1-4).

This conquest of coronation did not come easily though. There was a long war between the house of Saul and the house of David (2 Samuel 3:1). At first, only the tribe of Judah recognized David; but through a series of events that were completely outside of David's control, a former leader in the house of Saul, in a fit of anger, purposed that he would bring all the house of Saul under David which he did (2 Samuel 3:6-11). In the end, we read:

> Then all the tribes of Israel came to David at Hebron and said, "Behold, we are your bone and your flesh. Previously, when Saul was king over us, you were the one who led Israel out and in. And the LORD said to you, 'You will shepherd My people Israel, and you will be a ruler over Israel.'" So all the elders of Israel came to the king at Hebron, and King David made a covenant with them before the LORD at Hebron; then they anointed David king over Israel. David was thirty years old when he became king, and he reigned forty years (2 Samuel 5:1-4).

David had patiently trusted God to keep that first promise, the one that would make him king; and God did as He said.

David had patiently trusted God to keep that first promise, the one that would make him king; and God did as He said. However, there was another promise, a truly remarkable one, that came after David was made king.

WE NEED TO HAVE CLARITY IN THE COVENANT OF FAITH

As king, David had set his heart upon building a temple for the Lord, but the Lord told him no because he had been a man of warfare and bloodshed and it would not be appropriate for him to build the temple. Instead, the task would be given to his son. God also told David that rather than David's building a house for the Lord, the Lord would build up David's house forever.

When your days are complete and you lie down with your fathers, I will raise up your descendant after you, who will come forth from you, and I will establish his kingdom. He shall build a h.ouse for My name, and I will establish the throne of his kingdom forever (**2 Samuel 7:12-13).**

What an astonishing promise. David understood God to be speaking of an offspring who would not simply be on his throne for a long time but rather one who would have an eternal kingdom. He recognized this to be a promise of the coming Messiah who would reign on earth as God's appointed "eternal" King—the King of kings. In response, David prayed:

Now therefore, O LORD God, the word that You have spoken concerning Your servant and his house, confirm it forever, and do as You have spoken, that Your name may be magnified forever, by saying, 'The LORD of hosts is God over Israel'; and may the house of Your servant David be established before You (2 Samuel 7:25-26).

God did not give David this greater "second' promise" until after the lesser "first promise" had been fulfilled. Consequently, God built David's faith up so that the second promise—the one that benefits us all today—would be more fully believed. God nurtures our own faith in the same way.

David's life was perfect from then on—no, unfortunately, it was not. David later committed a terrible sin of adultery and tried to cover it up with murder. God confronted David with this great sin (2 Samuel 12:7-12); and when David made his confession, we find further evidence of faith in the promise of God.

WE NEED TO HAVE COURAGE IN THE CONFESSION OF FAITH

In David's psalm, we see how his heart was broken over his sin and concern over what would happen to God's great promises to him. He was concerned that God would remove His blessing and kingship and not allow David's offspring to rule as King forever.

> Create in me a clean heart, O God,
> And renew a steadfast spirit within me.
> Do not cast me away from Your presence
> And do not take Your Holy Spirit from me (Psalm 51:10-11).

David's words reflected his fears about the loss of the covenant promise God had made to him. In true repentance, David admitted he had sinned, and Psalm 51 shows that this confession was sincere.

God graciously forgave David; however, sin has unavoidable consequences. God allowed the child that was conceived in this terrible act of adultery to be taken from

David (2 Samuel 12:13-14), but he was given another son named Solomon (2 Samuel 12:24-25). It would be through Solomon that the promise God made would be kept.

Among the many other consequences of David's sin was the fact that from that day on, there would be trouble in David's household. His eldest son eventually rebelled against him and sought to draw the people to himself in order to dethrone his father.

God is faithful to His promises even when we are not as faithful to Him as we should be.

WE NEED TO BE CONSISTENT IN THE CRISIS OF FAITH

We can see something of this struggle when David was on the run from his son. As David sought to make his way out of the city to save his life and the lives of those in his royal household, Zadok, the priest, sought to bring the ark of the covenant from out of the temple. David would not allow it though and said: "Return the ark of God to the city. If I find favor in the sight of the LORD, then He will bring me back again and show me both it and His habitation. But if He should say thus, 'I have no delight in you,' behold, here I am, let Him do to me as seems good to Him" (2 Samuel 15:25-26).

God's favor was still upon David and the great kingdom promises were not withdrawn from him. David again had patience in God's promise and trusted that in God's time, the throne would be restored to him and the promise of God kept. When the rebellion was over, David was restored to the throne and wrote a song in which he declared of God:

267

He is a tower of deliverance to His king,
And shows lovingkindness to His anointed,
To David and his descendants forever (2 Samuel 22:51).

God is faithful to His promises even when we are not as faithful to Him as we should be.

WE NEED TO CONTINUE UNTIL THE CONCLUSION OF FAITH

In the course of time, David died; and his son, Solomon, was placed on the throne and built the temple of the Lord in place of his father David. After Solomon dedicated the temple, the Lord told him:

As for you, if you will walk before Me as your father David walked, in integrity of heart and uprightness, doing according to all that I have commanded you and will keep My statutes and My ordinances, then I will establish the throne of your kingdom over Israel forever, just as I promised to your father David, saying, "You shall not lack a man on the throne of Israel" (1 Kings 9:4-5).

God kept this promise for the angel spoke to Mary and told her:

Do not be afraid, Mary; for you have found favor with God. And behold, you will conceive in your womb and bear a son, and you shall name Him Jesus. He will be great and will be called the Son of the Most High; and the Lord God will give Him the throne of His father David; and He will reign over the house of Jacob forever, and His kingdom will have no end (Luke 1:30-33).

With David's last words, he affirmed God's blessing on those who feared Him and faithfully obeyed Him.

Truly is not my house so with God?
For He has made an everlasting covenant with me,
Ordered in all things, and secured;
For all my salvation and all my desire,
Will He not indeed make it grow (2 Samuel 23:5).

And God did. David's life was a life lived in humble and confident faith in God's promises, the greatest of which was the promise of the Savior, Jesus Christ—the Son of David and the King of kings. We live in the light of God's promises to David—both kept and still being kept. May we learn from David to trust our God to keep all of His promises!

---oooo---

When God is at work in your life,
even your enemies will know
that He has anointed your life
for great victory.

21

The Declaration of Faith

Speaking of the prophets of old, the writer of Hebrews states that "by faith [they] conquered kingdoms, performed *acts* of righteousness, obtained promises, shut the mouths of lions" (Hebrews 11:33). When we think of "shut the mouths of lions," we no doubt think of Daniel and the lions' den.

Daniel 6 is the famous chapter in which we find Daniel in and out of the lions' den. Nations are born, they live, they die. They rise and they fall with great regularity. When we look back to the empires of the Hittites, the Egyptians, the Assyrians, and finally the Babylonians, we find Daniel in the role of prime minister. Those empires were followed by the Medes and the Persians, the Greeks, and the Romans. All of them rose to power and then fell into oblivion.

On our own continent in the Western Hemisphere, we find tales of the Mayans, the Incans, and the great Aztec Empire; but little or no trace remains of them save for some archaeological artifacts. They have come and they have gone.

In more modern times, there are those who lived through the greatness of the days of England. Others remember the greatness of France and when Italy was a major power in the world and threatened to dominate Europe under the leadership of Benito Mussolini. Others remember Germany when Adolf Hitler with his Aryan philosophy thought he could conquer the world. We have seen the rise and fall of Japan as a mighty military power. China is now coming to the forefront while Russia seems to be in decline. Many devout spiritual leaders are wondering if we are watching the beginning of the fall of America.

Nations rise, nations fall; they come, they go. However, the Bible tells us in Acts 17 that the times of the nations are bound by the sovereignty of God. What is especially thrilling is that the coming and the going of nations have very little to do with the continuation of the people of God.

In Daniel 5, there could not be imagined a more cataclysmic event than had just happened. At the height of its glory as the greatest empire humanity had ever known, the Babylonian Empire, "the head of gold" as represented by the image in Daniel 2, had fallen. Without firing a shot, the Medes and the Persians entered the city; and the whole Babylonian Empire fell. What is amazing about it though is that it had little or no impact on what God did with His people for Daniel rode through the ebb and the flow of nations.

In Daniel 6, we enter the second of the four great empires, the Medo-Persian Empire which was represented by the image in Daniel 2 as the chest and the arms of silver. As we look at this empire, we do not see Daniel uninvolved; rather, we see him right at the heart of all that was taking place. He was the prime minister of Babylon as well as the prime minister of Medo-Persia.

This profound leadership theme is exciting. Across America and even around the world, there is a preoccupation among many Christians with the preservation of certain nations—even our own. Whether they realize it or not, they are attempting to equalize America with the Church or America with the plan of God; however, there is no biblical foundation for this. Nations come and go, yet God's work goes on. No nation is really significant when set against the backdrop of eternity and God's plan.

"Behold, the nations are like a drop from a bucket, and are regarded as a speck of dust on the scales" (Isaiah 40:15). Nations are like one speck of dust that spills out of a bucket; they are "inconsequential" and not a factor in the weighing at all. When God sets out to weigh the history of humanity, the nations are not the issue. When God pours out the floods of the flow of His redemptive plan, one drop is inconsequential. The nations are drops; they are dust.

Isaiah compares the nations to grass that withers and dies and fades away (40:7-8). We think back to Nimrod, Sennacherib, Nebuchadnezzar, Cyrus, Artaxerxes, Alexander, the Caesars, the Pharaohs, Napoleon, Churchill, Mussolini, Hitler, Mao, Khrushchev, Gorbachev, and on into our time. The leaders and the nations come and go yet God's work goes on.

"This sentence is by the decree of the *angelic* watchers and the decision is a command of the holy ones, in order that the living may know that the Most High is ruler over the realm of mankind, and bestows it on whom He wishes and sets over it the lowliest of men" (Daniel 4:17).

God rules in history even though nations may come and nations may go—even our own. However, God's redemptive plan as unfolded through His people will go according to schedule. The people of God go through the rise and fall of nations, and they transcend. That is a great hope for us, and we see this truth in Daniel for Babylon had fallen. The head of gold was crushed. The time of the

Gentiles was moved into phase two, but Daniel was right where God wanted him.

God rules in history even though nations
may come and nations may go — even our own.
However, God's redemptive plan as unfolded
through His people will go according to schedule.

The fact that Babylon had fallen was really quite amazing. Nebuchadnezzar had his name put on every brick used in the buildings of Babylon. In fact, thousands of bricks have been discovered with Nebuchadnezzar's name on them. He was trying to build a lasting empire. One brick which is now in the British Museum has the image and the name of Nebuchadnezzar with a dog's footprint over both of them. So it is with the world, but God's people and God's plan transcend all the nations of the earth.

OUR FAITH IN GOD MAY BRING US PROMOTION

"It pleased Darius to set over the kingdom [the Medo-Persian kingdom] an hundred and twenty princes, which should be over the whole kingdom; and over these, three presidents [this is the only place in the Bible the word president is ever used in the Hebrew or the Aramaic, and it appears to mean chief]; of whom Daniel was first: that the princes might give accounts unto them, and the king should have no damage. Then this Daniel was preferred above the presidents and princes, because an excellent spirit was in him; and the king thought to set him over the whole realm" (Daniel 6:1-3 KJV).

Darius is a very elusive person because there is no extra-biblical data in existence to tell us anything about him nor does there seem to be a place in the genealogical record of the kings of that time for a man named Darius. Most likely, Darius is another name for Cyrus. Also, the word Darius is a title like pharaoh or king or Caesar. "So this Daniel prospered in the reign of Darius" (Daniel 6:28).

Cyrus is best seen behind the name Darius. He was an intelligent and capable leader, an effective man in terms of organization and structure. He was powerful and influential with a commitment to his own god but not to the God of Israel although he did indicate great interest in the God of Daniel.

While Daniel 6:1 states that Darius appointed 120 princes and three presidents, Daniel 6:2 states that "Daniel was first"; and Daniel 6:3 states that "Daniel was preferred above the presidents and princes."

The word preferred means that he distinguished himself constantly over the others. Without question, he was the finest statesman in the entire Medo-Persian Empire just as he had been the finest statesman in the Babylonian Empire and perhaps the finest statesman ever to walk on the face of the earth.

"An excellent spirit was in him" (Daniel 6:3) speaks of Daniel's attitude; and, of course, attitude pervades everything we do. However, Daniel had more than an excellent attitude going for him; he also had experience. He had lived through the last regime as the prime minister and had wisdom like no one else.

Daniel also had a sense of history and a dynamic leadership ability if what he was able to do in the lives of Shadrach, Meshach, and Abednego was any indication of the model he set. He had administrative ability and was given responsibility on a wide and far-reaching basis. In addition to all of that, he had the ability to interpret dreams and visions that gave an idea of what was coming in the future which was invaluable to a monarch.

God placed Daniel right where He wanted him and allowed Darius to recognize his capability and put him in a very strategic place, a place of influence.

Daniel also had a sense of history and a dynamic leadership ability if what he was able to do in the lives of Shadrach, Meshach, and Abednego was any indication of the model he set.

In the first year of Darius's rule around 538 or 537 B.C., Darius made a decree that the Jews could go back to Judah after having been in Babylonian captivity for 70 years. Daniel was likely the one who was the great influencer on him in this matter.

By this time, Daniel was no longer a young man but was probably around 90 years of age; however, he was still God's man and God choice as well as the king's choice as prime minister. The power of a virtuous life extends into old age, and we are never too old to impact our world.

At the age of 83, William Gladstone became prime minister of Great Britain for the fourth time. At the age of 66, Michelangelo executed "The Last Judgment," perhaps the most famous painting in the world. John Wesley preached with almost undiminished eloquence at 87, ending at that remarkable age the most remarkable career of his time having traveled a quarter of a million miles in an age that knew neither electricity nor steam, delivered an estimated 4,000 sermons, and wrote some 400 publications.

Thomas Edison was still inventing into his 80s. At 90 years of age, Frank Lloyd Wright was still considered a creative architect and George Bernard Shaw was writing plays. Grandma Moses was painting at 80; and J.C. Penney, the great Christian, was working strenuously at his desk at 95. Some say, "I'm 55 years old; I've got to retire!" and thereby forfeit the richness of age. Daniel was pushing 90 and was still God's man. God put him right where He wanted him, and the politics of Medo Persia had little to withstand it.

OUR FAITH IN GOD CAN BRING US PROBLEMS

Daniel 6:4-9 demonstrates that whenever an individual is lifted up by the Lord to a place of prominence, that person falls into certain difficulty for there is always a price to pay. There is no exaltation, no success, and no prominence that is not paid for by a certain amount of slavery. The person who succeeds is a person who works, slaves, and labors—a person who is chained.

A musician is tied to an instrument, an artist to a canvas, an author to a manuscript, a physician to patients, and a preacher to prayer and study. Anyone and everyone who excels is a prisoner of sorts, slaving at the assignment and pouring life into it. There is a price to pay.

Another price to pay for being in a position of being blessed by God is that whoever is in that position will be dogged and hounded and followed by envy. When God lifts a person up, it is amazing how other people's hearts burn with rage, jealousy, and bitterness even when that individual has done them absolutely no injury or harm. How could anyone hate Daniel? How could anyone despise such a man? A tougher question is how could anyone crucify Jesus Christ? But they did.

"Then the presidents and princes sought to find occasion against Daniel concerning the kingdom; but they could find none occasion nor fault; forasmuch as he was faithful, neither was there any error or fault found in him"

(Daniel 6:4 KJV). Daniel had no skeletons in his closet so there was no way to indict him.

*When God lifts a person up, it is amazing
how other people's hearts burn with rage, jealousy,
and bitterness even when that individual has done
them absolutely no injury or harm.*

When a man is 90 years old and people in political office try to find something against him but come up with nothing, that is an honorable man. They found no fault, no corruption, and no error in Daniel. Corruption is the sin of commission, and error is the sin of omission. They could not find anything Daniel did that he should not have done nor anything that he did not do that he should have done. He was a virtuous man.

"Then said these men, 'We shall not find any occasion against this Daniel, except we find it against him concerning the law of his God'" (Daniel 6:5 KJV). When others cannot find anything against us but the fact that we are absolutely sold out to our God, then we are fulfilling the New Testament principle of suffering for righteousness sake. The only thing they said they would ever get Daniel on was the fact that he was totally committed to his God. What a commendation!

"All the presidents of the kingdom, the governors, and the princes, the counsellors, and the captains, have consulted together to establish a royal statute, and to make a firm decree, that whosoever shall ask a petition of any God or man for thirty days, save of thee, O king, he shall be cast into the den of lions" (Daniel 6:7 KJV).

They articulated that they wanted Darius to be God for thirty days. Now when someone can be elected to be God, that is bad theology; and when that someone is only God for 30 days, it is even worse theology. Yet they came to Darius and said something like: "We have consulted with all the governors, the princes, the presidents, the counsellors, and the captains; and everybody has agreed we ought to make a law. Because you are so wonderful and are worthy of being God for 30 days, we are going to give you that privilege. Consequently, we want to make a rule that whoever shall ask a petition of any god or man for 30 days, unless it is you, shall be cast into the den of lions."

These men came together and pulled it off. However, when they said "all the presidents," that was not true. There was one of them who did not agree and probably did not even know what they were doing, and that was Daniel. They wanted to make a statute and a firm decree. The double use of a royal statute and a firm decree showed how binding and strong they wanted it to be — that no one could worship or make a petition of anyone but Darius for 30 days.

Of course, Darius was flattered as any noble would be if a whole body of politicians came wanting to do that. It would be pretty difficult to resist, and Darius was swept away in the emotion of the whole deal.

"Now, O king, establish the injunction and sign the document so that it may not be changed, according to the law of the Medes and Persians, which may not be revoked" (Daniel 6:8). This meant that once a law of the Medes and Persians was enacted, it could not be changed.

These guys came along and hit the king at the point of his vulnerability — his ego, and "King Darius signed the document, that is, the injunction" (Daniel 6:9) which instantly meant that if anyone made a petition of any god but Darius, that person would be thrown into the lions' den.

OUR FAITH IN GOD WILL BRING US PERSEVERANCE

"Now when Daniel knew that the document was signed, he entered his house (now in his roof chamber he had windows open toward Jerusalem); and he continued kneeling on his knees three times a day, praying and giving thanks before his God, as he had been doing previously. Then these men came by agreement and found Daniel making petition and supplication before his God" (Daniel 6:10-11). Though they had made a law, Daniel went back to his room and did what he did every day.

When Daniel went up to pray, he faced toward Jerusalem because that was where the longing of his heart was — the people of God and the city of God which symbolized God to him.

When Daniel went up to pray, he faced toward Jerusalem because that was where the longing of his heart was — the people of God and the city of God which symbolized God to him. He would pray, no doubt, for the peace of Jerusalem, the restoration of the city, the confession of sin, and whatever else was on his heart; and he did it in just the same way he always had. Men may make laws; but when those laws violate the rules God has laid down, we do not worry about those laws.

We might think, "Well, couldn't Daniel have been a little more discreet? Couldn't he just have closed the window and prayed the same way?" Yes. "Couldn't he have just cooled it for 30 days and talked to the Lord standing up and walking around so he wouldn't have been as visible?" Yes, but any compromise at all would have been understood as self-serving; and it was not in Daniel's character to do that.

When Polycarp, a disciple of the Apostle John, was burned at the stake in Smyrna in A.D. 155, he had been a Christian for 86 years. Before the fire was lit, Polycarp was called upon to "deny the Lord and save your life." In quiet assurance and with a steady voice, Polycarp responded: "Eighty and six years I have served Him, and He has done me no wrong. How then can I blaspheme my King and Savior?" With praises on his lips and a quiet commitment to the Lord, Polycarp looked down at the flames and accepted them as God's will.

OUR FAITH IN GOD MAY BRING US PERSECUTION

"Then they approached and spoke before the king about the king's injunction." They had spied out Daniel. They saw what he did. "'Did you not sign an injunction that any man who makes a petition to any god or man besides you, O king, for thirty days, is to be cast into the lions' den?'" Now they put the monkey on the king's back. "The king replied, 'The statement is true, according to the law of the Medes and Persians, which may not be revoked'" (Daniel 6:12).

"Then they answered and spoke before the king, 'Daniel, who is one of the exiles from Judah...' They were forever throwing that at Daniel—that foreigner, that prisoner, that captive, not even of the right stock. '...[He] pays no attention to you, O king...' Was that true? Absolutely not. Daniel was a loyal and faithful servant as long it did not cause him to violate his principles. He regarded the king in the way a king should be regarded; and as the Lord said, he rendered "to Caesar the things that are Caesar's" (Mark 12:17). They continued, '...or to the injunction which you signed, but keeps making his petition three times a day'" (Daniel 6:13).

They confronted the king. Darius started out as god for a month and wound up as a fool in one day. "And the king, when he heard *these* words, was greatly displeased with himself" (Daniel 6:14 NKJV). At least Darius had the honesty to put the blame where it belonged. His own ego had entrapped him. Allurements are always going to be there, but we do not usually fall for them unless our own egos are involved. But Darius "set *his* heart on Daniel to deliver him; and he labored till the going down of the sun to deliver him" (Daniel 6:14 NKJV).

Assuming the edict was signed in the morning, the men hurried out to see what Daniel would do at noon; and there Daniel was—praying. They ran right back and told the king, and Darius labored all afternoon because according to their custom, execution was to come before nightfall. Darius exhausted every legal means possible to deliver Daniel. Perhaps he tried to find a loophole in the law or something in past Medo-Persian law that could undo his ruling; however, there was no way out.

Where was Daniel during all of this? Daniel never said a word, never took up his own cause, never defended himself for there was no defense. The only answer Daniel could have given was, "I was praying, and I'll keep on praying." He had had such confidence in God through all those years that he continued to commit himself to God.

OUR FAITH IN GOD MAY BRING US PENALTIES

"Then these men approached the king, and said to the king, 'Know, O king, that *it is* the law of the Medes and Persians that no decree or statute which the king establishes may be changed.' So the king gave the command,

and they brought Daniel and cast *him* into the den of lions" (Daniel 6:15-16 NKJV).

"The king spoke and said to Daniel, 'Your God whom you constantly serve will Himself deliver you'" (Daniel 6:16). Where did Darius get that idea? Daniel had no doubt spoken to him many times about God so it would seem apparent that Darius would have known what Daniel believed. Daniel had already been involved in miracles and in giving advice about the release of the Jews. Darius likely knew the story of Shadrach, Meshach, and Abednego's deliverance from the fiery furnace in Babylon so he knew that this God of Daniel's could do miracles which, in turn, showed that Daniel's evangelistic efforts were having results.

Darius likely knew the story of Shadrach, Meshach, and Abednego's deliverance from the fiery furnace in Babylon so he knew that this God of Daniel's could do miracles which, in turn, showed that Daniel's evangelistic efforts were having results.

"A stone was brought and laid over the mouth of the den" (Daniel 6:17). The den was most likely a cave in the side of a hill. On the lower side was the natural cave entrance where they would bring the lions in and out or do whatever they needed to do to feed them although the lions were purposely starved to be used as executioners. There would have been a stone there to cover the entrance. On the top of the hill, there would have been a hole with a grate over it where the executions could be viewed.

Then "the king sealed it with his own signet ring and with the signet rings of his nobles, so that nothing would be changed in regard to Daniel" (Daniel 6:17).

While we are thinking and praying over the truths of Daniel and the lions' den, it would be wise to think about the lions' dens of life. "Be sober, be vigilant; because your adversary the devil, as a roaring lion, walketh about, seeking whom he may devour" (1 Peter 5:8 KJV).

To be "sober" means to be mentally alert and self-controlled. To be "vigilant" means to be watchful, awake, and observant. Even though we understand that God is all-powerful and cares for us, we cannot afford to relax our guard spiritually. It is vital to recognize that Satan is relentless and wants to destroy us. We must be faithful in doing our part. There are times in life when an attack will come—not of our making or choosing—and behind the attack will be Satan, striving to devour us. Satan (the devil) is a false accuser and slanderer who walks about in a constant state of activity.

When we find ourselves in the lions' den of attack, we are to "resist stedfast in the faith" (1 Peter 5:9 KJV). "Steadfast" means standing firm without moving even under an attack from the enemy. Our response should not be panic, fear, or flight but a firm resistance through the faith of Christ in us—like facing an angry, charging lion in the wild. People who have studied lions in the wild will tell you never to turn your back and run from a charging lion. Lions are accustomed to their victims fleeing, but standing firm and facing them bewilders and confuses them. In most cases, the charging lion will stop short and turn away.

As true Christians, we stand fast "in the faith" because we have confidence in the One who is "greater . . . than he who is in the world" (1 John 4:4). Peter instructs us to stand steadfastly in "the faith"—to stand firm in our beliefs with a strong conviction about God's Word.

We oppose Satan's attacks by standing up to him. We cannot panic or take flight but rather should offer firm resistance. We must not allow him to get the better of us no matter the consequences (Revelation 12:10-11). We must never forget that our most insidious and treacherous enemies are Satan and his demons, the unseen rulers of this world.

OUR FAITH IN GOD CAN BRING US PRESERVATION

Afterwards, "the king went off to his palace" (Daniel 6:18). The Holy Spirit is so subtle. For example, if we were watching a film and it came to the climax where they threw Daniel into the lions' den and then cut to the king's palace, we would say: "What! We don't want to see the king's palace! We want to see what's going on in the lions' den!" Yet the Holy Spirit cuts to the palace, not saying what is happening in the lions' den.

Darius "spent the night fasting" (Daniel 6:18). Who cares? What happened in the lions' den? "And no entertainment was brought before him" (Daniel 6:18). He did not want any of that—no music, no dancers, no food, nothing. "His sleep fled from him" (Daniel 6:18). Darius probably paced the floor all night.

"Then the king arose at dawn, at the break of day, and went in haste to the lions' den" (Daniel 6:19). As soon as the sun was visible, he left the palace and hustled down to the den of lions to see what was going on. This action seems to indicate that he had some faith in the God of Daniel.

"When he had come near the den to Daniel, he cried out with a troubled voice" (Daniel 6:20). Darius was hoping for the best but perhaps believing the worst. "The king spoke and said to Daniel, 'Daniel, servant of the living God'" (Daniel 6:20). Where would Darius have learned the statement, "servant of the living God"? From Daniel, of course. "Servant of the living God, has your God, whom you constantly serve, been able to deliver you from the lions?" (Daniel 6:20).

God's angels are so powerful. One angel took care of 185,000 Assyrians and slew them all (2 Kings 19:35), so one angel would have been enough to shut the lions' mouths.

It seems a little late for that question. Was Daniel alive? Now to the crux of the matter: Was God able to deliver Daniel?

"Then Daniel spoke to the king, 'O king, live forever! My God sent His angel and shut the lions' mouths'" (Daniel 6:21-22). That had to mean that God took care of the lions' paws also since they could have ripped Daniel to shreds.

God's angels are so powerful. One angel took care of 185,000 Assyrians and slew them all (2 Kings 19:35), so one angel would have been enough to shut the lions' mouths. "My God sent His angel and shut the lions' mouths and they have not harmed me, inasmuch as I was found innocent before Him" (Daniel 6:22). That was not a proud speech but a true one; and if it is true it is not pride. "And also toward you, O king, I have committed no crime" (Daniel 6:22). Just to get the record straight.

It is interesting that Daniel only defends himself after he has given God the opportunity to put him through the test. He put his life in God's hands in a lions' den as though he were saying, "Now, God, I do not understand why I'm going into that lions' den, but maybe You have a reason. Maybe You know something in my life that is not right, and this is part of it." It was only after God delivered him that he could say, "I have done nothing; I am innocent." How do we know we are innocent? Because God had a perfect chance to chasten us and did not. Daniel waited for God's evaluation.

"Then the king was very pleased and gave orders for Daniel to be taken up out of the den" (Daniel 6:23). This is another indication that Daniel (then in his 80s) was in a pit, was probably dropped some ropes, grabbed onto the ropes, and up he came. "So Daniel was taken up out of the den and no injury whatever was found on him, because he had trusted in his God" (Daniel 6:23).

Daniel was saying it was a vindication of his great faith in God. He believed God, and God honored his faith. We must realize, however, that it does not always happen that way. Isaiah believed God, but he was sawn in half. Paul believed God also and laid his head on a block, and an axe head flashed in the sun and severed it from his body. Peter believed God, and he was crucified upside down.

Believing in God does not mean the lions will not eat us. There have been martyrs throughout all of history. The issue is that we accept God's will. If it is to live, it is to live; and if it is to die, it is to die. In either case, we are never defeated.

In fact, had Daniel been eaten by the lions, he would have been in the presence of God which would have been better than looking up at Darius and saying, "O king, live forever." He could not lose. We never lose. Had Daniel been torn to shreds, the angel who came would have carried him into the presence of the Lord to Abraham's bosom.

OUR FAITH IN GOD WILL BRING PUNISHMENT

"The king then gave orders, and they brought those men who had maliciously accused Daniel [the satraps, the princes, the presidents] and they cast them, their children and their wives into the lions' den; and they had not reached the bottom of the den before the lions over-powered them and crushed all their bones" (Daniel 6:24). Amazing! There must have been a tremendous number of lions.

Some might argue that Daniel was not eaten because the lions were not hungry; however, these were lions that were purposely starved to be used as executioners and were not old and toothless. They were so ferocious they shredded those who accused Daniel and their families before they ever hit the ground. A horrifying scene – the picture of retribution and the vengeance of God.

It is also a very interesting glimpse into pagan law. The law of the Medes and Persians said, "On account of the guilt of one, all his kindred must perish"; and so they did.

OUR FAITH IN GOD WILL BRING PROCLAMATION

"Then Darius the king wrote to all the peoples, nations and *men of every* language who were living in all the land: 'May your peace abound! I make a decree that in all the dominion of my kingdom men are to fear and tremble before the God of Daniel'" (Daniel 6:25-26).

One man, and he literally affected the entire empire. Now the entire Medo-Persian Empire had fallen under the decree to tremble and fear before the God of Daniel. It does not take a lot of people; it just takes the right kind and the right one. "For He is the living God and enduring forever, And His kingdom is one which will not be destroyed, And His dominion *will be* forever" (Daniel 6:26).

Nations come and go; and whether they be Babylonian or Medo-Persian, when God puts His men in the right place, His message gets through. God "delivers and rescues and performs signs and wonders in heaven and on earth, who has *also* delivered Daniel from the power of the lions" (Daniel 6:27).

Who received the glory in Daniel 6? Not Daniel — not for one minute. It was God who received the glory. One thread that runs through the Book of Daniel is the majesty of God who stands against the nations of the world and upholds His sovereignty.

One man, and he literally affected the entire empire. Now the entire Medo-Persian Empire had fallen under the decree to tremble and fear before the God of Daniel.

There can be no doubt that the declarations Daniel made about God were deposited into the life of Darius. In return, when Darius was about to put Daniel in the lions' den and later came back to check on him, he declared, "He is the living God and enduring forever, And His kingdom is one which will not be destroyed, And His dominion *will be* forever" (Daniel 6:26).

OUR FAITH IN GOD CAN BRING PROSPERITY

"So this Daniel enjoyed success in the reign of Darius and in the reign of Cyrus the Persian" (Daniel 6:28). It never ceases to amaze me how our Lord provides for us. As Daniel faithfully served the Lord, the Lord prospered Daniel.

The thought of prosperity is the last link in a long chain set through this chapter. We can see Daniel progressing along the path of being preferred, being plotted against, praying, praising, persisting, being persecuted, being protected, persevering, and enjoying prosperity.

One of the greatest blessings to come from Daniel 6 is to see the story unfold and point to Jesus Christ who was a man (1) without blame, faithful to God in all His ways, noted for prayer, and sent to His death because of the jealousy of those who wanted to prevent His exaltation; (2) condemned to death through the plotting of His enemies and the law of the land and thrown into a stone room meant to be his tomb; (3) who had a stone rolled over the opening of the tomb; however, in all its power and ferocity, death could not touch him; and (4) who came out victoriously on the morning the stone was rolled away glorifying God as did the pagans and whose enemies were judged.

Daniel prospered more than ever and was more in the favor of his prince and in reputation with the people which gave him a great opportunity to do good to his brethren. This great success began for Daniel because he "made up his mind that he would not defile himself" (Daniel 1:8). He gave his best to God in his early years, and God gave His best to him in his latter years.

As we walk out our faith, we need to declare the greatness of our God and live as one who obeys the living King of the Universe!

22

The Daybreak of Faith

I have no doubt that the Hebrew writer was thinking of Elijah when he wrote, "Women received back their dead by resurrection" (Hebrews 11:35). One of the most colorful characters of the Old Testament is Elijah whom God used in a mighty way at a time when spirituality was at an all-time low in the land of Israel. James tells us this about Elijah: "[He] was a man subject to like passions as we are, and he prayed earnestly that it might not rain: and it rained not on the earth by the space of three years and six months. And he prayed again, and the heaven gave rain, and the earth brought forth her fruit" (5:17-18 KJV). Elijah was an ordinary man who knew how to get hold of the extraordinary God and answer prayers on his behalf.

The opening of 1 Kings 17 shows a dreadful condition existing in Israel. As a result of Elijah's prayer, a terrible drought had hit Israel—a punishment sent by God due to the unlawful marriage of Ahab, a Jewish king, and Jezebel, a gentile woman. However, Jezebel was no ordinary gentile bride; she was a wicked, idol-worshipping woman who had many of the priests of the living God put to death and led the country in idol worship of Baal.

Elijah gave the pronouncement of the drought to Ahab and then went to the brook Cherith where he was fed twice daily by ravens. When the brook dried up, God sent him to Zarephath where he encountered a widow and her son—gentiles. While he is with the widow, the meal jar never emptied, and the oil never dried up.

The death bells had been ringing for three thousand years—from the death of Abel until the death of widow's son. No one had escaped death's chilly waters; that is, until 1 Kings 17:17-24.

WE WILL BE STRETCHED IN OUR TRIALS OF FAITH

"Now it came about after these things that the son of the woman, the mistress of the house, became sick; and his sickness was so severe that there was not breath left in him" (1 Kings 17:17).

"After these things" refers to the meal and the oil. There was a widow who thought life was over. She came out to get a few sticks to make a fire and prepare the final meal for her son and herself. Then the man of God came into their lives, and life was able to go on. Every time she opened the meal jar, there was meal. Every time she used the oil, there was still plenty. She had seen the Lord provide for her needs, and her hopes for the future must have been bright. Perhaps she thought that when the drought passed, the man of God would leave and her son would grow up and work in the fields. However, her son fell ill and died; and her pain had to have been overwhelming. The meal and oil had strengthened her faith, but now her faith went through a severe trial with the death of her son. Sickness, suffering, and death will and do come even to those who are living for God. We will never fully understand the fullness of God's economy.

If God does not step down into our lives and give us a good shake with a problem, a trial, or a disturbance, we can be sure we are not going to make very fast progress in the Christian life. Never think for one moment that prosperity is the only a sign of the blessing of God. Adversity is just as often a sign of the blessing of God.

If God does not step down into our lives and give us a good shake with a problem, a trial, or a disturbance, we can be sure we are not going to make very fast progress in the Christian life.

This story reveals the mysterious ways of God. When a tremendous calamity came the widow's way, she was called upon to pass the prosperity test. Her only son, apparently a very small lad because he could be upon her bosom, became ill very suddenly. In a matter of hours, the little boy was dead; and the light of this home, the star of her firmament, had suddenly gone out.

Psalm 30:6-7 says: "Now as for me, I said in my prosperity, 'I will never be moved.' O LORD, by Your favor You have made my mountain to stand strong; You hid Your face, I was dismayed." It is true that sometimes our mountain seems to stand so strong that it cannot be troubled or disturbed or moved, but it is often at that point that God begins to speak. Consequently, when the meal was there in the morning and the evening and the cruse of oil did not fail, Elijah, the widow, and her son lapsed into contentment and began to think that everything from then on was going to be all right.

When we experience God's blessings and provisions, particularly after some type of test or trial, there is always a subtle temptation for us to think we have passed the test and everything is going to be easier from then on. The worst is past, the storm is over, and it is going to be smooth sailing; but such an attitude ignores a basic truth that this world is not Eden nor the millennium. We should never expect from life in a fallen world what it simply cannot give and is not designed to give. We live in a fallen world where sin and Satan are ever active and where even nature, God's own creation, groans under the curse of the fall.

WE WILL NEED STABILITY IN OUR THINKING IN FAITH

"So she said to Elijah, 'What do I have to do with you, O man of God? You have come to me to bring my iniquity to remembrance and to put my son to death!'" (1 Kings 17:18).

The death of her son had touched a hidden spring that opened wide the door of her conscience, and her conscience reminded her of past sin although it is not known what the sin was. Nevertheless, this tragic event awakened a consciousness in her and reminded her of her past.

People sometimes seem to have no conscience until a great tragedy strikes, and then they want to call upon the man of God for answers. A good illustration is found in the lives of Joseph's brothers. It was not until they came to the place that they knew their father could not live if their brother Benjamin were to die in Egypt. This awakened their consciences: "Truly we are guilty concerning our brother" (Genesis 42:21). In addition to Joseph's brothers, it took hell itself before the rich man's conscious awakened. "And he said, 'Then I beg you, father, that you send him to my father's house—for I have five brothers—in order that he may warn them, so that they will not also come to this place of torment'" (Luke 16:27-28). He did not want his brothers to go to the place called hell.

Even though the Lord has richly blessed us in Christ and though He may meet our needs in marvelous ways, it never means we are immune to trials down the road or around the next corner.

When the widow spoke to him with grief and despair, he was moved in his spirit and said to her "'Give me your son.' Then he took him from her bosom and carried him up to the upper room where he was living, and laid him on his own bed" (1 Kings 17:19).

We Are Not Immune to Problems

Perhaps the widow thought that because the prophet was in her home, she was immune to problems. Some people think if they do the right things, follow the right principles, listen to the Bible, and live around other Christians, life will flow along smoothly. However, such an attitude is usually void of developing a real relationship with God where He alone becomes the sole source of strength and joy.

Even though the Lord has richly blessed us in Christ and though He may meet our needs in marvelous ways, it never means we are immune to trials down the road or around the next corner. Since He knows our hearts and the hearts of those around us, He certainly knows what we all need. The fact and presence of trials never mean God has removed His grace and love but prove He is at work preparing us for heaven and using us in His plan even now (Romans 8:28-29; John 15:2; Philippians 1:6; Hebrews 12:5).

As we so often do, the widow turned to Elijah, wanting to blame someone else. Her son had already been at the point of death a year before, and she had been resigned to that fact. She had said she was going out to cook the little bit of meal and oil that she had, and she and her son were going to eat their last meal and die. With Elijah's appearance, her hopes had been raised to tremendous heights but now were dashed. Consequently, she turned to Elijah and asked, "What do I have to do with you, O man of God?" (1 Kings 17:18). Amazingly, she said this right in the presence of the jar of meal and the jug of oil which God had supplied day after day for a year!

Making no reference to the jar of meal or the cruse of oil, she attacked the character of Elijah and made insinuations against his God asking if he and his God had come to curse her home. Her reaction was a believer's reaction in spite of its lack of faith. When something like this happens to unbelievers, they cannot understand it at all and do not respond with "What have I done wrong?" as this woman did. In the midst of her unbelief, she had a kernel of faith and acknowledged there was a God in heaven and that He did judge. Though it is contradictory, her faith and nonfaith mixed together are the response of a believer who is out of step with God—not the response of an unbeliever.

The mother's bereavement was not necessarily a judgment for sin. When she said to Elijah, "Art thou come unto me to call my sin to remembrance, and to slay my son?" (1 Kings 17:18 KJV), we might immediately think she was right and was now suffering because of her sin. However, the passage says nothing about that; and in the New Testament, this woman is singled out as an example of faith. Furthermore, when the account closes, we read that this widow gave a tremendous testimony to the glory of God through the prophet Elijah. Therefore, I am inclined to think the purpose of this testing was not a judgment at all but a deepening of her faith.

We Are Not Indicted by Our Past

Her reaction to Elijah suggests another aspect of her thinking that is common. She felt guilt and thought perhaps she was to blame for her son's death. Because she did not understand the scriptural teaching about suffering, she may have thought all suffering was caused by sin. Perhaps there were some skeletons in her closet. Surely the question, "What do I have to do with you, O man of God?" followed by the statement, "You have come to me to bring my iniquity to remembrance, and to put my son to death!" most likely means something like: "What have I done to displease you or your God" or "What did I do to deserve this?" or "Why has your God done this? Haven't I given you shelter?"

Elijah's response is one to notice. He did not say, "I'd like to take the pulpit now and have five minutes to defend myself." Many of us would not have had the mind of the prophet Elijah but would have said something like, "Why you old witch! You haven't got the brains of a bat! I've been here for one whole year, and it is because of me that you have lived to this point!" However, Elijah did not do that. He followed in the footsteps of the Great Prophet who, when He was reviled, reviled not again.

We Are Not to Become Indignant by Our Pain

Because her eyes were not on the Lord, her expectations were wrong, and she felt guilty thinking she perhaps was to blame in some way, her guilt and pain took the form of despair, anger or resentment, and then blame. She took the downward process. Pain is never wrong; it is natural. God expects and allows us to feel pain. The problem comes when we allow our pain to twist and deform us and cause us to react rather than respond to what God is seeking to do in us.

WE WILL NEED SECURITY IN OUR TESTS OF FAITH

"He said to her, 'Give me your son.' Then he took him from her bosom and carried him up to the upper room where he was living, and laid him on his own bed" (1 Kings 17:19).

She was reacting normally in this situation. She had dreams for her son, wanting to see him grow to manhood. With her son dead, she wanted to die also. She questioned God but could not reach Him; consequently, she hurled hot jabs to the closest one to God, Elijah.

Had it not been for Elijah, she would already be where her son was now; but it would have been by a slow, painful death of starvation. Her words revealed the evidence of the bitterness in her heart. Everyone, especially those in ministry, who has ever helped others has seen some of them — at one time or another — turn on them. Even our Lord Jesus had some of His disciples turn on Him. Perhaps some even heaped very bitter words on Him.

Yet Elijah showed true godly character. He did not blast her nor answer her charges but made a request of her. He wanted the privilege of helping one in need. Elijah had probably grown attached to the boy as perhaps the boy had also to the man of God.

Elijah lay the boy very gently upon the bed and turned to God saying, "O LORD my God, have You also brought calamity to the widow with whom I am staying, by causing her son to die?" (1 Kings 17:20). Evil in the Old Testament has a sense of calamity, and that is the sense of this scripture. He brought the problem to the only one who could solve it—God.

Then Elijah "stretched himself upon the child three times" (1 Kings 17:21). He got upon the bed—not to do mouth-to-mouth resuscitation—but to lie on top of the child and called out to God saying, "O Lord my God, I pray You, let this child's life return to him!" (1 Kings 17:21).

Because of the power of God that was sought in this room, the meal jar was never empty and the oil flowed freely. It was here that the man of God met with the God of man many times.

This event most likely took place in a small room on the second floor of the widow's house—a place of poverty except, that is, in this room. This was the place where Elijah had an audience with the King of Glory! Because of the power of God that was sought in this room, the meal jar was never empty and the oil flowed freely. It was here that the man of God met with the God of man many times. The great victories of faith are first hammered out on the anvil of prayer in the secret place. Many of our battles would turn into victories if we would seek out that secret place of prayer.

Our Lord's Providence

Elijah's question, "Have you also brought calamity," expresses his knowledge of God's sovereignty over all that happens in life; but the fact that he connected this death with his presence in the home of the widow suggests the realization of some special purpose of God for him in this tragedy. He focused on the Lord in terms of the revelation of God in Scripture. God had placed another bend in the road, and he was considering what God had done and what the Lord might want to do through him.

In this amazing story, we see the mystery of God's providence. If we had lived in Zarephath, looked all over the community, and wanted to pick out a home in which a calamity from God should come, the widow's home would have been the last one of all the homes in the region that we would have picked because the prophet of God was there.

Our Lord's Provision

Remember that this was the same prophet who told Ahab, king of Israel, that it would not rain for three years. Many months had now gone by, and every month that went by continued to prove that Elijah was a prophet of God. He had come into the widow's home because there was famine in the land; yet in that home, they were supplied day after day. Not only were they supplied because the prophet was there, but they were also supplied in miraculous fashion.

Look at the woman—healthy as an ox. Look at the boy and those pink cheeks—so healthy. How could this be? Their only provisions were a jar of meal and little jug of oil. Furthermore, the meal in the jar and the oil in the jug were close to the bottom also; but the widow and her son and Elijah were happy, healthy, and praising God. Of all the homes in the community, this was the last place anyone would have expected calamity to come. Yet it did.

WE WILL HAVE SUCCESS IN OUR TRIUMPH OF FAITH

"Elijah took the child and brought him down from the upper room into the house and gave him to his mother; and Elijah said, 'See, your son is alive.' Then the woman said to Elijah, 'Now I know you are a man of God and that the word of the LORD in your mouth is truth'" (1 Kings 17:23-24).

I imagine Elijah pacing and praying in the prophet's chamber. Elijah gets up and paces around the room. The Spirit of God takes hold of him again, and he lies upon the child on the bed and cries out, "O LORD God, I pray, let this child's soul come into him again!" He is in much anguish over this because a great deal seems to depend upon it. For him, the woman downstairs is very distraught and disturbed and obviously in the throes of unbelief.

We will never come to understand the God of our Lord Jesus Christ until we realize He is the God of the resurrection.

Elijah cries out again and looks at the child, and nothing happens. He paces around the room a little more. For the third time, the Spirit of God has burdened him deeply; and he goes over and lies down upon the child and cries out, "O LORD my God, I pray, let this child's soul come into him again!"

The boy's limbs begin move. His eyes flicker and begin to dilate. His pulse begins to beat. His soul returns. The prophet of fire has rekindled the dead ashes of the life of this boy. Elijah was no doubt thrilled in his heart as he picked up that little boy again and walked down the steps and into the room where the mother was. In the midst of her mourning and bereavement, he says, "Look! Your son's alive."

The woman looked at the child and then at Elijah and said, "Now I know that you are a man of God" (1 Kings 17:24). She had called him a man of God once before, but now she really knew he was a man of God and that the word of the Lord in his mouth was truth.

The widow learned grace as her needs were supplied through the jar of meal and cruse of oil, but she learned truth through the restoration of her son. She learned of the mercy and grace of God in that daily provision, but she learned something about the greatness of God and his power to raise the dead when her son was restored.

We will never come to understand the God of our Lord Jesus Christ until we realize He is the God of the resurrection. All throughout the Old Testament, what God is trying to get over to us is that He is the person who calls the things that be not as though they were, that He is the one who speaks to the dead, and that He quickens the dead and brings them to life. In the New Testament, the God of our Lord Jesus Christ is the God who raised Him from the dead.

Elijah most likely had told them he was fed by ravens twice a day. This woman knew of the unfailing supply of meal and oil. Now she saw the crowning miracle performed by God through his servant. She saw with her eyes that her son was alive. Imagine how she felt when she saw him. She probably ran and hugged him tightly. There was no question in her mind any longer that this was a man of God and that there was a God in heaven who cared about her. One of the most remarkable parts of this account is that the widow was a gentile.

One of the laws of Bible study is the law of first mention. There is an important truth we can glean from this first mention of a physical resurrection. Months turned into years and years stretched into centuries and centuries turned into a millennium, and it was in that millennium that the resurrection of Christ took place three days after his death.

The God of Elijah lives still. He is still as powerful as He was on that day when He raised the widow's son from the dead, and He is still raising those who are dead in trespasses and sins. God is still in the saving business.

Because He is the God who heals, there are times when He answers prayer and reaches down and touches a life where, humanly speaking, there is no hope. "The effective prayer of a righteous man can accomplish much" (James 5:16). That is why we need to pray when someone is sick because God might perform a miracle. There are also times in His will and His way that life is taken.

Why did Elijah stretch himself upon the body of the widow's son? To identify himself with that little child — in that child's sickness and death, especially his death. And just as the widow's son came to life and just as our Lord came to life, so we also shall come to life someday if we have put our trust in Him. Our Lord is touched with the feelings of our infirmaries as He has walked where we walk.

Elijah had the wonderful joy of returning that child to his mother, and there is going to be a reunion also of all who have put their faith and trust in Jesus Christ. We will experience resurrection, reunion, and rapture at the return of Jesus Christ! Even though in this life our sun does go down, it will come back up again. Nightfall will become a daybreak! We will be stretched in our trials of faith; we will need stability in our thinking in faith; we will need security in our tests of faith and we will have success in our triumph of faith.

We do not always need
to know where we are going,
but we do need to know
who we are following.

23

The Dilemmas of Faith

We cannot live the Christian life apart from faith for "the just shall live by faith" (Hebrews 10:38). Jesus said, "It shall be done to you according to your faith" (Matthew 9:29); and the writer of Hebrews said, "Without faith it is impossible to please [God]" (11:6).

We not only need to possess faith, but we also need a faith that possesses us.

We not only need to possess faith, but we also need a faith that possesses us. Occasionally, however, our faith seems to fail. We go to an outdoor event and pray, "Lord, give us beautiful weather," but the bottom drops out. We pray, "Lord, I want to marry that man; please give him to me as a husband," and then he marries our best friend. We have a loved one who is ill and we ask God to "heal my child" or "heal my wife"; but they get worse rather than better.

We have tried to believe, tried to trust; but faith seems to fail. We are ready to throw in the towel and say, "What's the use? It's not working." There are times when the answer does not come exactly as we think that it should. Trials, temptations, tribulations, heartaches, tears, and fears come, and faith does not seem to remove them.

The main reason Hebrews 11 was written was because there were some who were ready to throw in the towel and walk or run away. They were ready to hang it up for they had been serving the Lord under great persecution. To get a running start on Hebrews 11, we need to go back to Hebrews 10:36: "For you have need of endurance, so that when you have done the will of God, you may receive what was promised." We must learn to endure.

> And what more shall I say? For time will fail me if I tell of Gideon, Barak, Samson, Jephthah, of David and Samuel and the prophets, who by faith conquered kingdoms, performed acts of righteousness, obtained promises, shut the mouths of lions, quenched the power of fire, escaped the edge of the sword, from weakness were made strong, became mighty in war, put foreign armies to flight. Women received back their dead by resurrection; and others were tortured, not accepting their release, so that they might obtain a better resurrection; and others experienced mockings and scourgings, yes, also chains and imprisonment. They were stoned, they were sawn in two, they were tempted, they were put to death with the sword; they went about in sheepskins, in goatskins, being destitute, afflicted, ill-treated (men of whom the world was not worthy), wandering in deserts and mountains and caves and holes in the ground. And all these,

having gained approval through their faith, did not receive what was promised (Hebrews 11:32-39).

God said, "They get an A+ on their report card." They did it by faith. They did not escape; they endured. Some escaped by faith; some endured by faith. All had faith, but sometimes it seems as though faith seems to fail.

Many people have a superficial faith and a superstitious faith rather than a strong faith and a spiritual faith. They attend church until a crisis strikes or until the bottom falls out, and then they quit. They do not endure because they feel "it's not working." They have an immature faith, a superstition faith.

DEVELOPED FAITH BELIEVES IN THE ULTIMATE POWER OF GOD

If God does not do it, it is not because He cannot. Look again at Hebrews 11:32-35:

And what more shall I say? For time will fail me if I tell of Gideon, Barak, Samson, Jephthah, of David and Samuel and the prophets, who by faith conquered kingdoms, performed acts of righteousness, obtained promises, shut the mouths of lions, quenched the power of fire, escaped the edge of the sword, from weakness were made strong, became mighty in war, put foreign armies to flight. Women received back their dead by resurrection.

We love the story of Daniel in the lions' den. Daniel was told, "Don't pray or we'll throw you in the lions' den." He prayed anyway and they threw him in, but God gave the lions lockjaw. Daniel pulls up a lion, fluffs him up, and uses him for pillow while getting his Old Testament out and beginning to read between the lions.

We love the story of Shadrach, Meshach, and Abednego. The king told them to "bow down to the idol, or we'll cast you in the fiery furnace." They responded, "We're not going to worship your idol," so they were thrown into the furnace. They would not bend; they would not bow; they would not burn. The king looked in the fiery furnace and said, "I thought we threw three guys in the fire, but there are four in there now and the fourth is like the Son of God!" Jesus walked through the fire with them, and they came out without the smell of smoke on their clothes. What a mighty God they served!

The supernatural power of God is available to us, and mature faith believes that God can do anything but fail.

We love the story of David and Goliath which we have heard since we were children. Goliath was over nine feet tall; the NBA would have loved to have had him. Everyone else was afraid of Goliath except fair and ruddy-faced young David. Everyone else thought Goliath was too big to hit, but David thought he was too big to miss. Everyone else was thinking how much bigger Goliath was than they, and David was thinking how much smaller Goliath was than God. God gave David the victory over this giant, and our God is able to deliver us!

We love the story of Peter's deliverance from prison after being cast in by the wicked Herod. An angel came to lead him out saying, "Wake up; get dressed and put on your sandals." They did not sneak out but went out first class for the doors opened and Peter walked out of pris-on—a great jail break. As a matter of fact, Peter had more difficulty getting into the prayer meeting that was being held for his deliverance than he had getting out of jail.

For those of us who have walked with Jesus for a long time, we have a story where God miraculously, supernaturally, inexplicably worked in our hearts and in our lives. There is no way to explain it apart from God. The supernatural power of God is available to us, and mature faith believes that God can do anything but fail.

DEDICATED FAITH BOWS TO THE UNHINDERED PURPOSES OF GOD

There is God's supernatural power, but there is also God's sovereign purpose. God's ways are mysterious, but that does not mean they are weak.

> Women received back their dead by resurrection; and others were tortured, not accepting their release, so that they might obtain a better resurrection; and others experienced mockings and scourgings, yes, also chains and imprisonment. They were stoned, they were sawn in two, they were tempted, they were put to death with the sword; they went about in sheepskins, in goatskins, being destitute, afflicted, ill-treated (men of whom the world was not worthy), wandering in deserts and mountains and caves and holes in the ground. And all these, having gained approval through their faith, did not receive what was promised (Hebrews 11:35-39).

We love the exciting victories, but sometimes they do not seem to happen as "some were stoned to death" (Hebrews 11:37 God's Word Translation). Consider Zechariah: "At the command of the king they stoned him to death in the court of the house of the LORD

(2 Chronicles 24:21). Consider Stephen: They dragged him "out of the city and began to stone him" (Acts 7:58). Some would say, "He must not have been right with God," which would not be correct for he was filled with the Holy Spirit just as Peter was on the Day of Pentecost when 3,000 people were saved. Peter got souls while Stephen got stones, but both were filled with the Holy Spirit.

Some "were sawn in two" (Hebrews 11:37). This verse most likely refers to Isaiah for ancient Jewish-Christian tradition suggests that Isaiah was martyred by King Manasseh, son of Hezekiah. According to the tradition, Isaiah was tied inside a sack, placed within the hollow of a tree trunk, and then sawed in two. This story traces back to a first-century, noncanonical book called the *Ascension of Isaiah* which claims to tell the story of Isaiah's death.

God did not promise that we would never know difficulty, but He did promise that we would know ultimate victory and that He would never leave us or forsake us.

They "went about in sheepskins, in goatskins" (Hebrews 11:37). The ancients used to make delight and fun out of torturing godly people. The early Christians were sometimes dressed in animal skins and then turned loose in the woods so the dogs would bay after them in the hunt. At other times, they were fed to the lions. In Rome, Christians were tortured in the Coliseum. At the Circus Maximus, bloodthirsty crowds would scream, "Bring on the Christians! Bring on the Christians!" and the Christians would seal their fate with their lives.

If we get our theology from circumstances, we may come to the conclusion that God does not love us. Even though we read that "Jesus loved Martha and her sister and Lazarus" (John 11:5), Lazarus became ill and died; and Jesus said "to them plainly, 'Lazarus is dead, and I am glad....'" (John 11:14-15). If we try to reconcile these two statements without knowing the whole story, we would think this is very confusing; however, God had a greater plan for Lazarus.

God did not promise that we would never know difficulty, but He did promise that we would know ultimate victory and that He would never leave us or forsake us.

> Who will separate us from the love of Christ? Will tribulation, or distress, or persecution, or famine, or nakedness, or peril, or sword? Just as it is written, "For your sake we are being put to death all day long; we were considered as sheep to be slaughtered." But in all these things we overwhelmingly conquer through Him who loved us (Romans 8:35-37).

John the Baptist had been out by the River Jordan preaching repentance. He had a rock for a pulpit and a babbling brook for a choir. He called some of the people a bunch of rattlesnakes: "You brood of vipers" (Matthew 12:34). He was an outdoorsman, a rugged prophet, a man of God. However, he was eventually taken to prison and would be beheaded. He had been preaching a victorious Christ, the Messiah whose "winnowing fork is in His hand, and He will thoroughly clear His threshing floor; and He will gather His wheat into the barn, but He will burn up the chaff with unquenchable fire" (Matthew 3:12).

John the Baptist summoned "two of his disciples, [and] sent them to the Lord, saying, 'Are You the Expected One, or do we look for someone else?'" (Luke 7:19). John possibly asked the question because his disciples needed strengthening, and his faith may have waivered as a result of his being in Herod's prison. However, never mistake the moment for the man. This was not the whole story of John the Baptist, but he did have a doubting season even though Jesus had said of him, "Among those born of women there is no one greater than John" (Luke 7:28).

Jesus answered John's disciples and told them to "go and report to John what you hear and see: the blind receive sight and the lame walk, the lepers are cleansed and the deaf hear, the dead are raised up, and the poor have the gospel preached to them. And blessed is he who does not take offense at Me." (Matthew 1:4-6).

Jesus was telling John that He could open blind eyes, unstop deaf ears, cleanse lepers, and raise the dead. "If I have not taken you out of prison, it is not because I cannot. Don't become offended at me."

If we have prayed and asked God to do a miracle for us and He has not done it, it is not because He cannot nor is it because He does not love us. We must not become offended. It has been said that "faith is not receiving from God so much what we want as it is accepting from God what He gives or what He allows." Consequently, we need to have an "if not" clause in our faith.

Earlier we highlighted Shadrach, Meshach, and Abednego. The king said, "Look, if you don't bow down to this image, you're going to be cast into the fiery furnace. Now give me your answer" to which they replied:

> O Nebuchadnezzar, we do not need to give you an answer concerning this matter. If it be so, our God whom we serve is able to deliver us from the furnace of blazing fire; and He will deliver us out of your hand, O king. But even if He does not, let it be known to you, O king, that we are not going to serve your gods or worship the golden image that you have set up" (Daniel 3:16-18).

They had a **settled** faith; their minds were already made up. They had a **sure** faith; "Our God is able." And they had a **steadfast** faith; "Even if He doesn't, even if we're turned to bacon in that furnace, we're not going to worship your idol. Our God is able; but we know that if He does not, we are still not going to worship your idol."

Sometimes we are ready to quit just because God does not do the thing we ask of Him. We need an "if not" clause in our faith which does not mean our faith is weak but that it is stronger than ever. "God, I know You're able; but if You don't, I'm going to serve You anyway. I'm not going to make bargains with You." We do not always understand why God does things as He does, but a mature faith bows to His sovereign purposes.

When King Herod put James in prison and then killed him, everyone thought that was a good idea; consequently, he took Peter and put him in prison, planning to kill him also. However, God miraculously delivered Peter. Was James wrong and Peter right? Did God love Peter more than He loved James? Absolutely not! God had His own sovereign purposes in each of their lives.

Are we willing to let God be God? Are we willing to have an "if not" clause in our faith? Are we willing to dwell among the "and others" if necessary? That is not to diminish the supernatural power of God. We want the faith to escape, but do we have the faith to endure? We want to be healed; but if we are not, do we have the faith not to be healed and still serve and praise God saying, "Though He slay me, yet will I trust Him" (Job 13:15 KJV). Can we say that we will trust him "though the fig tree should not blossom and there be no fruit on the vines, though the yield of the olive should fail and the fields produce no food, though the flock should be cut off from the fold and there be no cattle in the stalls, yet I will exult in the

LORD, I will rejoice in the God of my salvation" (Habakkuk 3:17-18).

DETERMINED FAITH BUILDS ON THE UNMOVABLE PROMISES OF GOD

Every promise of God is yea and amen in the Lord Jesus Christ. "And all these, having gained approval through their faith, did not receive what was promised, because God had provided something better for us, so that apart from us they would not be made perfect" (Hebrews 11:39-40).

This means that God has a wonderful plan and is working on that plan—not only for the Old Testament saints and the early Christians but also for all of us. One of these days God will bring it all together and fulfill His promises to them and to us. God will keep His promises for He cannot lie nor can He fail. These people had faith; and if they did not have the answer in their hand, they had it in their hearts. They were basing their faith on the steadfast promises of God with an eye to the future.

Sometimes we expect too much of life and not enough of God. We measure life by eat, drink, and be merry; and then the stock market crashes and people jump off buildings because that is where their faith was. Even the good things of this life will ultimately fail us. We fall in love and get married; but sooner or later, we may sit in an empty family room looking at pictures on the wall. Life is fickle; and if we are looking for everything in this life, we will not find it. We must learn to rest on the eternal promises of God; and if things go upside down and our livelihoods are lost, we must remember that was not our greatest treasure anyway. If we never become famous, it is what God thinks about us that really counts. If we have a loved one in Jesus who dies, there is a homecoming in heaven.

God has not forgotten His promises. He gave the land of Israel to Abraham and every grain of sand there belongs to him and his descendants. They do not have it now, but they will. Jesus said, "Blessed are the gentle, for they shall inherit the earth" (Matthew 5:5). Be meek and see how much of it we get. We pray for our loved ones to be healed and yet they die. Was that prayer lost? No, it was heard because those in heaven are whole; we are sick. They are made like the Lord Jesus Christ.

Mature faith believes in the supernatural power of God, bows to the sovereign purposes of God, and is based on the steadfast promises of God.

In a prayer meeting, we often pray more for the sick than for the lost. We seem to be more interested in keeping the saints out of heaven than the lost out of hell. Jesus prayed, "Father, I desire that they also, whom You have given Me, be with Me where I am, so that they may see My glory" (John 17:24). We are the bride and He is the bridegroom, and the bridegroom wants the bride with him.

Paul said, "For to me, to live is Christ and to die is gain" (Philippians 1:21). We get things upside down sometimes and say, "The church is failing; there is scandal and problems on every hand," but Jesus said, "I will build my church and the gates of hell shall not prevail against it" (Matthew 16:18 KJV). The church of the Lord Jesus Christ is not dead; the promises of God are yea and amen.

It may be that we are asking something of our faith that God never really intended. Real faith is to center our lives on Almighty God. Mature faith believes in the supernatural power of God, bows to the sovereign purposes of God, and is based on the steadfast promises of God.

Sometimes we expect too much of life and not enough of God. We should expect more from God and life will have faith-filled meaning each day.

24

The Depiction of Faith

The world of our Lord was a world much like our own in that it made much of athletic competitions and endeavors. In New Testament times, there were three great games: the Olympian games held in Athens, the Pythian games at Delphi, and the Isthmian games at Corinth. These games were staggered so that the wealthy could attend them all.

The games had boxing, wrestling, and the throwing of the javelin and the discus as well as chariot races which in time gave way to car races at the Indianapolis Speedway. They also had foot races which is what the writer of Hebrews addresses.

> Therefore, since we have so great a cloud of witnesses surrounding us, let us also lay aside every encumbrance and the sin which so easily entangles us, and let us run with endurance the race that is set before us, fixing our eyes on Jesus, the author and perfecter of faith, who for the joy set before Him endured the cross, despising the shame, and

has sat down at the right hand of the throne of God (Hebrews 12:1-2).

To be an athlete in the New Testament era was an incredible opportunity and privilege. The athletes who competed in these games were the most popular people in the country. Cicero complained that an athlete would often receive more accolades and praise than a general who was returning home from a war.

The athletes competed in great amphitheaters larger than our stadiums. Some of the early theaters would be six times the size of one of our football stadiums.

At the end of the field would be an altar for a blood sacrifice to a pagan god. The athletes would bathe their hands in the blood of the animal, lift them to the heavens, and swear by the god they served that they would play by the rules, that their lives were pure, and that there was nothing against them that would keep them from running fairly. When the time came for the race to begin, the athletes would line up with every muscle stretched and every nerve at the ready.

All of us are in a race. Following are seven secrets to winning this race.

THE CONTEST BEFORE US

In ancient days, the emperor would arrive at his plush box at the stadium where he would sit and look down at the games while thousands and thousands and thousands of people, tier upon tier upon tier of them, did the same. God has a race set for us; and just as the emperor was looking down at those runners so long ago, our Lord in heaven is watching us as we run our race.

In the spiritual realm, we are runners and there is a goal for each of us. However, we are not running against one another for we are not in competition. Rather, we are in a pilgrimage with one another.

Our race is against sin, against self, and against life itself. The goal is not heaven nor is salvation the reward at the end of the race. Salvation is what puts us in the race. It is not a reward for the righteous but a gift for the guilty. We must come to our Lord and trust Him and be born again in order to qualify to get into the race. "So then it does not depend on the man who wills or the man who runs, but on God who has mercy" (Romans 9:16). Thank God for His mercy that puts us in the race.

God has a race set for us; and just as the emperor was looking down at those runners so long ago, our Lord in heaven is watching us as we run our race.

Our word for "race" is the Greek word "agon" from which we also get "agony." The writer of Hebrews is talking about a marathon, a race that is grueling and agonizing— not a stroll. God has a race for each of us to run.

THE CROWDS AROUND US

Now here is the second step to winning the race are the crowds. There are those in the grandstand to cheer you on. In chapter 11 we have studied about all of the heroes of the faith; a gallery of the great. There they are, all of the saints in heaven. They are what is called "a great cloud of witnesses." They are watching us. They are looking down upon us. Does that bother you that those up in heaven are watching you? Well the Lord is watching you. They're made one with Him.

They are aware of us, just as those runners were running, so long ago. There were countless eager eyes watching them; these heroes of the past. I wonder if there was a multitude watching them, what a great multitude are watching us. The crowds are cheering us on in the race. They are inspiring us to run at our best.

THE CONDITIONING WITHIN US

"Therefore, since we have so great a cloud of witnesses surrounding us, let us also lay aside every encumbrance [or weight in KJV] and the sin which so easily entangles us, and let us run with endurance the race that is set before us" (Hebrews 12:1).

In running a race, we cannot afford to let anything slow us down. There has to be discipline if we are going to run to win, but there are encumbrances that slow us down and sins that trip us up, either of which is bad. There are things that are not necessarily bad in and of themselves. There is nothing wrong with an overcoat; but a runner would not be wise to wear one in a 100-yard dash. A runner strips down to the bare necessities (sometimes almost to the point of indecency). Nevertheless, we are to "lay aside every weight." Good things can be bad things if they keep us from the best things.

"All things are lawful for me, but not all things are profitable" (1 Corinthians 6:12). When we think of the word "expedient," we often think of an expedition, a journey undertaken by a group of people with a particular purpose. Paul is saying that if something does not help us go to the place we are supposed to go, it is wrong for us. There are certain things I have laid aside in my own partic-ular life, not because they are bad in and of themselves but simply because they are excess baggage. I do not have time to read good books because I have not read the best ones. A good book may be considered recreational, and God does want us to have recreation; but so many times, we are simply wasting time. We must lay aside every weight—the good things that may be bad things if they keep us from the best things.

We must lay aside every weight—the good things that may be bad things if they keep us from the best things.

A good exercise would be to write down the things in our lives that would allow us to move faster down the track if we laid them aside—for example, the things we spend time, money, thought, and energy on. At our devotional time, we could pull the list out and pray over it.

Good things become bad things when they keep us from the best things. Life would be simpler if it were simply a choice between good and bad, but it is often a choice between good and best. "Let us lay aside every weight" and strip down to the bare necessities for our race.

"Let us also lay aside every encumbrance and the sin which so easily entangles us" (Hebrews 12:1). There are sins which must be laid aside, sins that trip us up. We must deal with sin or sin will deal with us. Our "pet" sin is no friend. We must be ruthless with that sin and have NO MERCY on it for sin will have no mercy on us. It will entangle us, and we will fail to win the prize.

THE COURSE BEFORE US

"Therefore, since we have so great a cloud of witnesses surrounding us, let us also lay aside every encumbrance and the sin which so easily entangles us, and let us run with endurance the race that is set before us" (Hebrews 12:1).

God has marked out a course for each of us to run from which we must never turn aside; however, each of our races is different. When the Apostle Paul came to the end of his life, he said: "I have fought a good fight, I have finished my course" (2 Timothy 4:7). Paul's course took him to a Philippian jail where he had revival at midnight, to a Roman jail where he brought a slave to Christ, and to Caesar's prison where he set up a little piece of heaven right in the prison. Let us not complain about the race that is set before us for God knows where we are and put us there or allowed us to be there. If we get off course, we will be disqualified.

THE COMPLETION AHEAD OF US

"Therefore, we have so great a cloud of witnesses surrounding us, let us also lay aside every encumbrance and the sin which entangles us, and let us **run with endurance**" (Hebrews 12:1). The meaning of endurance is the ability or strength to continue or last despite fatigue, stress, or other adverse conditions; to bear up under pressure. When I was in high school and college, I ran a lot so I know what it is to run until my lungs are aflame and my muscles ache! It hurts! If we are looking for a cheap, easy, or lazy way to serve Jesus Christ, it does not exist.

Many people think they have done God a big favor when they come to church on Sunday morning and listen to a sermon. They call it their "service." Church is not a service; church is a filling station. Serving the Lord Jesus costs. We must pray over it, study over it, and weep over it. God does business with those who mean business. We will never, ever win a race unless we mean business.

While we may eventually leave some sermons unfinished, some songs unsung, some houses unbuilt, some flowers unplanted, or some needlework undone, we are immortal until our work on earth is done. We run with endurance and must not quit. No matter how far ahead we may be, we will lose the race if we quit. We must run with endurance the race that is set before us.

―――――――――― ❊ ――――――――――

The meaning of endurance is the ability or strength to continue or last despite fatigue, stress, or other adverse conditions; to bear up under pressure.

―――――――――― ❊ ――――――――――

THE COACH TO US

"Looking unto Jesus the author and finisher of our faith" (Hebrews 12:2 KJV). We look to Jesus because He is the creator of our faith. It is not primarily great faith we need but faith in a great God and Savior. He is the author of our faith and the finisher or "completer" of our faith.

Salvation is a gift at the beginning of the race, and Jesus is the one who gives us the strength to run the race. Running the race does not save us. As stated earlier, salvation qualifies us for the race. Unfortunately, there are those who start the race and never finish. They do not finish either because they quit due to backsliding or died before their race was complete. We are called to complete the race our Coach has marked out for us.

Our relationship to this "Coach" is "looking unto Jesus"…not "looking at Jesus." What is the difference? Imagine someone in financial difficulty who is unable to pay their mortgage with the possibility that they might lose their home. However, a friend says, "Look to me."

He does not mean, "look at me." "Look to me" means "depend upon me. I will see you through; I will take care of you."

"Looking unto Jesus" is having faith in Jesus, not just having facts about Jesus. The Greek word that says "looking unto Jesus" is a word that means looking away from everything else and looking at something else. It is not looking at Jesus and other things. We must look away from everything else and put our eyes upon Jesus.

We must look away from everything else
and put our eyes upon Jesus.

We must not put our eyes upon Satan for he will terrify us or entice us. We must not put our eyes upon the sins of those for whom Jesus died. We must get our eyes off of hypocrites and look to the Lord Jesus Christ. We must not put our eyes upon ourselves. So many people are guilty of morbid introspection. They open themselves up, pull their innards out, and stuff them back in again. That gets us nowhere. We must take our eyes off of ourselves and off of our sins, confess our sins and put them in the sea of God's forgetfulness, and look to the Lord Jesus Christ. We must quit saying, "What a fool I was!" and start saying, "What a fool I am for what a fool I was." We must get our eyes off all of that and put our eyes upon the Lord Jesus Christ.

The devil is diabolical and deceptive. He will get us to look at anything rather than Jesus. He will even get us to look at our faith, wondering if it is strong enough. We must forget about our faith and look to Jesus. We must not put faith in faith; we must put faith in Jesus. The devil used to tell me, "Your faith is not good enough"; but I learned how to deal with him by saying, "That's right, but isn't Jesus wonderful?" Look away from everything else and look to the Lord Jesus Christ. He is the Coach; he is the Author of our faith and the Finisher of our faith.

THE CROWN FOR US

"Fixing our eyes on Jesus, the author and perfecter of faith, who for the joy set before Him endured the cross" (Hebrews 12:2).

In the New Testament era, the name of an athlete who ran in the Olympic games and won would be proclaimed throughout the whole country. His family and kinsmen would be announced and honored. There would be a parade; the athlete's pathway would be scattered with flowers and he would be presented with costly gifts. If he was from Athens, his expenses would be paid for the rest of life. Poets of national repute would write poems about him; and sculptors would make statues of him. The athlete who won would also win a crown. There was a crown for the Lord Jesus as well, and we are the prize that He ran for.

We are in a race and must lay aside every weight and every sin that would trip us up.

Every runner runs to win a prize: "Do you not know that those who run in a race all run, but only one receives the prize? Run in such a way that you may win" (1 Corinthians 9:24). Paul talked about his prize: "For who is our hope or joy or crown of exultation? Is it not even you, in the presence of our Lord Jesus at His coming?" (1 Thessalonians 2:19).

When we go to heaven, will we take anyone with us? Will we have a crown, a soul-winner's crown? We must answer seriously, soberly, and somberly for there will be a reward when we meet the Lord: "Behold, I am coming quickly, and My reward is with Me, to render to every man according to what he has done" (Revelation 22:12). We are in a race and must lay aside every weight and every sin that would trip us up.

I would like to motivate those who have perhaps strayed from the course, fallen on the track, or dropped out of the race to make a brand-new resolve and get back in the race.

Conclusion

The number one debilitating fear of people is "having lived a meaningless life." Do you know what your mission in life is? How can you know if you are making progress unless you have a purpose? The purpose is the compass, and the progress is the coordinates for your life and ministry. In a sense, you have an "ambidextrous calling." You will have to remain faithful to the Word of God and still minister in an ever-changing world.

Do you know what your mission in life is? How can you know if you are making progress unless you have a purpose? The purpose is the compass, and the progress is the coordinates for your life and ministry.

Whether you are just beginning you walk with God or have been walking for some time, let me ask you one question: Why do you do what you do in life? Do you pray with purpose and minister with a mission? Do you know your God-given patent for existence? The early disciples knew what their mission was from Christ. Their mission was the Great Commission. Their goal was world evangelization. In your life you are either leading or being led.

Your faith-filled calling is to be *providential*. It has a sense of divine destiny about it. The call of the Apostle Paul began before the creation of the world (Galatians 1:15). God knew Jeremiah before he was formed in the womb of this mother (Jeremiah 1:5). When Christian leaders do not know their divine call, they will eventually settle for "whining" rather than "winning." We cannot live with constant change unless there is a changeless core inside of us. The key to the ability to change is a changeless sense of who you are, what you are about and what you value. A divine sense of who you are will provide direction for what you are to do. If money was not an issue and time did not matter, what would you like to do the rest of your life? Would you be willing to do it without charge?

Your faith-filled calling is *purposeful*. Abraham was called to be the "father of the faithful." Joseph was called to be a leader in Egypt during a time of famine. Moses was called to lead the Israelites out of Egyptian bondage. Joshua was called to lead his people into Canaan. The Old Testament prophets were called to proclaim the "Word of the Lord." Jesus was called to die for the sins of the world (John 3:16). Peter was called to be a fisher of men (Luke 5:10). Paul was called to preach the gospel to the Gentiles (Acts 9:15; cf. Galatians 3:15-16). When Christ calls individuals, He has a unique purpose for them in the church and in the world. Why does your life exist? Until you are able to answer that question adequately, you will not be clear in your decision-making, what you should do and should not do, and the direction in which you are going.

What are your roles and goals in life? Your roles provide your direction and your goals determine your destiny. For example, you have a role as a Christian, but your goal is heaven. If you are in Bible college, then you have the role of a student, no doubt with a goal to graduate. You may have a role as a husband or wife, but your goal is to build a healthy marriage.

What is your vision and mission ? Your vision will flow out of your mission. Your mission is born from above while your vision is lived here below. Vision is cultivated by (1) looking above you (what does God expect of you?), (2) looking within you (what do you feel?), (3) looking behind you (what have you learned?), (4) looking around you (what is happening to others?), (5) looking ahead of you (what is the big picture?), and (6) looking beside you (what resources are available to you?) If your vision and mission are fuzzy in your mind, your morale will be low. All great leaders know where they are going and are able to persuade others to follow them.

The mission is not just a profession but a divine act of God. God has not called you to live someone else's mission.

Your faith-filled calling is *personal*. Numerous Old Testament prophets (Moses, Isaiah, Jeremiah, and others) and New Testament apostles (Peter and Paul) were personally called to proclaim the Word of God. The mission is not just a profession but a divine act of God. God has not called you to live someone else's mission. A lot of Christians live "unlived" lives before God. Your true identity or self-worth before God is much greater than your present level of ministry.

Your faith-filled calling is *practical*. For a calling to be right, it must fit our abilities. What are your gifts or talents? One of the reasons many of us don't recognize our gifts as gifts is because they seem so natural to us. Why do you suppose God gave those gifts to you? There is a God-given purpose for the unique gifts in your life. It is our responsibility to recognize them, use them, and expect fair wages for the use of them in our service to God (Matthew 20:1-13; 25:29). Do not mystify God's calling on your life.

The Protestant Reformation reshaped the landscape of Europe and theological minds throughout the centuries.

Your faith-filled calling is *powerful.* A divine call provides both the passion for the necessary creativity and the power for the passion for the necessary creativity and the power for the renewed energies of the daily preaching grind. If your mission holds no personal passion, it is not your path. Enthusiasm comes from the root words 'en' and 'theos' — which means 'in God.' What are you enthusiastic or 'in God' about?" Do people have to prime your emotional pump, or does your passion for your mission get you up when everything else in life is down? Are you seeking success or significance in your life? There is a vast difference between these two concepts. Success is timely and dies when you die. Significance is timeless and lives on after you die. What is your all-encompassing goal in life?

The Reformer, Martin Luther, is one the greatest faith-filled Christian leaders, to ever lived on this earth. When he nailed his famous 95 Theses on Castle Church Door, on October 31, 1517, it became named in the top ten historic days of all time. The Protestant Reformation reshaped the landscape of Europe and theological minds throughout the centuries.

On November 1, 2017, our ministry was fortunate to host the Wittenberg 2017 in Castle Church; exactly 500 years later when the Protestant Reformation began. More than 600 influential leaders join us from around the world. At the gravesite of Martin Luther, who is buried inside Castle Church, all of the leaders together, launched FINISH 2030. FINISH 2030 is synergistic, missional thrust to complete the Great Commission by the 2000th Birthday of the Church.

How did this historic event come to pass? In February 2015, Dr. Leonard Sweet, a renowned Christian author, and I were talking on the phone about the upcoming 500th Anniversary of Martin Luther nailing 95 Theses on Castle Church Door. During the conversation, Dr. Sweet asked, "I wonder if anyone will take the time to celebrate it? This question kept swirling around in my mind. I researched the answer thoroughly and discovered that nothing significantly was scheduled in the Christian world to celebrate the 500th anniversary.

With the above in mind, after praying about it, I took a leap of faith. I made personal phone call to Castle Church to arrange a meeting with the person, who managed the schedule for events at Castle Church. Once the meeting date was set, I immediately flew to Berlin and took a train to Wittenberg. Upon my arrival, I met the President of the Wittenberg Seminary, who was also the Castle Church scheduler of sacred events. During our meeting, I shared with her our desire to host a global conference in Berlin, with its final day convening in Castle Church on November 1, 2017. She picked up her diary and said to me, "We do not have anything scheduled on that day. I do not see any reason why you could host your conference on this day."

I could not believe what I was hearing. I said to her, "Please double check your diary. 500 years in the making does not come very fast. Surely, someone has already booked Castle Church for this day." She looked at me with a smiled and said, "I am the only one who schedules special events in Castle Church. I know that this date is available." After short series of protocols and meetings, we were confirmed to host our Wittenberg 2017 Congress in Castle Church. We were the only ministry to have this sacred church on the actual 500th Anniversary of Martin Luther nailing the 95 Theses on Castle Church Door! It all happened because of a leap of faith!

Martin Luther was born on November 10, 1483 in Eisleben, Germany to Margaret and Hans Luder. Hans worked in the mining industry, even owning a few copper mines, but he wanted something better for his son. Martin was sent off to boarding school and then to the University of Erfurt.

After this divine revelation, Luther began to write page after page regarding what it meant to be justified by faith and not by works.

He was an excellent student. He soon earned both a bachelor's and master's degree and seemed to be well on his way to success as a law student. But about a month into his legal studies, on the 2nd of June in 1505, Luther was on his way back to school from his parent's home when he was caught in a violent thunderstorm. The storm grew more intense and Luther became afraid for his life. Suddenly, a lightning bolt struck near him, throwing him violently to the ground. At that very moment, he committed to become monk.

As a monk, Luther sought earnestly to find acceptance from God. Like others in his day, Luther believed the Catholic Church's teaching on how people are to be saved: not by God's grace alone, but by God's grace enabling you to do the work necessary to earn your own salvation. But Luther had no confidence in his ability to remain in a state of Grace. He was terrified of God's wrath and was wracked with uncertainty about his ability to earn God's favor through his works.

As indicated above, on October 31, 1517, Martin Luther nailed his 95 Theses to the door of the Castle Church in Wittenberg, Germany. This single act, though not particularly unusual or defiant, would reverberate across countries, across continents and across centuries. This was the act which sparked the Protestant Reformation, and it was the Protestant Reformation that brought light into darkness and recovered the core truths of the gospel obscured by medieval religion.

Luther was not trying to cause trouble. This was an academic and theological issue, and his 95 Theses were written in Latin, not the language of the people. Without his knowledge or permission, these Theses were translated by some of his students from Latin to German and distributed. Thanks to the new technology of the printing press, within 2 weeks nearly every village in Germany had a copy. The ideas soon took hold, and storm clouds began to loom on the horizon.

As tensions mounted with the church authorities, Luther's inner turmoil about sin and salvation continued. All at once, as if reading it for the first time, Luther came to understand the full meaning of Romans 1:17:

> "For in it [the Gospel] the righteousness of God is revealed from faith for faith, as it is written, "The righteous shall live by faith."

Four times in Scripture we read, "the just shall live by faith (Hab. 2:4; Rom. 1:17; Gal. 3:11; Heb.10:38). In Habakkuk 2:4, faith produces the *character* we need in the face of huge adversaries. Habakkuk learned how to have high times in hard times. In Romans 1:17, faith provides the *conversion* needed to be born again in a sinful world.

In Galatians 3:11, faith prepares the *consecration* needed to produce the fruit of the Spirit. Last, in Hebrews 10:38, faith precipitates the *courage* needed not to shrink back in the face of persecution.

After this divine revelation, Luther began to write page after page regarding what it meant to be justified by faith and not by works. He articulated that he had truly been born again. Salvation is by grace through faith – not by prayers or fasting or pilgrimages or sacraments. Righteousness before God was not earned by our works but was a gift from God to us received by faith! It is Christ's righteousness, applied to us through faith.

Luther was overjoyed – But this Gospel truth of salvation by grace alone through faith alone (and not of works) immediately brought Luther into even greater contention with Catholic doctrine. What was he to do? Should he ignore Scripture to obey the church, or should he challenge the church to obey Scripture? Rather than being subject to both sacred Scripture and sacred tradition, as the church taught, Luther believed that we are to be subject to Scripture alone – and that Scripture has the authority to correct the traditions when they are in error.

To protect his life, his friends kidnapped him and hid him away in Wartburg Castle. Here he hid for ten months in disguise. (He grew a beard and took the name Junker Jorge, or Knight George). During his time in exile, Luther undertook the translation of the New Testament into the language of the German people.

Remember, at this time Scripture was only available in Latin. Whether you were English, or German, or French, or Spanish, your Bible was in Latin – The Latin Vulgate, the Bible that Jerome had produced in A.D. 380. But the people couldn't speak Latin, and the clergy were not well trained in Latin. Reading and studying Scripture was something reserved only for the academics and the elite.

Luther did not simply take the Vulgate and translate the Latin into German. He translated his German New Testament out of the original Greek. Within three months Luther had translated the whole of the New Testament. This is an amazing feat and is even more so considering the monumental impact that this translation would have on the German people. For the first time, an ordinary believer could read the Bible for themselves.

All of the faith visionary leaders we have studied throughout this entire book saw the promises and welcomed them from a distance. They confessed that they were strangers and exiles on the earth, seeking a country of their own.

Luther immediately set to work on translating the Old Testament. The first five books, the Pentateuch, appeared in 1523 and the Psalms were finished in 1524. By 1534 the entire Bible had been translated. This was not the first German translation, but it was the finest and became the primary Bible of the German people. Luther knew that for the people to return to the truth of the Gospel – that we are saved by grace through faith in Jesus Christ, they needed Scripture in their own language.

If Luther had done nothing else, his translating of Scripture into German would have propelled the Reformation onward. The people consumed the Word at a phenomenal rate. One Wittenberg printer sold about a hundred thousand copies in 40 years, which is an enormously large number at that age, and these copies were read and reread by millions of Germans.

All of the faith visionary leaders we have studied throughout this entire book, saw the promises and welcomed them from a distance. They confessed that they were strangers and exiles on the earth, seeking a country of their own. They desired a better country, that is, a heavenly one. All of them heard "the voice, saw "a vision" and stepped out into "victory." God wants to give you a promise, a path, a plan, a people and a possession. This is your greatest moment, reach out by faith and take hold of it!

About the Author and
His Resources

Dr. James O. Davis is the founder of Cutting Edge International and Global Church Network, a growing coalition of more than 2,600 Christian ministries and denominations synergizing their efforts to build a premier community of pastors worldwide to help plant five million new churches for a billion soul harvest and to mobilize the whole body of Christ toward the fulfillment of the Great Commission. With more than 700,000 churches, the Global Church Network has become the largest pastors' network in the world.

Christian leaders recognize Dr. Davis as one of the leading networkers in the Christian world. More than 80,000 pastors and leaders have attended his biennial pastors' conference and leadership summits across the United States and in all major world regions. Dr. Davis is considered to be in the *Top Ten Christian Influencers in the World.*

In October 2017, Dr. Davis spearheaded and hosted *The Wittenberg 2017 Congress* in Berlin, Germany. The Wittenberg 2017 Congress celebrated the 500th anniversary of Martin Luther's nailing his 95 Theses on Castle Church door in Wittenberg, Germany. This historic congress brought together more than 650 influential leaders from more than 80 different denominations and every world region.

Dr. Davis served 12 years leading 1,500 evangelists and training thousands of students for full-time evangelism as the National Evangelists' Representative at the National Office of the Assemblies of God. Ministering more than 45 weeks per year for 40 years, Dr. Davis has now traveled over 10 million miles to minister face-to-face to millions of people in more than 130 nations.

Dr. Davis earned a Doctor of Ministry in Preaching at Trinity Evangelical Divinity School and two master's degrees from the Assemblies of God Theological Seminary.

Dr. James O. Davis' Books and Resources

- *We Are The Church: The Untold Story of God's Global Awakening* (coauthored with Dr. Leonard Sweet)
- *The Forgotten Baptism: Your Visionary Path To Success* (coauthored with Dr. Kenneth Ulmer)
- *How to Make Your Net Work: Tying Relational Knots for Global Impact*
- *Scaling Your Everest: Lessons from Sir Edmund Hillary*
- *Gutenberg to Google: The Twenty Indispensable Laws of Communication*
- *The Great Commission Study Bible* (coauthored with Dr. Ben Lerner)
- *The Billion Soul Story*
- *12 Big Ideas*
- *The Pastor's Best Friend: The New Testament Evangelist*
- *Living Like Jesus*
- *The Preacher's Summit*
- *What to Do When the Lights Go Out*
- *It's a Miraculous Life!*
- *Signposts on the Road to Armageddon*
- *Beyond All Limits: The Synergistic Church for a Planet in Crisis* (coauthored with Dr. Bill Bright)
- *Winning Qualities Of High Impact Leaders*

- *The Adrian Rogers Legacy Collection*
- *The Ed Cole Legacy Collection*
- *The Elmer Towns Legacy Collection*
- *The Stephen Olford Preaching Collection*

His quotes and articles have appeared in scores of magazines, newspapers, and blogs.

Dr. Davis resides in the Orlando area with his wife, Sheri, and daughters, Olivia and Priscilla. They have two children, Jennifer and James, who reside in heaven.

Faith Notes

Faith Notes

Faith Notes

Faith Notes

Faith Notes

Faith Notes

Faith Notes

Faith Notes

Faith Notes

Faith Notes

Faith Notes

Faith Notes

Faith Notes

Faith Notes